# Excerpt of What Readers Are Saying

I wholeheartedly congratulate Jim for providing God's people with a wonderful roadmap, of the book of Revelation, to help them on their spiritual journey.      Tyler Cole – Asheboro, NC

Jim Harman has done a marvelous job of giving us searched out insight into one of the most complicated books of our Bible...Jim's life and writings, through the years, have helped us much...      Joan Olsen – Edmond, OK

*Calling All Overcomers* is wonderful "out of the box" insight into the unsealed book of Revelation. It is a great read and forces you out of your "religious," sometimes confident understanding of "what will soon take place."
      Richard Fowler – Winter Park, FL

*Calling All Overcomers* challenges many traditional religious teachings, and it should challenge the reader to discern for themselves what the Bible really teaches. (Act 17:11)
      Lynn Navarre – Jensen Beach, FL

What sets this book apart from the hundreds of others is Jim Harman's great understanding of the important truths surrounding the accountability of believers... More importantly, Jim is able to explain these things in an easy-to-understand, down to earth manner that is often missing in commentaries...
      Pastor Joey Faust – Theodosia, MO

For the serious student of the book of Revelation, Brother Jim Harman's latest work, *Calling All Overcomers*, will prove to be a thought provoking read.      Charlie Dines – Marshfield, MO

Jim Harman has dedicated his life
for the fulfillment of all scriptures
labor to prepare the church for thi

*Calling All Overcomers* gives great encouragement to all believers to become Overcomers who are prepared and looking for Christ's return. I encourage all believers to read this edifying book – you will be blessed!

Judith Stack – Missionary in Central
America with Christ for the City Int'l

James Harman has a very unique gift from the Lord of making what could be considered difficult to understand, very simple. I recommend this book for reading enjoyment, study groups or a reference tool. Pastor Marcus L. Jackson – Baton Rouge, LA

I have always been inspired by Jim Harman's writings. His love for the Lord and the Word mixed with his insight and wisdom resonates throughout this remarkable book.

Pastor Jeff Philips – Orlando, FL

Author James Harman does an amazing job exploring the mysteries of this important book of Revelation, while revealing God's heartbeat for His children to know, love and walk with His Son, and to be overcomers through the presence and power of the living Christ in their daily lives.

Pastor Tom Myers – Longwood, FL

The complete comments by the above readers start on page 239.

# CALLING
# ALL
# OVERCOMERS

An Interpretation of the Book of Revelation

## James T. Harman

Prophecy
Countdown
Publications

# CALLING ALL OVERCOMERS

Copyright © 2015, James T. Harman

Prophecy Countdown Publications, LLC
P.O. Box 941612
Maitland, FL 32794
www.ProphecyCountdown.com

ISBN: 978-0-9636984-7-6

All references from Scripture are from the King James Version unless noted otherwise: AMP – Amplified Bible, copyright ©1987 Lockman Foundation
        ESV – English Standard Version®, copyright ©2001 Crossway
        NAS – New American Standard Bible, copyright ©1960
        NLT – New Living Translation, copyright ©1996
        NIV – New International Version, copyright ©1973
        NKJV- New King James Version, copyright ©1982
        YLT – Young's Literal Translation, copyright ©1898

Scripture abbreviations as used throughout this book are from the Blue Letter Bible (www.BlueLetterBible.org), and they are summarized on p. 186. Numerical references to selected words in the text of Scripture are from James H. Strong Dictionaries of the Hebrew and Greek words.

Words in bold emphasis are authors and not in original Scripture. Certain words such as Kingdom and Judgment Seat of Christ are capitalized to emphasize their importance, but not in accordance with traditional fashions. Certain numerical values are used for clarity or emphasis in presentation and not in accordance with guidelines recommended by all traditional practices.

---

### NOTE TO READER

The purpose of this writing is not to provide a verse-by-verse commentary of the entire book of Revelation. Many other authors have provided such works. The main objective of this book is to focus on helping the reader learn to be a faithful and obedient overcomer when the Lord returns or calls him home.

Throughout this book, bibliographical references will be provided in the comments on selected texts with the commentators last name in parenthesis (without page numbers) since the references cited are the same chapter and verse found in the biblical text.

# Prologue

The Bible is one of the most popular-selling books of all times. The book of Revelation is probably one of its most enthralling sections and literally thousands of commentaries and interpretations have been written on this most captivating part of Holy Scripture. So why write another commentary when so many other excellent and more scholarly ones already exist?

Since coming to know Jesus Christ as my Lord and Savior 37 years ago, I have been fascinated and intrigued by the book of Revelation. After coming to Christ, I was on fire for the Lord and actively witnessing about what Jesus means to me. About that time, I ran across a clipping in the *Wall Street Journal* regarding the 10th nation joining the European common market, and in my fervent naivety, I was convinced that the tribulation period was about to begin! Having read the book of Revelation several times I wanted to alert everyone. I even had a license plate made for my car that read: ***DON'T ACCEPT 666.***

After several decades of reading and studying the Scriptures (with several learned and experienced mentors to guide me), I have matured in my faith and my understanding of God's Word. Realizing the book of Revelation is supposed to be a *"revealing,"* I became perplexed by the many different interpretations that have been offered by so many commentators. Its message and meaning have been so widely debated that it has become a book shrouded in mystery and confusion. To most readers it is a mystifying and baffling book that is avoided because it seems too difficult to understand.

In 2009, I wrote one of my most popular books, **The Kingdom**, which has been widely distributed from our website where it can be freely downloaded and e-mailed to others. Two years later, the Lord prompted me to write a sequel on the subject of the Sermon on the Mount, which we titled, **Overcomers' Guide**

*To The Kingdom* (it can also be freely downloaded from our website). While writing this sequel was originally intended to help believers prepare for the coming Kingdom, the Lord showed me that I needed its message as much as anyone else!

After writing the above sequel, the Lord prompted me to write my most challenging work, which you are currently holding in your hands. I have diligently studied the book of Revelation since becoming a believer and have immersed myself in numerous commentaries over the last several decades.

While starting this current manuscript, I was once again confronted by the Lord with another personal revelation that I needed the message in this book just as much as the audience I was writing it for! The Holy Spirit graciously revealed areas in my life that needed to be addressed and I was humbled to admit as the Apostle Paul did:

> *"O wretched man that I am! Who will deliver me from this body of death?"* (Rom 7:24 – NKJV)

I could also relate to how Paul was concerned for his own spiritual well being of not qualifying for the prize:

> *"Otherwise, I fear that after preaching to others I myself might be disqualified."* (1 Co 9:27 – NLT)

The book of Revelation is a prophecy of God's future plans for planet Earth. Jesus Christ will be returning very soon and believers must be properly prepared before He arrives. When Jesus comes, He will be looking for a faithful remnant of believers who will be qualified to rule and reign with Him. The purpose of this book is to help you learn to be the overcomer Jesus will be looking for at His return.

> *"He that **overcometh** shall **inherit all things**; and I will be his God, and he shall be my son."* (Rev 21:7)

# Dedication

This book is dedicated to:

1) The called, chosen and faithful followers of our Lord who are learning to be genuine overcomers in order that they may be qualified to be included as part of Christ's final army:

> *"These shall make war with the Lamb, and the Lamb shall **overcome them**: for he is Lord of lords, and King of kings: and they that are with him are **called, and chosen, and faithful.**"* (Rev 17:14)

2) While the following men of God are no longer with us, this book is also fondly dedicated to three accomplished friends who I was fortunate to have as pastor and personal mentors:

> Pastor Gary Whipple
> Ray Brubaker
> Lyn Mize

―――――――――――――――――――――

*"If I have seen further than others, it is by standing upon the shoulders of giants."* Sir Isaac Newton

# 7's Found in Book of Revelation[1]

1. 7 Churches
2. 7 Spirits
3. 7 Candlesticks
4. 7 Stars
5. 7 Lamps
6. 7 Seals
7. 7 Horns
8. 7 Eyes
9. 7 Angels
10. 7 Trumpets
11. 7 Thunders
12. 7 Thousand
13. 7 Heads
14. 7 Crowns
15. 7 Plagues
16. 7 Vials (Bowls)
17. 7 Mountains
18. 7 Kings
19. 7 Beatitudes
20. 7 Patterns of the 7 Letters
21. 7 Promises to Church of Philadelphia
22. 7 "I am's" of Christ
23. 7 Doxologies in Heaven
24. 7 Earthquakes
25. 7 Divisions of Book of Revelation
26. 7 Visions between Trumpets and Vials
27. 7 Voices between Vials and final 7 Visions
28. 7 Final Visions

The number 7 has always been associated with spiritual perfection or completion. It's the sum of 4 which represents the number of the world combined with 3 which signifies divine perfection. Added together, 7 epitomizes the end of a matter which notably attests to the fact that this significant book is God's final word to the world.

# Table of Contents
## Summary

# Table of Contents – Detailed

# Table of Contents – Detailed

# Foreword

It is with deep gratitude to James T. Harman that I have been allowed to review his book, *Calling All Overcomers*, prior to its publication. The contents of this book are the product of many years of devoted Christian living, a copious prayer life, and extensive study in God's Word. More importantly, this book stresses the importance of being an "Overcomer," a unique interpretation of the soon coming Rapture-Tribulation-Kingdom of Christ, and how each are interrelated.

This book is the third in a trilogy of works—the others being *The Kingdom* and *Overcomers' Guide to the Kingdom* — that outline and stress the overwhelming biblically-based importance for Christians to live a Spirit-filled life in order to be qualified to rule and reign with Christ in His soon coming Kingdom, the thousand year Messianic Era.

Although preceded by many authors who have originated a wide spectrum of interpretations of the book of Revelation, Jim Harman strongly believes he offers several revealing truths, which will clarify the identity of various individuals and the order of events of this, the last and most encouraging and promising book of the New Testament.

I enthusiastically salute Jim in this endeavor and, along with him, wish to encourage all believers in Jesus Christ to study and seriously consider his interpretation of individuals and events that comprise this most auspicious book in God's Word. More than this, it is my hope and prayer that every Christian who turns its pages will become an Overcomer for Christ in this life—the salvation of his soul—obtaining a spiritually exciting and stimulating hope for what is to soon come.

Charles F. Strong – Harlingen, TX
Bible One Ministry  www.bibleone.net

# Introduction

We are about to start our journey into one of the most unique books in God's Word. One of its main themes is God's magnificent plan to restore the world with Jesus Christ returning as the victorious King and to establish His righteous Kingdom over all the Earth.

When Jesus came the first time, He established his Church and in his Sermon on the Mount he taught how the Kingdom of God can be manifested today in the lives of believers' hearts. When He returns again, He will bring with Him all overcoming believers (Rev 17:14) to defeat Satan and all of his evil cohorts and to rule and reign with His faithful followers during the Millennium.

A central message in the book of Revelation is that God is calling all believers to be genuine overcomers. This message has been obscured from most in the Church because the book of Revelation is often thought to be too difficult to comprehend for the average believer. All the many signs, symbols and metaphors used throughout John's extraordinary vision have cloaked this vital message. As a result, most pastors, teachers and believers miss this central theme or avoid the book entirely.

Being a true overcomer is what being a Christian is all about. Learning to be an overcomer is perhaps the most difficult thing to do. Through the trials of this life, the overcomer's faith is put on trial and thereby confirmed as evidence before a mighty God, it is authentic. For those who would like to familiarize themselves with the subject of being an overcomer, readers are encouraged to read Appendix 6, prior to starting Chapter 1.

The purpose of this writing is to encourage all believers with the crucial understanding that God's desire is for them to be authentic overcomers. Being a faithful, obedient overcomer is vital to the believer's well being and future destiny.

God is calling all those – who bear the testimony of Jesus Christ – to allow His life to reign in their lives so that they too can overcome, just as Jesus overcame for us.

**Calling All Overcomers** is more than the title to this book. For all those who know Jesus Christ as their Savior, it is the personal call from God's own heart. As we will discover in the following pages, God is promising incredible blessings to those who will heed this important call.

Many of the ideas developed in this short work may seem foreign to modern believers who have been indoctrinated by the many traditional teachings of today. Readers are encouraged to try to keep an open mind and desire to understand what the Scriptures say, even if what is presented here may differ with what we have all been taught.

This writer has experienced several paradigm shifts in his thinking as the Holy Spirit helped shed the many error-filled "sacred cow" teachings that have become traditions for most of today's church.

This writer prays that this endeavor will help illuminate those with teachable hearts down a glorious trail that will help them become the overcomers that God is calling them to be.

---

"Do not go where the path may lead,
go instead where there is no path
and leave a trail."
Ralph Waldo Emerson

# Chapter 1 – 7 Letters to Churches

**Opening Vision**

> *"The Revelation of Jesus Christ, which God gave Him to show His bond-servants, the things which must soon take place; and He sent and communicated it by His angel to His bond-servant John, who testified to the word of God and to the testimony of Jesus Christ, even to all that he saw."* (Rev 1:1-2 – NAS)

The last book in the word of God begins by telling us that it is a direct communication from God, which He gave to Jesus Christ. It states that it is a "Revelation" of Jesus Christ by using the Greek word for Apocalypse (#602 *apokalypsis*), which literally means an uncovering or disclosure of truth. It is a message given from God to Jesus, which He then gave to His angel to give to its author, the Apostle John, who testifies to its validity. In other words, it represents God's final word to mankind and contains an important message of the things that Jesus will accomplish to bring God's plan to fulfillment.

*Beatitude for Overcomers*

After telling us what we are about to read, John instructs us with the first of seven important blessings (see Appendix 5) that are provided to those who read this most vital book:

> *"**Blessed** is he who **reads** and those who **hear** the words of this prophecy, and **keep** those things which are written in it; for the time is near."* (Rev 1:3 – NKJV)

It is imperative for the reader to understand that this blessing to be received from God is based upon **reading**, **hearing** and **keeping** those things which are written in the book. After reading and hearing the message, we need to make sure that we are **keeping** the things that we are admonished to keep. The Greek word for "keeping" (#5083 *tereo*) means to guard, keep or to hold firmly. This same word is also used in the Lord's conditional promise to the church of Philadelphia for keeping or holding firmly: *"Because you have **kept** My command to persevere, I also will keep you from the hour of trial which shall come upon the whole world..."* (Rev 3:10 – NKJV) As the steadfast Philadelphian believers are assured of escaping the final "hour of trial," the faithful overcomer who keeps all of the things that God tells us will receive a remarkable blessing, as we will discover in the pages that follow.

The first of seven Beatitudes found in the book of Revelation promises to bless faithful believers who read, hear and keep the things that God instructs us to. The other remaining Beatitudes have similar admonitions; however, the audience that each blessing is addressed to is not the same. As outlined in Appendix 5, the 1st, 6th, and 7th Beatitudes are addressed to the overcomer in general, with the other four beatitudes referring to the following groups:     2nd – the Martyrs, 3rd – the Watchful, 4th – the Bride of Christ, and 5th – Part of 1st Resurrection. As we will see when we address each of the Beatitudes, there is a great distinction as to the importance and timing of each group.

While all of the seven Beatitudes refer to overcomers, the point needs to be remembered that God will abundantly bless those who are found faithfully obeying Him.

The opening vision continues with a beautiful fourfold salutation in verses 4 to 6 – stating it is from John, God the Father, the Holy Spirit and Jesus Christ. Verse 7-8 then announces the Second Coming: *"Behold, **He is coming** with clouds, and **every eye will see Him**, even they who pierced Him. And all the tribes of the earth will mourn because of Him. Even so, Amen. I am the Alpha and the Omega, the Beginning and the*

*End,"  says the Lord, "who is and who was and **who is to come,**
the Almighty."* (Rev 1:7-8 – NKJV)

At the second coming, the entire world will see Jesus Christ
returning and mourn in fulfillment of Zechariah 12:10.  This
event is also proof that the Lord will keep the promise he made
to his disciples to return again: *"And if I go and prepare a place
for you, I will come again and receive you to Myself; that where
I am, there you may be also.*  (Jhn 14:3 – NKJV)

In verses 9 to 11, John relays the vision that he received while
being exiled on the island of Patmos because of his faith in
Jesus.  He heard a loud voice like a trumpet say:

> *"Write on a scroll what you see and send it to the seven
> churches: to Ephesus, Smyrna, Pergamum, Thyatira,
> Sardis, Philadelphia and Laodicea."* (Rev 1:11 – NIV)

When John hears the voice he turns to see who is speaking to
him. Verses 12 to 18 describe the vision John sees of Christ.

> *"Then I turned to see the voice that spoke with me. And
> having turned I saw seven golden **lampstands**, and in
> the midst of the seven lampstands One like the Son of
> Man..."* (Rev 1:12-13 – NKJV)

The lampstands symbolize the 7 churches, which represent the
witness of the Church as Jesus taught in his Sermon on the
Mount:

> *"**You are the light of the world**. A city that is set on a
> hill cannot be hidden. "Nor do they light a lamp and put
> it under a basket, but **on a lampstand, and it gives light
> to all**..."* (Mat 5:14-15 – NKJV)

The Church is God's witness upon the earth during the present
age. The One in the midst of the seven lampstands *"like unto
the Son of Man"* is Christ himself.

John then continues the remainder of chapter 1 to describe the magnificent vision that he saw of Jesus Christ. The vision of Christ given in chapter 1 is remarkably similar to the description of Christ in chapters 2 and 3. This can be visibly seen by comparing the narratives side by side[1]:

| Description of Christ Chapter 1 | Description of Christ Chapters 2 & 3 |
|---|---|
| 'And he had in his right hand seven stars..in the midst of the lampstands one like unto a son of man.' Rev 1:16,13 | '...he that holds the seven stars in his right hand, he that walks in the midst of the seven golden lampstands.' Rev 2:1 |
| 'I am the first and the last and the living one, and I was dead, and behold, I am alive for ever-more.' Rev 1:17,18 | '...the first and the last, who became dead, yet lived." Rev 2:8 |
| 'And out of his mouth proceeded a sharp two-edged sword.' Rev 1:16 | 'he that has the sharp two-edged sword.' Rev 2:12 |
| '...his eyes were as a flame of fire, and his feet like unto burnished brass.' Rev 1:14-15 | '...his eyes like a flame of fire, and his feet are like unto burnished brass.' Rev 2:18 |
| '...and from seven spirits that are before his throne...and he had in his right hand seven stars.' Rev 1:4,16 | 'he that has the seven spirits of God and the seven stars.' Rev 3:1 |
| 'the faithful witness...I..have the keys of death and Hades. Rev 1:5,18 | '...he that is true, he that has the key of David.' Rev 3:7 |
| '...Jesus Christ, the faithful witness, the first-born of the dead, and the ruler of the kings of the earth.' Rev 1:5 | 'the Amen, the faithful and true witness, the beginning of the creation of God.' Rev 3:14 |

John's vision of Jesus caused him to fall to the ground at Christ's feet in reverent adoration and fear. Jesus told him not to be afraid, but to write: *"things which you have seen, and the things which are, and the things which will take place after this."* The **things which are** correspond to the accounts of the churches outlined in chapters 2 and 3, which are examined next.

As we begin our review of the 7 churches, the reader may want to pause for a moment and read Appendix 1, which surveys the five various methods of interpreting the book of Revelation. This writing will take the eclectic view and we agree with Robert Mounce's assessment that each approach has some important contribution to help us understand it.

We believe that the 7 churches can be viewed three different ways: literally, figuratively and prophetically. The 7 churches were actual literal churches that existed when John wrote his visions. They also figuratively represent 7 different categories which every believer can fall into. Finally, because Revelation is a prophecy, we believe they can symbolize the 7 types of churches that have existed from the beginning until the end of the church age at Christ's second coming (see Appendix 1).

Regarding the millennium (Appendix 2), our view is a merging of the Dispensational view with the Historic Premillennial view. This is because we believe in a phased rapture: with one rapture at the very beginning of the tribulation for those who are properly prepared (Firstfruits), followed by one rapture at the end of the tribulation for the remainder of the church (Main Harvest). To learn more about this method of interpreting the rapture, please read: *The Coming Spiritual Earthquake* which can be freely downloaded from our website. This view was also held by such noted teachers as: Govett, A.B. Simpson, Lang, Panton, Dahl, Brubaker and Mize.

---

**7 Patterns of The 7 Churches**

On the following page is a chart to assist in reviewing the 7 churches.     This chart is fairly self-explanatory with each church listed across the top in order to analyze the following patterns: 1) Addressed to, 2) Attribute of Christ, 3) Commendation, 4) State of Each Church, 5) Warning Given, 6) Exhortation, and 7) Promise to Overcomers. These patterns will provide useful insights as we explore each church in greater detail.

## The 7 Patterns of The 7 Churches

| Addressed to | Angel at Ephesus | Angel at Smyrna | Angel at Pergamos | Angel at Thyatira | Angel at Sardis | Angel at Philadelphia | Angel at Laodicea |
|---|---|---|---|---|---|---|---|
| Attributes of Christ | Holds 7 Stars | First & Last Dead > Alive | Sharp Two Edged Sword | Eyes - Flame Feet - Bronze | 7 Spirits & 7 Stars | Holds Key of David | Faithful Witness |
| Commendation | Have Zeal Works | Know Your Tribulation | Did Not Deny My Name | Know Your Endurance | Few Worthy | Kept Word Not Denied | |
| State of Church | Lack 1st Love for Christ | Willing to Die for Christ | Stumbling Block | Tolerate False Teaching | Reputation Alive-But Dead | Willing to Live for Christ | Lukewarm Christ Outside |
| Warning | Repent Do 1st Works | Faithful Unto Death: Crown | Repent Sword | Repent | Wake Up Watch! | Hold Fast | Buy Gold & Garments |
| Exhortation | Hear What Spirit Says | Hear What Spirit Says | Hear What Spirit Says | Hold Fast | Do Not Soil Your Garments | Don't Loose Crown | Knocking on Door |
| Promise to Overcomers | Grant to Eat Tree of Life | Will Not Be Hurt 2nd Death | Give Hidden Manna | Authority Over Nations | Clothed In White Raiment | Pillar - Temple New Name | Sit on Throne |

**Church of Ephesus (Rev 2:1-7)**

> *"...To him who overcomes I will give to eat from the **tree of life**, which is in the midst of the Paradise of God."*
> (Rev 2:7 – NKJV)

The promise to the overcoming church member in Ephesus is to eat from the tree of life in the middle of Paradise! This should be the aspiration of every believer. Let's see what we can learn from the church in Ephesus to help us be the overcomer that Jesus will be looking for.

### Old Testament (O.T.) Reference

First of all, we should remember that Adam and Eve were banished from the Garden of Eden because they disobeyed God's command not to eat from the tree of knowledge. Because of their disobedience, God could not let them eat from the tree of life – for if they did, they would have lived forever in a sinful state (see Gen 2:16-17 and 3:22-24). The tree of life allows man to live forever and God will finally permit people to have the right to eat from the tree of life:

> *"Blessed are those who do His commandments, that they may have the right to the tree of life..."*
> (Rev 22:14 – NKJV)

Here we see that the promise given to the overcomer in the church of Ephesus will ultimately be fulfilled. This is the 7th Beatitude in the book of Revelation and it is God's promised blessing to all obedient overcomers. Because of man's disobedience in the garden, the right to the tree of life was taken away. God will restore that right for their obedience to Christ.

### Commendation

Jesus commends the church of Ephesus for its zeal: *"I know your works, your labor, your patience, and that you cannot bear*

*those who are evil. And you have tested those who say they are apostles and are not, and have found them liars; and you have persevered and have patience, and have labored for My name's sake and have not become weary.... But this you have, that you hate the deeds of the Nicolaitans, which I also hate."*
(Rev 2:2-3, 6 – NKJV)

These church members were exemplary when it came to doing many fine works for Jesus. They worked hard to hold up the true doctrines of the faith and would not tolerate false teachers who tried to invade their congregations. They were very patient in both their service and suffering for the Lord and had not grown tired. Despite this wonderful report, Jesus found a major flaw:

> *"Nevertheless I have this against you, that **you have left your first love**. Remember therefore from where you have fallen; repent and do the first works, or else I will come to you quickly and remove your lampstand from its place--unless you repent."* (Rev 2:4-5 – NKJV)

What does Jesus mean by *"left your first love?"* How did this happen? It seems apparent that in their zeal for holding up correct doctrine, and performing good works, these members had forgotten to love. Not only had their love for Jesus been detracted by their zest for serving Him, they had also forgotten to show the love of Christ to others. Both their pure devotion to Jesus, and their compassion for others, had waned because they were so concerned with upholding sound doctrine. The sweet affection for Jesus and proper fellowship with others had died. The Apostle Paul fully recognized this defect: *"...but our competence comes from God. He has made us competent as ministers of a new covenant–not of the letter but of the Spirit; for the **letter kills, but the Spirit gives life.**"* (2 Co 3:5-6 – NIV)

The zeal for knowledge and truth can quench the flame of love.

The eagerness for building the Church and performing many great and important activities can become efforts of the flesh rather than loving deeds of the Spirit.

In order to be the overcomer that Jesus will be looking for, we should apply the lessons learned from the church of Ephesus. We need to ask ourselves if our passion for knowledge, our fervor for good works, or our zeal for upholding sound doctrine have distracted us from totally loving Jesus and showing His compassion to others? The overcomer will want to prayerfully examine his or her heart and ask the Lord for help in correcting and changing any grievous ways. As David so aptly prayed:

> *"Search me, O God, and know my heart! Try me and know my thoughts! And see if there be any grievous way in me, and lead me in the way everlasting!"*
> (Psa 139:23-24 – ESV)

From our review of the church of Ephesus, we can glean some valuable lessons. To be the overcomer that will be pleasing to the Lord, we want to make certain that we are obedient to Him and his Word. As disobedience caused Adam and Eve to be banished from the paradise that God had created for them, disobedience can cause the believer to forfeit the blessing that is promised to the overcomer.

In addition, the overcomer will assess his or her relationship with the Lord to make sure their love for Him is genuine. Our devotion to Him must be foremost – as it was when we first came to know Him as our Saviour. While our works, labor and desire to uphold sound doctrine are still be important, they can never be allowed to replace that rich love we first experienced when we came to Christ.

> *"He who has an ear, let him hear what the Spirit says to the churches..."* (Rev 2:7 – NKJV)

## Church of Smyrna (Rev 2:8-11)

*"He who overcomes shall **not be hurt by the second death.**"* (Rev 2:11 – NKJV)

Jesus promises the overcomers in the church of Smyrna that they will not be hurt by the second death. This is a vital promise that is important for every believer to understand. It should motivate us all to be the overcomer that Jesus wants us to be. Before we learn more about this church and what the second death is all about, let's look back in the Old Testament to the time when the first death occurred at the Fall of man.

### O.T. Reference

As we learned from our review of the church of Ephesus, Adam and Eve were banished from God's Paradise because of their disobedience. Let's see what the reason behind it was and the momentous consequences. Right after God told Eve not to eat from the tree of knowledge; Satan came along and told her: *"Then the serpent said to the woman, '**You will not surely die.**' So when the woman **saw** that the tree was good for **food**, that it was **pleasant** to the eyes, and a tree **desirable** to make one **wise**, she took of its fruit and ate..."* (Gen 3:4, 6 – NKJV)

The monumental change in man's destiny is primarily the result of **deception**. Satan told Eve a great lie and due to her own lust (food, pleasure and wisdom), she believed the lie. Eve was deceived because she listened to, and believed, a lie. Because of deception, mankind's fate has been death: *"...return to the ground, For out of it you were taken; For dust you are, And to dust you shall return."* (Gen 3:19 – NKJV) Ever since the garden, mankind has been faced with death (Heb 9:27).

While the first death came about because of deception that led to man's disobedience, the good news is that Jesus conquered death for all men: *"Christ suffered for our sins once for all time.*

*He never sinned, but he died for sinners to bring you safely home to God. He suffered physical death, but he was raised to life in the Spirit.*" (1 Pe 3:18 – NLT)

All those who acknowledge Christ as their personal savior should have no fear of death because he paid the penalty for all of our sins and has abolished death once for all! (2 Ti 1:10)

### Commendation

This good news was important to the church of Smyrna because they were under tremendous persecution and were facing the likely prospect of martyrdom:

> *"I know your works, tribulation, and poverty (but you are rich); and I know the **blasphemy** of those who say they are Jews and are not, but are a synagogue of Satan. Do not fear any of those things which you are about to suffer. Indeed, the devil is about to throw some of you into prison, that you may be tested, and you will have tribulation ten days. Be faithful until death, and I will give you the crown of life.* " (Rev 2:9-10 – NKJV)

The church of Smyrna is commended for its work and ability to stand up under the many tests and trials it faced. It was financially very poor, but spiritually quite wealthy (the exact opposite of the church of Laodicea, which we will discuss later in this chapter). The fact that Jesus acknowledges its spiritual wealth is wonderful praise that will certainly be acknowledged when its members stand before Him at the Judgement Seat.

This church was severely slandered [(#988) *blasphēmia* Greek word for *blasphemy*] by the Jews. Members were persecuted and killed by those who believed that they were doing service for God as Jesus predicted would happen (Jhn 16:2). These oppressors may have been born Jewish, but they were not true Jews in the spiritual sense as the Apostle Paul rightly describes:

*"For he is not a Jew who is one outwardly, nor is circumcision that which is outward in the flesh.* **But he is a Jew** *who is one inwardly; and* **circumcision** *is that which is* **of the heart**, *by the Spirit, not by the letter; and his praise is not from men, but from God."* (Rom 2:28-29 – NAS)

True Jews are those who have experienced a change in their heart by the Spirit of the living God. In other words, a true Jew is one who has been born again. These false Jews were the ones slandering and killing those in this church. Jesus encouraged them with this great assurance: *"Be faithful until death, and I will give you the* **crown of life**.*"* (Rev 2:10 – NKJV)

The **crown of life** is promised to all those who face martyrdom. This crown is God's award to the faithful believer who is willing to die for his faith when confronted with death. While being a martyr is one way to receive this crown, James tells us that this great reward can also be obtained by being a faithful and obedient believer in his or her daily living:

> *"Blessed is the man who remains steadfast under trial, for when he has stood the test he will receive the* **crown of life**,[2] *which God has promised to those who love him."* (Jas 1:12 – ESV)

In this life, all believers experience trials and temptations. Those who overcome these tests are given the wonderful promise of receiving this precious crown. By dying to self and allowing the Spirit of God to help win the daily battles, the believer is granted this magnificent reward.

## Second Death

Jesus continues his letter to the members in Smyrna by assuring those who overcome that they will not be hurt by the second death. The second death is defined as being cast into the Lake of Fire (see Rev 20:14). By being faithful martyrs, they have the

Lord's guarantee that they will not be harmed by the second death. Being loyal overcomers assures them the crown of life and Christ's word that they will not be hurt by the second death.

Let's review what we have learned from the church of Smyrna. The believers in this church were faced with the trial of their faith, which required them to either renounce Christ or face death. Because Christ conquered death, they believed He would bring them safely home to God. Being a successful overcomer assured them the *crown of life* and Christ's pledge that they would not be hurt by the second death. This same *crown of life* is available to all believers today who are victorious over the many trials and temptations in this life. This *crown of life* is God's great reward to those who demonstrate steadfast faithfulness when faced with either death or the trials of daily living.

Satan will continue to use deception to attempt to divert us from these truths. Satan deceived Eve by telling her that she would not die if she disobeyed God. Satan attempts to deceive believers today by telling us that all believers will receive rewards no matter how we live our lives. The carnal believer wants to satisfy his or her own personal desires and readily accepts the adversary's false claims. Being as shortsighted as Eve, they don't realize the consequences of their actions and they will be sorely disappointed if they do not wake up and die to their carnal lifestyle and allow Christ to reign in their life.

The overcomers, however, will not accept Satan's lies and will defeat him by relying upon Jesus and their love for him and his Word. By so doing, they are learning to die to self on a daily basis. They are devoted to Him and want to please him by allowing His life to reign in theirs.

> *"He who has an ear, let him hear what the Spirit says to the churches"* (Rev 2:17 – NKJV)

## Church of Pergamos (Rev 2:12-17)

> *"To him who overcomes I will give some of the **hidden manna** to eat. And I will give him a white stone, and on the stone a new name written which no one knows except him who receives it."* (Rev 2:17 – NKJV)

The promise to the overcomer in the church of Pergamos is twofold: hidden manna to eat and a white stone with a name that no one else knows. These honors are special rewards to those who are able to overcome the degraded state present in the church of Pergamos. Before we review the condition of this church we need to explore the Old Testament for insight into the unique award of hidden manna offered to these overcomers.

### O.T. Reference

The reference to the hidden manna goes back to when God provided bread from heaven when Moses led the people of Israel in the wilderness: *"And the whole congregation of the children of Israel **murmured** against Moses and Aaron in the wilderness"* complaining that God brought them out of Egypt to starve (Exo 16:2). God provided the people with bread from heaven which they named *"**Manna**"* and they ate for 40 years until they arrived at the border of Canaan. (Exo 16:3-4, 31, 38)

During their 40 year journey though the wilderness, the people of Israel continued to test God with their continued murmuring, idolatry and immorality. The Apostle Paul reminds us: *"Nevertheless, with most of them God was **not pleased**, for they were **overthrown in the wilderness**. Now these things took place as examples for us...they were written down for our instruction..."* (1 Co 10:5-6, 11 – ESV) The writer of Hebrews tells us: *"Do not harden your hearts as in the rebellion, In the day of trial in the wilderness, Where your fathers tested Me, tried Me, And saw My works forty years. So I swore in My wrath, '**They shall not enter My rest.**'"* (Heb 3:8-9,11 – NKJV)

*"Let us, therefore, **make every effort to enter that rest**, so that no one will perish by following their example of disobedience. For the word of God is alive and active. Sharper than any **double-edged sword**, it penetrates even to **dividing soul and spirit**, joints and marrow; it judges the thoughts and attitudes of the heart."* (Heb 4:11-12 – NIV)

Israel's passage through the wilderness represents a type of the church in this present age. Their unfaithfulness of murmuring, idolatry and immorality caused all but Caleb and Joshua to be excluded from entering into the Promised Land. This speaks of believers failing to participate in the coming millennial rest if we fail to learn from their mistakes. The allusion of *"the word of God...sharper than any double-edged sword"* relates to the attribute of Jesus (Rev 2:12) addressed to the church in Pergamos. Jesus (the Word of God) is able to penetrate and judge our innermost thoughts. The overcomers will allow the Word of God to judge our hearts in this current age – helping us make every effort to reach that coming rest (Mat 6:33).

### Commendation

The church of Pergamos was situated in a city of great wealth with many pagan temples for worship of heathen gods and Roman Emperors. Despite the fact that they were located at the heart of Satan's domain, they were commended for remaining loyal to Jesus, and not denying their faith, even when one of their leaders was martyred. While this church did remain faithful, they were guilty of some of the same vices exhibited by the nation of Israel in their trek through the wilderness:

*"But I have a few things against you, because you have there those who hold the doctrine of Balaam, who taught Balak to put a **stumbling block** before the children of Israel, to **eat things sacrificed to idols**, and to commit **sexual immorality**. Thus you also have those who hold the **doctrine of the Nicolaitans**, which thing I hate."* (Rev 2:14-15 – NKJV)

The church in Pergamos had compromised their faith with the false doctrines of Balaam and the Nicolaitians. Balaam was a prophet who led God's people into fornication and idolatry for his own financial gain (see Num 22-24, 25:1-3, and 31:16). Some of the members in Pergamos had adopted his teachings by attending heathen festivals and participating in idolatry and fornication. They also had established the teachings of the Nicolaitans, which placed a clerical hierarchy over the congregation who then tolerated and allowed these worldly practices, which are offensive to God (Mize, Ladd).

Many false practices are present in today's worldly church with such deceptive beliefs as 1) Ultra-Grace teaching where grace[3] is emphasized in place of the proper principle that salvation is by grace, but rewards are based upon works (Eph 2:8-9 **and** 10), 2) the "Prosperity gospel," which teaches believers false claims about money and 3) the hierarchy of the Clergy over the people.

From the church of Pergamos we have learned that worldly compromise based upon false doctrine is poisonous to the health of the church. These incorrect teachings have blinded its members from the real source of our strength as believers. Jesus Christ is the *"bread of life"* (Jhn 6:35) and our God is a jealous God who hates compromise. The distractions of untrue teachings can cause believers to overlook fellowship with Jesus and the proper nourishment provided by Him through the word.

To be an overcomer when surrounded by a worldly, corrupt church requires us to be sanctified by the Word (Jhn 17:17) on a daily basis. The overcomer will be feeding on Jesus as the true manna and not be guilty of murmuring, or of practicing idolatry or immorality. They will be making every effort to enter the rest of God where they are promised the hidden manna to eat.

> *"He who has an ear, let him hear what the Spirit says to the churches"* (Rev 2:11 – NKJV)

**Church of Thyatira (Rev 2:18-29)**

> *"And he who overcomes, and keeps My works until the end, to him I will give power over the nations. He shall rule them with a **rod of iron**; They shall be dashed to pieces like the potter's vessels – as I also have received from My Father; and I will give him the morning star."* (Rev 2:26-28 – NKJV)

The overcomers in the church of Thyatira are given the promise of ruling the nations if they are able to be found keeping the Lord's works faithfully to the end of their life.   We will be given a *"rod of iron,"* which is a picture of strength and power which comes from God to govern the people.   Let's look into the Old Testament for insight into this significant reward offered to those who successfully endure and **overcome** the **apostasy** associated with this church.

### O.T. Reference
The *"rod of iron"* granted the overcomer is pictured for us when Moses goes to the top of the hill and uses the **rod of God** to defeat Amalek:   *"And Moses said to Joshua, "Choose us some men and go out, fight with Amalek. Tomorrow I will stand on the top of the hill with the **rod of God** in my hand...And so it was, when Moses held up his hand, that Israel prevailed; and when he let down his hand, Amalek prevailed... But Moses' hands became heavy; ...And Aaron and Hur supported his hands...and his hands were steady until the going down of the sun. So Joshua **defeated Amalek** and his people...And Moses built an altar and called its name, The-LORD-Is-My-Banner"*(Exo 17:9,11-13,15 – NKJV)

Moses was able to defeat Amalek using the *"rod of God"* to prevail over his enemies.   While Moses became weary holding up the rod throughout the fight, he had help in carrying out the defeat.   At the end of the battle, Moses built an altar, revealing that he recognized it was God who defeated Israel's enemy. He named it *"The Lord Is My Banner"* and it prefigures our Lord's cross, which was lifted high on the hill at Calvary. Lee notes that the altar named by Moses "signifies the cross as a memorial of our victory…through the cross…as our banner, our victory."[4] The rod of iron represents God's power provided to the overcomer in order to rule in the coming age.

### Commendation

The church of Thyatira had much to be commended. It was praised for its works, love, service, faith and patience; and its works increased as time passed. These believers worked hard and demonstrated their faith by many charitable endeavors aimed at helping others. These many fine attributes are very commendable and will not go unrewarded. Christ, however, is very displeased that they had allowed doctrines and practices completely inappropriate for His church: *"Nevertheless I have a few things against you, because you allow that woman Jezebel, who calls herself a prophetess, to teach and **seduce** My servants to commit sexual **immorality** and eat things sacrificed to **idols**."* (Rev 2:20 – NKJV)

This evil woman encouraged the congregation to participate in rituals that have no place in the church. Her strong influence created a heretical condition that has continued to this day. Many writers recognize the church of Thyatira as the Roman Catholic Church and is laden with false doctrines and practices.

Those in this church who continue in this heretical system are called to repent; and if they fail to do so, they will be cast into great tribulation: *"Indeed I will cast her into a sickbed, and those who commit adultery with her into **great tribulation**, unless they repent of their deeds… and all the churches shall know that I am He who searches the minds and hearts. And I will give to each one of you according to your works."* (Rev 2:22-23 – NKJV)

Prophetically, these verses tell us that those who fail to withdraw from these practices will be cast into the tribulation period. This should be a somber warning to those who have been captivated by its seductive teaching. Fortunately, there are some in this church who do not follow these beliefs: *"But to the rest of you in Thyatira who do not hold this teaching, who have not learned what some call the deep things of Satan, to you I say, I do not lay on you any other burden. Only hold fast what you have until I come."* (Rev 2:24-25 – ESV)

Both the churches of Pergamos and Thyatira are guilty of promoting false teachings that Jesus is not pleased with. Like Pergamos, those in Thyatira are blinded from seeing their real need, which is Jesus, the true source of our hope and strength as believers. Jesus wants us to come to him:

> *"Come to me, all who labor and are heavy laden, and I will give you rest. Take my yoke upon you, and **learn from me**, for I am gentle and lowly in heart, and you will find **rest for your souls**. For my yoke is easy, and my burden is light."* (Mat 11:28-30 ESV)

To be the overcomer that Jesus desires, we need to learn to come to Him on a daily basis and ask him to teach us.[5] If we do, He promises to give us rest for our souls without heavy burdens.

Ironically, the Catholic Church desires to rule over its people by its many false teachings and practices. Instead of being distracted by its icons, indulgences and relics, the believers will lift high the banner of the Lord Jesus in their hearts to obtain the crucial victory over religion. Those who do not believe or follow its false doctrines can be the overcomer who Jesus will bestow the remarkable opportunity of ruling the nations and be given His mighty **rod of iron**.

> *"He who has an ear, let him hear what the Spirit says to the churches."* (Rev 2:29 – NKJV)

## Church of Sardis (Rev 3:1-6)

> *"He who overcomes shall be **clothed in white garments**, and I will not blot out his name from the Book of Life; but I will confess his name before My Father and before His angels. "* (Rev 3:5 – NKJV)

The church in Sardis has a reputation of being alive, but it is viewed as dead by the Lord who is calling out members to be overcomers. Those who hear his call are given the promise that they will be clothed in white garments and never be blotted out of the Book of Life. These precious pledges by Jesus can be appropriated by believers if we are able to grasp what He is calling us to do. To help us gain the necessary understanding, let's turn to the Old Testament for clues about what these white garments represent.

### O.T. Reference

In God's design, the Priests were to wear holy garments made of fine linen, which sanctified them for serving in their priestly office. (Exo 28:2-3, 39, 42) The prophet Zechariah records the vision of Joshua, who was given the position of High Priest: *"1)Then he showed me Joshua the high priest standing before the angel of the LORD...3) Now Joshua was standing before the angel, **clothed with filthy garments**. 4) And the angel said to those who were standing before him, 'Remove the filthy garments from him.' And to him he said, 'Behold, I have taken your iniquity away from you, and **I will clothe you with pure vestments**.'* (Zec 3:1,3-4 – ESV)

Joshua came standing in *"filthy garments,"* which is a picture of how we appear to God in our flesh: *"But we are all like an unclean thing, And all our righteousnesses are like filthy rags..."* (Isa 64:6 – NKJV) Joshua was given pure robes, which would allow him to serve before the Lord. This also speaks prophetically of Christ's righteousness, provided by faith.

*"Even the righteousness of God which is by faith of Jesus Christ unto all and upon all them that believe..."* (Rom 3:22) This is the imputed righteousness provided by Christ that is obtained by faith. Faith in Jesus Christ is the only thing that will justify a person before God. The believer receives the righteousness of God by faith in Jesus Christ + nothing. By God's marvelous grace we are saved and provided our robe:

> *"I will greatly rejoice in the LORD, my soul shall be joyful in my God; for he hath clothed me with the garments of salvation, he hath covered me with the **robe of righteousness**... "* (Isa 61:10)

While believers receive Christ's **robe of righteousness** when they are saved, the overcomers will want to be certain they also have their wedding dress prepared: *"For the marriage of the Lamb has come and **His bride has made herself ready....**to clothe herself in **fine linen, bright and clean**; for the **fine linen is the righteous acts of the saints"** (Rev 19:6-8 – NAS)

The righteous acts or deeds of the saints are the things that set the bride of Christ apart. While she already has obtained her *"robe of righteousness"* by faith, she makes herself ready for the wedding by obtaining her *"**fine linen**,"* which represents her righteous life that she leads (conduct, acts, and deeds). Now let's look at the condition of the saints in the church of Sardis.

### Commendation

The church in Sardis does not have very much to be commended for: *"...I know your **works**, that you have a name that you are alive, but **you are dead**. Be watchful, and strengthen the things which remain, that are ready to die, for I have **not found your works perfect before God**. Remember therefore how you have received and heard; hold fast and repent. Therefore if you will **not watch**, I will come upon you as a thief, and you will not know what hour I will come upon you."*

> *"You have a few names even in Sardis who have **not defiled their garments**; and they shall walk with Me in white, **for they are worthy**."*
> (Rev 3:1-4 – NKJV)

For the most part, the works of the members in this church are found lacking. While all the members had once received their own *"robe of righteousness,"* very few appear to be working on their own wedding dress of *"fine linen."* It appears that most of the members have fallen asleep and are not watching as Jesus taught in his Olivet Discourse in Matthew 25:1-13. The 5 wise virgins are prepared and ready because they have their extra supply of oil, which is a picture of them being *"filled with the Spirit"* (Eph 5:18), while the 5 foolish virgins lack this extra measure of oil.    An accurate, literal word-for-word paraphrase of Matthew 25:5 might be: *"While the bridegroom tarried, they all **beckoned or slept**."*   The wise virgins were *"**beckoning**"* for the Lord to return, while the foolish virgins were sleeping.[6]

A few members in Sardis (pictured by the 5 wise virgins) have allowed the Holy Spirit to fill their lives, thereby providing them with undefiled garments. The vast majority of the church of Sardis, however, has fallen asleep and is not watching for the return of the Bridegroom. Jesus admonishes them to repent and start watching or else they will be taken by surprise when He returns.

Jesus promises the few members who have not defiled their garments that they will walk with him in white because they are worthy (Rev 3:4). Their "worthiness" is attributed to the fact that they have remained pure and their works are considered complete (Osborne). As the Apostle James reminds us:

> *"Pure religion and undefiled before God and the Father is this.... **to keep himself unspotted from the world**."*
> (Jas 1:27)

Our brief survey of the church of Sardis has given us a great deal of insight into what Jesus will be looking for when he returns. Remember, Jesus will be returning for His bride. He expects her to be without spot or wrinkle and to be holy and without blemish (Eph 5:27).

While the church in Sardis was considered mostly dead, it did have a few members who had not defiled their garments. They had been able to keep them spotless without any wrinkle or blemish. Because of this, they were considered worthy.

Jesus is showing us that the overcomers will not allow their wedding garments to become soiled or dirty by this dark and dying world. This would include staying away from anything that would cause us to get our dress wrinkled or spotted. In order to do this, we must always remember that this can only be accomplished by relying upon the Holy Spirit to direct and empower our lives. We can do this by yielding to his direction and trusting Him to keep us fully separated from the things of this world so we can remain holy and pure.

### Book of Life

The promise to the overcomers in this church also includes not having their name blotted from the Book of Life. In our book, **The Kingdom** we devote chapter 9 to this important subject (this book can be freely downloaded from our website). For purposes of this discussion, it is important to note that successful overcomers will **not** have their names blotted from the Book of Life. While commentaries on this verse vary widely, the prudent believer who has been personally convicted of the possibility that they have not been leading the life of a genuine overcomer should heed Christ's admonition to repent and begin watching for the Lord now, while time still remains.

> *"He who has an ear, let him hear what the Spirit says to the churches."* (Rev 3:6 – NKJV)

### Church of Philadelphia (Rev 3:7-13)

> *"He who overcomes, I will make him a **pillar in the temple** of My God, and he shall go out no more. I will write on him the **name of My God** and the **name of the city** of My God, the New Jerusalem, which comes down out of heaven from My God. And I will write on him **My new name.**"* (Rev 3:12 – NKJV)

Of all the churches in the apocalypse, Philadelphia stands out as the one most admired by Jesus. It is the only church that is not rebuked and is even granted seven notable promises by the Lord (four of which are included in the above verse). To fully appreciate the importance of what being a pillar in the temple is, we need to explore the Old Testament for additional insight.

### O.T. Reference

The first instance of the term "pillar" in a positive aspect is found in the story of Jacob's dream at Bethel (Gen 28:10-22). After being sent out by Isaac, Jacob rests his head on a stone to sleep for the night. In Jacob's dream he is given the vision that God wants to build His house on the earth as a precursor to the time when He will bring the New Jerusalem as the future dwelling place of God (Rev 21:2, 22).

The stone Jacob uses to rest his head represents Christ, who promises to give us rest: *"Come unto me…I will give you rest."* (Mat 11:28) Christ is also the cornerstone (Isa 28:16) and the ladder that bridges heaven with earth. When Jacob awakes from his dream, he sets up the **stone as a pillar** and pours oil on it, signifying how the Triune God (Father, Son and Holy Spirit) wants to dwell with man in a place for our mutual abode: *"…And this stone, which I have **set for a pillar**, shall be **God's house**…"* (Gen 28:19,22) Also: *"…**If a man love me**, he will **keep my words**: and my Father will love him, and we will come unto him, and **make our abode** with him."* (Jhn14:23)

The pillar represents the basic material and support for God's house and Jesus promises to come and dwell with those who love him and keep his words. Remember, it is the overcomer who loves God and keeps His words. Jesus' vow to the overcomers in the church of Philadelphia is for us to be a very pillar in His Holy temple!

After Jacob awakens from his sleep, the first thing that he says is, *"surely the LORD is in this place...How **awesome** is this place!"* (Gen 28:16-17 – NKJV) Upon realizing the significance of God's pledge to the overcomer in the church of Philadelphia, we might add: how **awesome** is this promise! As the leading apostles were called "pillars" in the early church (Gal 2:9), the overcomer will be regarded as a "pillar" in the coming millennial temple.

### Commendation

In addition to the four immense promises mentioned above in Rev 3:12, Jesus praises the church in three more areas:

*1) "I know your works. See, I have set before you an **open door**, and no one can shut it; for you have a little strength, **have kept My word, and have not denied My name**."* (Rev 3:8 – NKJV)

The members of this church are faithful believers who keep Gods word and do not deny Jesus before men. Even though they have little strength, they are loyal followers who exhibit Christ to others in their daily walk. Because of this, he grants them an open door, which is a picture of their entry into the coming Kingdom, as a reward for their faithfulness in keeping His word.

*2) "Indeed I will make those of the synagogue of Satan, who say they are Jews and are not, but lie—indeed I will **make them come and worship before your feet**, and to know that **I have loved you**."* (Rev 3:9 – NKJV)

The church of Philadelphia suffered oppression by these false Jews. Remember, those in the church of Smyrna (see pp. 27-28) also underwent repression by a group of Jews. The Lord promises that he will make these Jews come and worship before their feet and to let them know that He loves them.

3) *"Because thou hast **kept the word of my patience**, I also will **keep thee from the hour of temptation**, which shall come upon all the world, to try them that dwell upon the earth."*(Rev 3:10)

This wonderful promise to the members of this church is the Lord's guarantee that because they have patiently kept his word, they can be assured of being **kept from** the coming tribulation period (Beirnes, Lang, Lee, Mize, Newell and Seiss). These believers did not compromise the word and they were faithful in obeying what it teaches. As James instructs us, they were *"**doers of the word**, and not hearers only..."* (Jas 1:22) Because of their commitment to holding firmly to his word, Jesus will remove them from the earth before the hour of testing begins.

Finally, Jesus gives these faithful church members one last word to encourage them: *"Behold, I am coming quickly! Hold fast what you have, that no one may take your crown."* (Rev 3:11 – NKJV) When Christ returns, it will happen very suddenly. The possibility of losing one's crown (reward) always exists, even for committed believers. Remember, the great Apostle Paul was concerned that he could be disqualified for the prize (1 Co 9:24-27) so the Lord's reminder is an encouragement to remain diligent and steadfast to the very end.

Our brief study of this most dedicated church of Philadelphia has shown us how important it is to be the overcomer that Jesus is calling us to be. Devoted believers who are found keeping God's word will be richly rewarded for their loyalty to Christ. Obedience to Jesus is of utmost importance and overcomers desire to please the Lord in everything that they do. For them, compromise is not an option. Even though we may be tested every single day, we always need to keep our eyes on Jesus and come to him whenever we realize we cannot continue in our own strength. We need His help in order to finish our race:

> *"...let us also lay aside every encumbrance and the sin which so easily entangles us, and let us run with endurance the race that is set before us, **fixing our eyes on Jesus**, the author and perfecter of faith, who for the joy set before Him endured the cross, despising the shame, and has sat down at the right hand of the throne of God."* (Heb 12:1-2 – NAS)

Living in our modern, fast-paced world, surrounded by materialism, corruption, depravity and immorality, is a most formidable challenge for the average believer. Jesus is calling out to those who really love him and asking us to uphold his teachings that will be noticed by others and motivate them to seek the true answer to life's numerous difficulties.

If we are successful in our walk with him, we will be rewarded with matchless honors including: an open door into reigning with Jesus in the coming millennial Kingdom, becoming a pillar in God's temple, and if we should be alive before he returns for His bride, the promise of escaping the rapidly approaching tribulation period that will soon engulf this planet in horrifying and tumultuous times, which will be described more fully in the chapters to follow. Because escape from this terrible period is promised to those who are successful overcomers, they will be praying the prayer Jesus taught us to pray on a regular basis:

*"Watch ye therefore, and pray always, that ye may be accounted worthy to escape all these things that shall come to pass, and to stand before the Son of man."* (Luk 21:36)

> *"He who has an ear, let him hear what the Spirit says to the churches."* (Rev 3:13 – NKJV)

### Church of Laodicea (Rev 3:14-22)

> *"To him who overcomes I will grant to **sit with Me on My throne**, as I also overcame and sat down with My Father on His throne."* (Rev 3:21 – NKJV)

When we reach the final church, it has become degraded to the point that Jesus is pictured standing outside the door knocking to try to get in!  Prophetically, this represents the modern church of today, which is not commended for even one thing. It is described as lukewarm with Jesus getting ready to cast it into the tribulation period, if it does not repent in time.

For the believer who overcomes, Jesus promises the incredible opportunity of being able to share Christ's throne in the coming millennial Kingdom.

### O.T. Reference

To better understand what is being offered to those who are able to overcome, let's look into the Old Testament for additional consideration.  Just prior to being stoned for his faith in Jesus, Stephen gives a lengthy testimony that is recorded for us in Acts 7:1-53. At the very end of his speech, Stephen instructs the Jews on how God does not dwell in man-made temples:

> *"However, the Most High does not dwell in temples made with hands, as the prophet says:*
> > *"**Heaven is My throne**, And earth is My footstool. What house will you build for Me? says the LORD, Or what is the place of My rest? Has My hand not made all these things?"'* (Act 7:48-50 – NKJV)

Stephen ended his quote from Isaiah 66:1-2, without finishing the entire passage, because he realized they were: *"...stiffnecked and uncircumcised in heart and ears, ye do always resist the Holy Ghost..."* (Act 7:51) If he had finished the passage it says:

> *"...But on this one will I look: On him who is poor and of a contrite spirit, And who trembles at My word."*
> (Isa 66:2 – NKJV)

Stephen realized that these Jews would not comprehend what the Prophet Isaiah meant. God no longer desires people to require a material man-made temple in order to worship him. He is looking for a people who have a *"poor and contrite spirit"* in which He can come and dwell. The throne in this new temple is the throne of the person's heart: *"...Christ Jesus himself being the cornerstone, in whom the whole structure, being joined together, grows into a **holy temple in the Lord**. In him you also are being **built together into a dwelling place for God by the Spirit**."* (Eph 2:20-22 – ESV) The type of believer God is looking for is one who has a reverence for God's holy Word that comes to him with a humble and contrite heart in submission to Him. This is the type of person Jesus is looking for in the overcomer. The successful overcomer is then given the magnificent reward to share Christ's throne in the same manner that He shares the throne with God on His throne!

## Commendation

As mentioned earlier, the church of Laodicea had nothing to be commended for by the Lord. *"**I know your works**, that you are neither cold nor hot. I could wish you were cold or hot. So then, **because you are lukewarm**, and neither cold nor hot, **I will vomit you out of My mouth**. Because you say, 'I am **rich**, have become wealthy, and have **need of nothing**'–and do not know that you are **wretched, miserable, poor, blind, and naked**..."* (Rev 3:15-17 – NKJV)

These are rather scathing remarks by Jesus. Many have commented that these must not even be true believers, however, this is reputed by the Lord's comment: *"As many as I love, I rebuke and chasten..."* (Rev 3:19 – NKJV) Jesus only chastens and rebukes his own (Heb 12:5-6 and Pro 3:11-12).

Yes, these are genuine believers who have deceived themselves into thinking that they are model Christians. They think they have it all together and that they don't need anything. They don't realize that Jesus views them as being:

**Wretched** – Their love and worship of mammon, instead of loving and worshiping Jesus, has made them quite despicable.
**Miserable** – They are truly unhappy because of their false deception of being rich; when in fact they are very poor, from a spiritual standpoint.
**Poor** – Whereas the church of Smyrna was very poor financially, but spiritually rich, the church of Laodicea is very materially rich, but spiritually bankrupt.
**Blind** – Because those in this church appear to not read or know the Scriptures (Christ outside), they are spiritually blind to truth.
**Naked** – While these believers have obtained their robe of righteousness provided by Christ, Jesus says that they are naked because they have not been preparing their wedding garment of fine linen (see discussion of Sardis, pp. 37-39 and Rev 19:6-8).

Because of their destitute spiritual state, Jesus tells them to come to Him to acquire what they truly need (Rev 3:18–NKJV):

*"I counsel you to buy from Me gold refined in the fire, that you may be rich..."* Gold tried in the fire is a picture of the believer undergoing the trial of their faith: *"That the trial of your faith, being much more precious than of gold that perisheth, though it be tried with fire, might be found unto praise and honour and glory at the appearing of Jesus Christ..."* (1 Pe 1:7)

Believers who are able to undergo such trials and successfully overcome them with the Lord's help will be considered truly rich and be rewarded when they appear at his Judgement Seat.

*"...white garments, that you may be clothed, that the shame of your nakedness may not be revealed..."* Jesus wants believers to prepare their own wedding garments of fine linen as described

above and in the discussion of the church of Sardis. They are currently viewed by Jesus as naked and he wants them to acquire the necessary fine linen while time still remains.

*"...anoint your eyes with eye salve, that you may see."* The Holy Spirit is the one that comes to the believer when they are saved. Apparently, the carnal life of these believers has quenched the Holy Spirit and caused the terrible blindness that they have. Jesus wants them to be filled once again (Eph 5:18) so that they can be guided into all truth (Jhn 16:13) and be given the spiritual sight they so desperately need.

Jesus then finishes his admonitions and instructions with a most startling invitation:

*"As many as I love, I rebuke and chasten. Therefore be zealous and repent." "Behold, I stand at the door and knock. If anyone hears My voice and opens the door, I will come in to him and dine with him, and he with Me."* (Rev 3:19-20 – NKJV)

Sadly, Jesus is pictured outside the church knocking on the door to come in. He wants to come dine with them, if they will only open the doors of their hearts. Remember, Jesus is the bread of life (Jhn 6:35) and he wants to provide the members of the church with their proper nourishment and intimate fellowship. (Many believe this verse pictures the need for salvation, however, this claim was addressed earlier in discussing how Jesus only chastens his own).

From our review of the church of Laodicea, we have discovered what happens when the members take their eyes off of Jesus and become satisfied with the artificial success they perceive as being the result of God's blessing. Jesus is so displeased, he is seen knocking on the door, trying to come in. He is calling for them to repent now, before it is too late, or they will be cast into the coming tribulation period.

Jesus is crying out to those believers who have an ear to hear his voice. He wants to come reside on the very throne of our heart. Those who come to him with a humble and contrite spirit can be the overcomer that Jesus is looking for.

> *"For thus saith the high and lofty One that inhabiteth eternity, whose name is Holy;* **I dwell in the high and holy place, with him also** *that is of a contrite and humble spirit, to revive the spirit of the humble, and to revive the heart of the contrite ones."* (Isa 57:15)

God wants to revive our spirits and fill our hearts with the very presence of his Spirit. The power of His life in ours allows us to be triumphant when faced with the many trials and tribulations that will come to test our faith (Jas 1:2-4, 12). The working of his life in ours by the Spirit will help us accomplish the works that God prepared in advance for us to do (Eph 2:10), providing our wedding garments of fine linen (Rev 19:7-8). Our great love and reverence for His word will provide us with a lamp to guide every step of our journey in this life (Psa 119:105). Because of our immense love for Him, and to acknowledge our gratitude for his presence in our heart; we will present our very lives as a living sacrifice as our way of worshiping him like the Apostle Paul taught (Rom 12:1).

Today, God is calling all believers to be overcomers. Those who are successful will be granted the unsurpassed opportunity to share the Lord's throne in the coming millennium.

*"Therefore, as the Holy Spirit says,* **"Today, if you hear his voice, do not harden your hearts**...*For we have come to share in Christ, if indeed we hold our original confidence firm to the end."* (Heb 3:7-8, 14 – ESV)

> **"He who has an ear, let him hear what the Spirit says to the churches."** (Rev 3:22 – NKJV)

# Chapter 2 – 7 Seals

## Throne in Heaven (Revelation 4)

> *"After these things I looked, and behold, a door standing open in heaven. And the first voice which I heard was like a trumpet speaking with me, saying, 'Come up here, and I will show you things which must take place after this.' Immediately I was in the Spirit; and behold, **a throne set in heaven**, and One sat on the throne. And He who sat there was like a jasper and a sardius stone in appearance; and there was **a rainbow around the throne**, in appearance like an emerald."*
> (Rev 4:1-3–NKJV)

John finishes describing the *"things which are"* (Rev 1:19) with the promise for the overcomer to share Christ's throne in heaven, and he is immediately taken up to heaven where he is given a rare glimpse of God the Father sitting on his throne. The vision that John records is strikingly similar to the one given to the prophet Ezekiel, which also pictures the awesome majesty of God sitting on his throne, overseeing all of creation.[1] As the Psalmist David declares:

> *"**The LORD has established his throne in the heavens**, and **his kingdom rules over all**. Bless the LORD, O you **his angels, you mighty ones who do his word, obeying the voice of his word!**"* (Psa 103:19-20 – ESV)

Yes, God is in control and He reigns over the entire universe! This is certainly an encouragement to think of when we are faced with all the trials, tests and tribulations that we encounter in our daily living in this fallen world. Whenever we may feel down or that life's challenges are about to get the best of us, we need to remember that God is in control and that we can conquer any situation with His help. Yes, He will help us be the overcomer that he is calling us to be. And those who are successful overcomers will be granted the remarkable privilege of sharing in the Lord's throne – ruling and reigning with Him.

### 24 Elders

John continues his description of the throne room by telling us who is seated around God's throne: *"Around the throne were twenty-four thrones, and on the thrones I saw* **twenty-four elders** *sitting, clothed in white robes; and they had crowns of gold on their heads."* (Rev 4:4 – NKJV)

The identity of who these 24 elders are has been highly debated and misunderstood. The fact that they are seated on thrones, wearing white garments with crowns on their heads, has led many to believe that they represent redeemed men (Beirnes, Hendriksen, Mize, Morris and Seiss). Some feel they represent the bride of Christ, while others believe they include men from both the Old and New dispensations, symbolized by the 12 patriarchs and the 12 apostles. This author once held the view they are men, however, upon further study and investigation, their true identity is found to be 24 angelic beings around God's throne (Bullinger, Chitwood, Ladd, Lang, Lee and Mounce).

These 24 elders are seen sitting on their thrones **before** Jesus has even entered the picture. Remember, Jesus told his disciples that they would sit on their heavenly throne **after** he sits on His throne (Matthew 18:28). Jesus does not take His throne in heaven until the very end of the tribulation period (Rev 11:15 and Rev 19:6) therefore those qualified to share the Lord's throne cannot do so until He takes his own seat. Once Jesus completes his mission described in the rest of John's vision and assumes His throne, **then** the overcoming saints will take their thrones. Until then, these 24 highly exalted elders are angels who will continue to serve God as elders in the divine **rule of the universe**[2] as noted above: **"...*you mighty ones who do his word, obeying the voice of his word!"*** (Psa 103:20 – ESV)

Further proof that these 24 elders must be angelic beings will be provided below in their song of praise.

## Living Creatures

After the elders are introduced, John paints a magnificent picture of the throne room where he sees 4 living creatures:
*"And from the throne proceeded **lightnings**, **thunderings**, and **voices**. Seven **lamps of fire** were burning before the throne, which are the seven Spirits of God. Before the throne there was a sea of glass, like crystal. And in the midst of the throne, and around the throne, were **four living creatures** full of eyes in front and in back. The first living creature was **like a lion**, the second living creature **like a calf**, the third living creature had **a face like a man, and the fourth living creature was like a flying eagle**."* (Rev 4:5-7 – NKJV)

These 4 living creatures have the appearance of a lion, a calf, a man and an eagle. These descriptions are quite similar to those in Ezekiel's vision (Eze 10:14) where these beings are depicted as **cherubim**, which lends support that these 4 living creatures are highly exalted angelic beings who surround the throne of God. These creatures are seen leading the praise and worship of God; extolling His holiness, greatness and omnipotence: *"...they rest not day and night, saying, Holy, holy, holy, Lord God Almighty, which was, and is, and is to come."* (Rev 4:8)

## Song of Praise for Creation

*"And **when** the **living creatures** give glory and honor and thanks to Him who sits on the throne, to Him who lives forever and ever, **the twenty-four elders** will fall down before Him who sits on the throne, and will worship Him who lives forever and ever, and **will cast their crowns** before the throne, saying,*
> *'Worthy are You, our Lord and our God, to receive **glory** and **honor** and **power**; for **You created all things**, and because of **Your will** they existed, and were created.'"* (Rev 4:9-11 – NAS)

The 4 living creatures are seen leading the praise and worship of the Almighty God who created the entire universe. This is an awesome scene that is worth taking the time to meditate upon. When the living creatures sing, the 24 elders fall down before God in adoration and praise; giving Him all glory, honor and power for the creation of all things. In their reverence and exaltation of our great God, John tells us that they: *"will cast their crowns before the throne."*

Here we see that these 24 elders will eventually cast their crowns before God's throne. This is an important event that will take place just before Jesus takes His throne and presents the overcoming saints with their crowns as they take their thones.[3] Right before these events transpire, the 24 angelic elders will relinquish their crowns before the throne in order that Jesus may award the redeemed saints with their crowns and thrones. These divine heavenly events are significant proceedings that represent the **transfer** of the **rule of the universe** from the angelic hosts to Jesus and the redeemed *"sons of God,"* which the Apostle Paul states all of creation is eagerly anticipating:

*"For I consider that the sufferings of this present time are not worthy to be compared with the **glory which shall be revealed in us. For the earnest expectation of the creation eagerly waits for the revealing of the sons of God.** "* (Rom 8:18-19 – NKJV)

Once the angelic elders relinquish their crowns, Jesus will reveal the *"sons of God"* who will be granted the incredible opportunity to rule and reign with him.

Until this glorious revealing of the *"sons of God"* takes place, John's vision of the throne in heaven shows us a remarkable picture of the majestic regality of our great God surrounded by angelic beings, giving unceasing praise and worship for his vast creation.

**Scroll and the Lamb (Revelation 5)**

After John describes the previous scene, he is shown God holding in his right hand a scroll that is written on both sides of the paper sealed with 7 seals. An angel laments that no one in heaven or earth is worthy to open the scroll – then an elders tells John:

> *"Stop weeping; behold, **the Lion** that is from the tribe of Judah, the Root of David, **has overcome** so as to open the book [scroll] and its seven seals."* (Rev 5:5 – NAS)

John is told that the Lion from the tribe of Judah has **overcome** and is therefore considered **worthy** to open the sacred writing. Jesus is described by the elder as a Lion, which is a portrayal of his mighty power and strength capable of defeating his enemies. John probably remembered the Lord had previously told the disciples: *"These things I have spoken to you, so that in **Me you may have peace**. In the **world you have tribulation**, but **take courage; I have overcome the world**."* (Jhn 16:33 – NAS)

Yes, Jesus has defeated our great enemy Satan by His death and resurrection. Because of his great victory of conquering the grave we can have peace and take courage in all the many trials and tribulations that may come our way. Jesus has overcome our greatest enemy – we have nothing to fear because of this.

While John did not see the Lion that the elder reported, he looked and saw Jesus (as a Lamb) standing between God's throne and the elders: *"And I saw...a **Lamb standing**, as if slain, having seven horns and seven eyes, which are the seven Spirits of God, sent out into all the earth."* (Rev 5:6 – NAS)

John had witnessed the Lord's death, but now he sees him having 7 horns, which represent divine power (omnipotence) and 7 eyes that stand for his all-knowing Spirit over everything (omniscience). No enemy can defeat the all-powerful strength of Jesus. Nothing can escape His ever-watchful notice. These attributes of our Lord provide the believer with added confidence in his ability to help us, no matter what we may face now or in the future.

Jesus then approaches the throne and takes the scroll out of the right hand of God the Father. This a beautiful picture of how God holds complete sovereignty over the entire realm of history. The 7 sealed scroll represents both the inheritance of the righteous and the judgement of the wicked. God holds the future in his hand and in the transfer of the scroll to Jesus gives him complete authority over mankind's destiny. Recognizing how solemn this action is, the entire angelic hosts fall down in reverent worship:

> *"And He came and **took the book** out of the right hand of Him who sat on the throne. When He had taken the book, the four living creatures and the twenty-four elders **fell down before the Lamb**, each one holding a harp and golden bowls full of incense, which are the prayers of the saints."* (Rev 5:7-8 – NAS)

In this solemn scene, the 24 elders are seen holding bowls filled with the prayers of the redeemed. This should invigorate our prayer life when we realize that all of our appeals to God are coming before the One who is able to answer our pleadings. When we go into our prayer closet (Mat 6:6), we can rest assured that God does hear and answer all of our prayers.

After falling down in recognition of the fact that all power in heaven and on earth has been given to God's Son (Mat 28:18), the heavenly hosts sign a new song:

### New Song of Redemption
*"And they sang a **new song**, saying, "Worthy are You to take the book and to break its seals; for You were slain, and **purchased for God with Your blood men** from every tribe and*

***tongue and people and nation. You have made them to be a kingdom and priests*** *to our God; and they* ***will reign*** *upon the earth. "* (Rev 5:9-10 – NAS)[4]

This new song of redemption is different from the song that the elders sang in the previous chapter. There they were praising God for all that he had done in the creation of the universe. Here they are signing praises for the fact that Jesus has sacrificed his very life's blood to redeem all of mankind and to ransom us from the power of sin and death. Those who are called, chosen and faithful (Rev 17:14) will become priests of God, ruling and reigning in the coming Kingdom. This is an awesome promise that warrants a new song to be proclaimed before the heavenly throne.

John finishes his description of the throne room by telling us that innumerable angels sing praise, followed by all of creation joining in the praise and worship:

> *"Worthy is the Lamb that was slain to receive power and riches and wisdom and might and honor and glory and blessing. ... 'To Him who sits on the throne, and to the Lamb, be blessing and honor and glory and dominion forever and ever. "'* (Rev 5:12-13 – NAS)

The four living creatures appropriately end this section by adding *"Amen."* The opening of the seals is about to commence.

Before we begin to observe the opening of the 7 Seals, we should pause for a moment to evaluate an overview of the entire book. Readers may want to turn back to the "Detailed Table of Contents" (pp. x and xi.), which provides a good picture of the majority of the book. The reader will notice that the entire book of Revelation can be divided into 7 major sections with 7 key divisions within each of these 7 sections.[5] In addition to this amazing aspect, you will notice that the 2nd section through the 6th section share a unique feature: there is a distinctive pause between the 6th and 7th divisions. This remarkable detail can be summarized as follows:

| Section | | Pause<br>(Time-out) | |
|---------|---------|-----------------------|----------|
| 2 | Seal 6 | Interlude<br>(Rev 7) | Seal 7 |
| 3 | Trumpet 6 | Interlude<br>(Rev 10-11) | Trumpet 7 |
| 4 | Vision 6 | Beatitude<br>for Martyr's | Vision 7 |
| 5 | Vial 6 | Beatitude<br>for Watchful | Vial 7 |
| 6 | Voice 6 | Beatitude<br>for Bride | Voice 7 |

Notice that in section 2 and 3, there is a major pause in the action between the Seals and the Trumpet Judgments. These significant breaks in the proceedings appear to be designed in order that the reader can gain further perspective and insight into how the first 6 events are about to come to a close with the final judgments.

For the 4th, 5th, and 6th sections the pause in the action is quite brief; allowing significant Beatitudes to be inserted in order to alert the reader that things are about to come to their ultimate conclusion. It is worth noting that each of the Beatitudes offer appropriate promises to those groups in relation to the circumstances that are being experienced in that section.

**Seal #1: White Horse (Rev 6:1-2)**

> *"And I saw when the Lamb opened one of the seals, and I heard one of the four living creatures saying, as it were a voice of thunder, 'Come and behold!' and I saw, and lo, **a white horse**, and he who is sitting upon it is having a **bow**, and there was given to him a **crown**, and he went forth overcoming[3528], and that he **may overcome**.[3528]"* (Rev 6:1-2 – YLT)

The much anticipated opening of the sealed scroll has arrived. The Lion from the tribe of Judah who John saw as a Lamb had overcome (Rev 5:5 - #3528)[6] and is considered worthy to open the seals of this sacred writing, which is about to reveal how the inheritance of the righteous and the judgement of the wicked will be carried out. Once the Lamb opens the first seal, one of the angelic living creatures tells John to come and observe a white horse coming forth. But who is the person riding on this majestic white horse?

The popular tradition in the church today is that the rider on the white horse is the Antichrist, who is getting ready to emerge on the scene. This teaching has permeated much of modern culture and this author had been captivated by this belief for most of his life. Breaking from such a steeply engrained tradition is very difficult. Most will scoff and reject any teaching that does not match popular thought. A similar situation surrounds the traditional teaching that this same Antichrist is getting ready to confirm and then break a 7-year peace treaty halfway through. This author broke from this traditional view in 2007 and the reader can learn more about this topic in Appendix 3.

The reader is encouraged to keep an open mind with a teachable heart as we delve into what the Scripture has to say about the true identity of the rider on this white horse John saw coming forth at the opening of this 1st seal. In order to properly analyze

John's vision, let's first look into the Old Testament for additional insight about who the rider really is.

### Horses

As the first four seals are opened, John sees 4 horses riding forth. The Prophet Zechariah also had visions of 4 horses that can be read in Zec 1:7-11 and 6:1-8. In the first vision, the prophet sees a man standing among the trees who many believe was the pre-incarnate Jesus Christ (John 1:14) i.e., he was an angel of the Lord who was also the rider on the first horse.[7] It is important to note that these four horses were sent out by the Lord to patrol the earth: *'These are they whom the LORD has sent to patrol the earth.'* (Zec 1:10 – ESV) Here we have a picture of God sending out 4 horses to traverse the earth. The rider on Zechariah's 1st horse represents Christ, while the remaining 3 horses are assisting with the mission of patrolling the earth. In like manner, the rider on the 1st horse in John's vision has just been sent out from the throne of God to carry out the specific (albeit different) mission noted earlier. The contention of this book is that Christ is also the rider of the first horse with the other 3 horses also serving the purposes that are being directed from the throne in heaven.

Some may object that Zechariah's 1st horse is **red**, while John's 1st horse is **white**. While the two visions are similar, but not identical, this objection can be answered by noting that Christ had not yet conquered the grave and was therefore riding on a red horse in Zechariah's account. After Christ's conquest of death, he is seen riding on a **white** horse, which signifies not only holiness, purity and righteousness, but also **victory** as evidenced by the word *nikao* #3528, which is used twice in describing the purpose that this horse was sent out from heaven.

### Bow

In addition to Christ being the more likely candidate as the first horseman in John's vision, it also states he carries a bow with no mention of any arrows.  This depiction has led people to believe that this represents the Antichrist, who supposedly is going to bring peace and therefore will not need any arrows. Instead of trying to force this picture to say something, let's look into the Scriptures to help us with the true interpretation.

We need to remember that one of the main purposes of these seals is to bring the righteous into God's kingdom and judgment on the wicked in an attempt to bring them to repentance.  The rider on the white horse carries a bow, and Psalm 45 also shows Christ riding with a bow, conquering people with truth and righteousness as revealed in the following:

*"And in Your majesty **ride** prosperously because of truth, humility, and righteousness; And Your right hand shall teach You awesome things. Your arrows are sharp in the heart of the King's enemies; The peoples fall under You. **Your throne, O God, is forever and ever; A scepter of righteousness is the scepter of Your kingdom.**"* (Psa 45:4-6 – NKJV)

In the Greek Septuagint, verse 5 reads: *"**And in thy majesty ride, and bend the bow**, and prosper and reign..."* That the psalmist is referring to Christ is confirmed by other Scripture:
> *"**But to the Son He says**: "Your throne, O God, is forever and ever; A scepter of righteousness is the scepter of Your kingdom."* (Heb 1:8 – NKJV)

Psalm 45 therefore shows Christ riding out **conquering men's hearts** with righteousness, which is precisely what the rider on John's white horse is doing.  In addition, the Prophet Isaiah tells us: *"For when the earth experiences Your judgments The inhabitants of the world learn righteousness."* (Isa 26:9 – NAS)

The bow then represents the Word of God (*cf.* Hab 3:8-9), which is able to conquer men's hearts – one of the rider's main objectives.

From our brief review of the foregoing examples we see two distinct pictures of Christ riding forth on horses, carrying out either a direct mission from heaven, or one of conquering men with truth and righteousness. Both of these argue in favor of Christ being the rider on the 1$^{st}$ horse in John's vision. The cherished tradition that the 1$^{st}$ horseman is the Antichrist lacks even one comparable reference from Scripture to support it!

### Crowns

One of the objections raised regarding Christ as the rider on the 1$^{st}$ horse is that he is wearing a crown in Rev 6:1-2, while Christ is shown in Rev 19:11-15, on a white horse wearing many crowns. These differences need to be understood in light of the context of when these events are taking place.

In Rev 6, Christ is beginning his ride on the white horse after his triumph over the grave. As previously shown he is the victorious Lamb; and with the opening of the 1$^{st}$ seal he takes his seat on the white horse with the mission of **overcoming men's hearts** with the Gospel so they may also **be overcomers**. The crown Christ is wearing here is a victor's wreath (#4735 – *stephanos*), while in Rev 19, Christ is wearing many crowns (#1238 – *diadema*). The first worn by Christ is symbolic of his victory over death. Christ overcame death and is seen wearing a crown signifying his heavenly glory as the victor. For almost 2,000 years, Christ has been riding this white horse, conquering men's heart. Those who have crowned Him as their King will wear similar crowns as an emblem of his conquest in their life.

When Jesus returns in Rev 19, he will be wearing many crowns, signifying his regal power and authority because at that time he will be returning as the "KING OF KINGS, AND LORD OF LORDS." (Rev 19:16) These crowns are distinctive; revealing His stately regal position at that time. When understood in proper context, seemingly dissimilar crowns augment the contention that Christ is the rider on both horses.

The interpretation that Christ is the rider on the white horse under the 1st seal is not a new idea being advocated by this book. In fact, one of the oldest explanations available is that of Irenaeus, who was taught by Polycarp, a direct disciple of the Apostle John, the actual writer of the prophecy. In the 2nd century, Irenaeus stated in his **Against Heresies**: "For to this end the Lord born, the type of whose birth he set beforehand, of whom also John says in the Apocalypse: '**He went forth conquering, that He should conquer.**'"

In addition to being supported by the early church, various noted and respected scholars have advanced this same teaching down through the centuries. While various approaches to the book of Revelation have been developed, the teaching that Christ is the rider of the 1st horse has been held by expositors in each of the five methods. See Appendix 1, to discover the many well-regarded scholars who were proponents of this belief.

Before moving on to the 2nd seal, we need to remember that Jesus is indeed advancing and conquering the hearts of men open to hearing his Word and responding by crowning Him as the ruler of their hearts and lives. Because He overcame, he gives us the ability to also overcome. As the Apostle John said: **"...he went forth overcoming,** and that he **may overcome"** (Rev 6:1-2 – YLT)

One of the central messages in the book of Revelation is that God is indeed calling men out of this world to be genuine overcomers. This message is epitomized in the proper interpretation that Christ is the one riding the 1st horse in John's vision. Jesus Christ has been sent out from the throne of God to conquer men's hearts with the good news that he is the sacrificial Lamb that overcome death and has risen in victorious life. All men who come to embrace Him as the King of their heart will also be able to overcome any obstacle, trial or test that they may be faced with in this life.

**Seal #2: Red Horse (Rev 6:3-4)**

With the opening of the seals, God is revealing his magnificent plan to bring about the restoration of the world with Jesus Christ as the central means. He is the **Lion** from the tribe of Judah, the sacrificial **Lamb** who conquered death to redeem mankind from sin – worthy to open the seals on the scroll – and the majestic **Rider** on the 1st white horse, riding across the world for almost 2,000 years, conquering men's hearts with the Gospel. The remaining seals, trumpets and vials are all agents used by God to establish his righteous Kingdom. Remember, judgments are sent so men can learn righteousness (Isa 26:9).

The next 3 seals are represented by 3 horses that appear after Christ begins his ride of conquest. These horses symbolize the tests and trials being allowed by the throne in heaven to accomplish their objective of bringing men into God's righteous domain. These trials are experienced throughout the entire history of the world and will continue until Jesus returns to establish his Kingdom.

> *"And when He broke the **second seal**, I heard the second living creature call out, Come! And **another horse** came out, flaming red. And its rider was empowered to take the peace from the earth, so that* **men slaughtered**[4969] *one another; and he was given a huge* **sword**.[3162] *"* (Rev 6:3-4 – AMP)

When the 2nd seal is broken the 2nd living creature announces that **another**[8] horse appeared. John only uses the term another with the introduction of this horse which intimates that the first horse is different from the later three (the 1st rider being Christ with the 3 remaining riders being set apart since their purposes are to carry out other objectives of the throne).

The identity of the remaining 3 horses and their riders has been widely interpreted with varying ideas as to what they represent. The traditional view is that the 2$^{nd}$ horse represents **war**; the 3$^{rd}$ horse stands for **famine**, with the 4$^{th}$ horse used to bring a recapitulation of the prior judgments of war and famine with the addition of **pestilence** and **wild beasts**. This author once held the above views, however, upon further examination; the 2$^{nd}$ and 3$^{rd}$ horses appear to have slightly distinctive characteristics than what is held under this conventional teaching.

Jesus gives us a clue to a more accurate interpretation of the next two horses when he told his disciples:

> *"Think not that I am come to send peace on earth: I* ***came not to send peace****, but a **sword**."* (Mat 10:34)

The opening of the 2$^{nd}$ seal brings out the rider on the red horse, who came to take peace from the earth. The text does not mention war – only the removal of peace. Also, the sword the rider is yielding is used for men to **slaughter** #4969 (*sphazo*) one another. With one exception, this word is only used by John to indicate the death of Christ or the execution of believers (Hendriksen). The one exception is found in Rev 13:3, which refers to the supposed death of the Antichrist (as we will learn when we get to chapter 4, this man of sin does not even really die).

The primary use of slaughter is related to believers. This seems to indicate that **religious persecution** is what John is describing in the 2$^{nd}$ seal. This becomes even more apparent when we discover that Jesus' word for **sword** in Mat 10:34, is *machaira* (#3162), which actually means "a short sword or dagger." This type of short sword is primarily used in sacrifices and the persecution of believers. The rider on **the red horse** brings the slaughter of believers – red signifying the blood of the saints. His weapon (also a *machaira*) is not the type used in war, but to spill the blood of believers for upholding Christ. (*cf.* Rev 6:9)

An entirely different sword is used for war, as we will see when we review the sword used by the rider of the pale horse when the 4th seal is opened. The point is that the rider on the red horse is bringing the slaughter of believers. After Jesus rides out on the 1st white horse, the 2nd red horse brings the sword of persecution of believers; exactly as Jesus told his disciples would happen.

The persecution of believers has been taking place throughout the history of the church. Religious persecution has been well documented down through the centuries, beginning with the Apostles and the early church (see church of Smyrna) down to today, with such atrocities recently witnessed in Iraq with the slaughter of believers by ISIS (Islamic State in Iraq and Syria).

While persecution will always be with us, the overcomer can rest assured that Jesus overcame death, and we need not even fear death (Rev 2:10 and 12:11).

### Seal #3: Black Horse (Rev 6:5-6)

> *"When He broke open the **third seal**, I heard the third living creature call out, Come and look! And I saw, and behold, a **black horse**, and in his hand the rider had a pair of scales (a balance). And I heard what seemed to be a voice from the midst of the four living creatures, saying, A quart of wheat for a denarius [a whole day's wages], and three quarts of barley for a denarius; but do not harm the oil and the wine!"* (Rev 6:3-4 – AMP)

These verses have been widely interpreted as representing famine, however, if this is what John meant, why didn't he just say "famine" as he did when describing the judgments under the 4th seal? The most plausible explanation is that these conditions do not indicate famine, but rather severe scarcity affecting the very poor who cannot afford the basic necessities, while the rich continue to enjoy their many luxuries (Ladd, Mounce, and Hendriksen). Hendriksen goes further to suggest that the poor represent believers who are suffering religious persecution for their stand for Christ.[9] While some believers may face persecution by the rider on the red horse, others may be faced with situations that require them to uphold principles of righteousness, which result in economic loss and hardship.

The rider on this black horse appears to be sending out tests from God to determine if the believer will uphold values of truth and righteousness, or succumb to the temptation, and relinquish them in order to avoid monetary loss. Both the **red** horse (martyrdom) and the **black** horse (financial hardship) represent **religious persecution** by the world, which hates Jesus Christ. But always remember that these trials are only allowed under the sovereignty of the throne room and the overcomer who remains steadfast will rejoice because of these trials:

> *"Count it all joy, my brothers, when you meet trials of various kinds, for you know that the testing of your faith produces steadfastness."* (Jas 1:2-3 – ESV)

### Seal #4: Pale Horse (Rev 6:7-8)

> *"When the Lamb broke open the **fourth seal**, I heard the fourth living creature call out, Come! So I looked, and behold, an ashy pale horse [black and blue as if made so by bruising], and its rider's **name** was **Death**, and Hades (the realm of the dead) followed him closely. And they were given authority and power over a fourth part of the earth to kill with the **sword**[4501] and with **famine** and with **plague** (pestilence, disease) and with **wild beasts** of the earth."* (Rev 6:7-8 – AMP)

The 4th and final horse of the Apocalypse rides out and is ashy pale in color, which fits with the rider's ominous name: **Death**.

While the 2$^{nd}$ and 3$^{rd}$ horsemen are delivering trials aimed at believers, this final rider brings death and destruction to all of mankind – ever since our Lord's departure around 32 AD. The instruments this horseman uses to bring his anguish are: the sword (war), famine, plagues and wild beasts. These are the same afflictions mentioned in Eze 14:21 and they are judgments allowed by God to impact one fourth of the earth.

This horseman uses the sword as his first method of bringing death. A different word for "sword" is used than in the 2$^{nd}$ seal. There the sword was a *machaira* (#3162), which is a short sword or dagger used primarily in sacrifices and the persecution of believers. Here John uses the word *rhomphaia* (#4501), which represents a large sword or spear used in warfare. This same word is used in the Greek Septuagint translation of Eze 14:21 mentioned above. The 2$^{nd}$ horseman wielded the short sword (*machaira*) for religious persecution; the 4$^{th}$ horseman carries a large sword (*rhomphaia*) for war (*cf.* Rev 2:16; 19:21).

Mankind has experienced the devastation of war down through the centuries, and it will continue until the Prince of Peace returns. The second manner of bringing death is famine, which has also been responsible for untold misery throughout history. Millions upon millions of people have died because of the lack of food, despite efforts by many aimed at relieving this dreadful affliction. War and famine are frequently followed by plagues caused by pestilence and disease; and a land that is ravaged by such desolations would certainly be fertile ground for invasion by wild animals.

While believers were the target of the horsemen on the red and black horses, this pale horse causes suffering for all of mankind. God allows these judgments for the sanctification of believers and to teach unbelievers righteousness. In his great love for men he permits afflictions so they will learn to look to the Lamb and to trust in Him for the solution to all of their many woes.

## Seal #5: Martyrs under Altar (Rev 6:9-11)

*"When He opened the fifth seal, I saw under the altar the souls of those who **had been slain**[4969] for **the word of God and for the testimony which they held**. And they cried with a loud voice, saying,*
> *'How long, O Lord, holy and true, until You judge and avenge our blood on those who dwell on the earth?'*
*Then a white robe was given to each of them; and it was said to them that they should **rest a little while longer**, until both the number of their fellow servants and their brethren, who would be killed as they were, was completed."* (Rev 6:9-11 – NKJV)

The 5th seal is fairly self-explanatory. These souls that are seen under the heavenly altar are the martyrs down through the history of the church, who were slain #4969 (*sphazo*) for religious persecution described under the 2nd seal. They cry out to the Lord to vindicate the shedding of their blood, and they are told they will need to wait a while longer.

The white robes given to these martyrs are also referred to in the great multitude of martyrs that are seen coming out of the great tribulation (*cf.* Rev 7:9, 13-14). This is why the martyrs under the altar are instructed to wait a little longer. There will be more martyrs coming from the tribulation period that is about to begin once the events under the 6th seal get underway.

## Seal #6: Great Earthquake (Rev 6:12-17)

The opening of the 6th seal brings us to the time when dramatic changes are about to take place. The events portrayed in the next six verses have never been experienced before on the earth. While they were predicted to occur by the prophets, the degree of calamity about to engulf this planet will affect the lives of mankind far beyond what anyone has ever encountered or imagined. The Great Tribulation is about to begin.

### Great Earthquake – Sun / Moon

*"And I beheld when he had opened the sixth seal, and, lo, there was a **great earthquake**; and the **sun became black** as sackcloth of hair, and the **moon became as blood...**"* (Rev 6:12)

When the Lamb opens of the 6th seal, a great earthquake takes place.   This earthquake will be unlike any the earth has undergone before – creating widespread volcanic eruptions throughout the earth.   Plumes of volcanic ash will be dispersed over a widespread area, causing the sun to become darkened and the moon to appear as blood red.

On the day of Pentecost, the Apostle Peter predicted this day would come when he quoted the Prophet Joel (*cf.* 2:30-31):

> *"And I will shew wonders in heaven above, and signs in the earth beneath; blood, and fire, and vapour of smoke: The **sun shall be turned into darkness, and the moon into blood**, before that **great** and notable **day of the Lord** come..."* (Act 2:19-20)

Peter is telling us that these events associated with the opening of the 6th seal will take place **before** the great day of the Lord begins.   The great earthquake will cause major disruptions, creating widespread panic and fear. On the heels of this earthquake, John records more dramatic calamities that are difficult to imagine:

### Heavens Vanish – Mountains & Islands Move

*"And the heaven departed as a **scroll** when it is **rolled together**;[10] and every **mountain and island were moved** out of their places."* (Rev 6:14)

We need to understand that the judgments described under the 6th seal, the trumpets and the vials will all take place over a period of 3 ½ years.   The 6th seal introduces the initiation of the tribulation, which will progress in ever increasing magnitude.

The preceding verse states that every mountain and island is moved out of their places. This may be difficult to comprehend, however, a recent event occurred in 2004 that gives us an idea about how this event could take place.

Readers may recall that on December 26, 2004 the Great Tsunami took place in which close to 250,000 people were killed. This tsunami was caused by an underwater **earthquake** that measured 9.3 on the Richter scale. Scientist who studied the effects of this disaster determined that in places the earth's crust moved between 10 to 15 meters (50 feet) and the entire island of Sumatra was reported to have moved 100 feet.[11]

The earthquake that began the Great Tsunami was a precursor to the Great Earthquake predicted to unveil the 6th seal. It will be more enormous than any the earth has experienced; and yet, as the tribulation period progresses, the trumpets and vials will continue to build into a great crescendo with the 7th vial:

> *"And there were voices, and thunders, and lightnings; and there was a **great earthquake**, such as was not since men were upon the earth, so mighty an earthquake, and so great."* (Rev 16:18)

So while the earthquake that inaugurates the tribulation period will be great, the final earthquake scheduled to bring the final climax will be even more tremendous. One can now easily understand how *"every **mountain and island were moved** out of their places,"* as predicted in John's vision.

John also sees the *"stars of heaven"* falling to earth. How can this be?

### Falling Stars

*"And the stars of heaven **fell unto the earth**, even as a fig tree casteth her untimely figs, when she is shaken of a **mighty wind**."* (Rev 6:13)

Interpretations by commentators are not in agreement as to how this portion of the vision will be fulfilled. Some believe the falling stars represent heavy meteor showers (Morris, Seiss and Thomas) while others see them as a shower from the tail of a comet passing by the earth (Bowman).[12] While either comets or meteors falling to the earth could be what the prophet saw, there is also another possible explanation to what could cause such a phenomenon.

Space scientists regularly monitor solar flares for their effect on our planet. In December 2013, it was reported that the earth experienced a "near miss" of a solar super storm that occurred in July 2012.[13] Evidently, a major CME (coronal mass ejection) took place that passed though the Earth's orbit one week ahead of the time our planet reached that point. Had this CME been one week later, the results could have been catastrophic. Scientists agree that intense storms from the surface of the sun could **disrupt satellites**, communications and power grids on earth and even endanger astronauts. These CME's are caused by twisted magnetic fields in the sun that suddenly snap and release tremendous amounts of energy.

Could satellites falling from the sky be what John witnessed in his vision under the 6th seal? Scientists believe strong "solar winds" could disrupt the orbits of the satellites. Are these the mighty winds that God will use to make the "stars" fall to the earth? If so, then this portion of the 6th seal could be far worse than a meteor shower.

Remember that the action described from the 6th seal, through the trumpets, and then the vials, happen over an extended period of time. As we will observe when the 7th seal is opened, it contains all of the 7 trumpets, and the 7th trumpet includes all of the 7 vials. The 6th seal sets everything in motion that continues until the 7th trumpet, and 7th vial all conclude about the same time at the very end of the tribulation period.

The fact that the 6th seal initiates end time events can also be observed by the reaction of mankind once it begins.  We are told in Rev 6:15-16 that people will want to hide in caves to seek shelter from the coming furry under which no one will be able to stand up against when God's wrath arrives.

> *"For the **great day of his wrath** is come; and who shall be able to stand?"* (Rev 6:17)

This verse confirms that the day of the Lord's wrath comes **after** the 6th seal has been opened.  While God's final wrath does not actually begin with the first great earthquake under the 6th seal, it does begin when the 7 angels pour out the **vials of his wrath**, which takes place under the 7th trumpet:

> *"And I heard a great voice out of the temple saying to the **seven angels**, Go your ways, and **pour out the vials of the wrath of God** upon the earth."* (Rev 16:1)

### Seal #7: Silence in Heaven (Rev 8:1-6)

But before the final calamites begin, and the angels prepare to sound their 7 trumpets, the Lamb opens the 7th and final seal, which produces a great **silence in heaven**:  *"And when he had opened the **seventh seal**, there was **silence in heaven** about the space of half an hour...And the seven angels which had the seven trumpets prepared themselves to sound."* (Rev 8:1, 6)

This silence in heaven is a rather ominous time.  The final judgments of the tribulation period are about to be unleashed.  The scroll is now completely open, the final days have arrived.

---

**Summary of 7 Seals, 7 Trumpets and 7 Vials**
At this point in our review of the first 6 chapters of the book of Revelation, the reader my feel a little overwhelmed.  To give us a better perspective, the chart on the following page was developed.  Please refer back to it as we continue our study.
(A full-color 8½ x 11 copy of this chart is available on our website.)

---

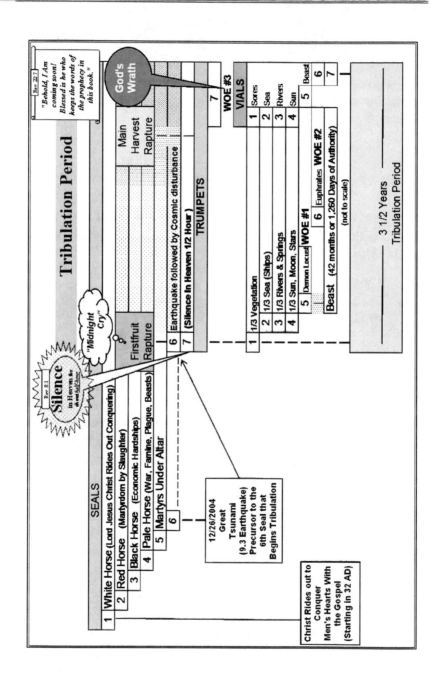

---

**Summary of 7 Seals, 7 Trumpets and 7 Vials**

The chart on the facing page gives a comprehensive overview of how these judgments take place over the history of the church, from the time Jesus rides out to conquer men's hearts in order to enable them to be the overcomers He is calling them to be. The reader will notice that the seals continue throughout the entire age with the 6th seal ushering in the tribulation period as the 7 trumpets (p. 79) are introduced. As the 7th trumpet sounds, God **then** pours out the final 7 vials (p.117) of his wrath on the earth.

The Firstfruit rapture occurs prior to the start of the tribulation with the removal of the **overcoming** believers found worthy to escape (p.106). The remaining believers will be faced with an additional period of trials and testing, but will be removed from the planet in the Main Harvest rapture, just before God pours out his wrath (pp.110-115).

God is **calling overcomers** to be part of the 1st assembly.

---

## Interlude: 144,000 & Great Multitude (Rev 7)

Chapter 7 was inserted between the 6th and 7th seals to give the reader additional information before the final seal is opened. It's as if we are allowed to take a short intermission before the concluding judgments begin. In this brief interlude, we are given the details of two different groups of people and God's plans for their lives.

### 144,000 Children of Israel Sealed

John first sees four angels standing on the four corners of the earth, holding back the winds so they would not blow. These angels are empowered to harm the earth and the sea, but they are told by another angel, who has the *"seal of the living God,"* not to harm the earth, the sea, or the trees until God's servants are sealed on their foreheads. They then seal the 144,000 from all of the tribes of the children of Israel (see Rev 7:1-8).

The identity of these 144,000 individuals is highly debated with some believing they represent believers (Beasley-Murray, Bowman, Hendriksen, Ladd, Mounce and Osborne) because they represent the new Israel or the spiritual Israel who will all be sealed for protection before the angels are allowed to sound their trumpets of destruction on the earth.

Others believe they represent a literal 144,000 servants from the 12 tribes of Israel who will be given the responsibility of witnessing for Christ during the tribulation period (Bullinger, Mize, Lang, Lee, Seiss and Thomas). We would agree that this group is a literal 12,000 individuals from each of the 12 tribes listed by John. They are a faithful remnant of the descendants of Abraham, Isaac and Jacob who will be used to witness for the Lord during the world's darkest hour. They are given the seal of the living God on their foreheads in order to protect them (*cf.* Rev 9:4) from the calamites about to engulf planet earth.

### Great Multitude in Heaven

After John tells us that the 144,000 children of Israel will be given the seal of God's protection during the impending hour of trial, he tells us that he saw a great multitude standing before the throne in heaven and before the Lamb.

> *"After these things I looked, and behold, a **great multitude** which no one could number, of all nations, tribes, peoples, and tongues, **standing before the throne** and before the Lamb, clothed with **white robes**, with palm branches in their hands..."* (Rev 7:9 – NKJV)

The debate and controversy over the identity of this great company of people is almost as intense as the dispute surrounding the 144,000 discussed above. While most view this massive assembly as redeemed individuals, the major contention stems around when this scene is taking place and how they arrive before the throne.

The answer is given by one of the elders who says:

> *"...These are they which **came out of great tribulation**,*
> *and have **washed their robes**, and made them **white** in*
> *the blood of the Lamb."* (Rev 7:14)

This shows us that this **great multitude** from every nation around the world had to **wash** their **robes** in order to make them **white** again. This reveals a great deal about them. First, it tells us that they had white robes at one time, which means that they were indeed believers (Isa 61:10).

Second, it tells us they somehow soiled their robes. This is a picture of the believer too caught up with the things of this world (*cf.* Jas 1:27). They had soiled their garments by not living the blameless, holy lives they had been called to live.

Remember, those few in the church of Sardis had not defiled their garments, and were able to walk with the Lord dressed in white because they were worthy (see pp. 38-39). Had the great multitude heeded the Word of God, they would not have found themselves in the tribulation period. They did not keep God's word as the church of Philadelphia had (see p. 42), and therefore they were not kept from the hour of testing.

Also notice this great multitude will be required to become overcomers.

> *"And they overcame him [Antichrist] because of the*
> *blood of the Lamb and because of the word of their*
> *testimony, and they did not love their life even when*
> *faced with death."* (Rev 12:11 – NAS)

The main thesis of this book and what has been expounded so far is that all believers are called to be overcomers. Some will be successful overcomers prior to the time when the tribulation period begins, because these believers have kept God's word and pleased him by their righteous lives (*cf.* Rev 3:10 & 19:8). They will be found blameless, holy and worthy before God; thereby proving to be overcomers in God's sight.

The great multitude, on the other hand, will enter into the tribulation period because they had not been genuine overcomers prior to when it began. They will finally become overcomers when they are required to stand up for Christ during their final hour of testing. They will be required to refuse the mark of the beast and be martyred for Jesus. Their act of obedience unto death is viewed as washing their soiled robes in the precious blood of the Lamb.

The brief interlude provided by chapter 7 between the 6th and 7th seals alerts mankind: **God is providing deliverance** to two groups of people as the world is cast into its darkest period.

### 144,000 Witnesses
A small remnant from the children of Israel will be protected by the seal of the living God to be faithful witnesses for Him.

### Great Multitude
God wants all of mankind to call on the Lord before he returns. The call of His heart is for believers to be overcomers **now**, before the final hour of testing commences. All those who answer this call will be abundantly rewarded (Firstfruit rapture). Those believers who fail to respond will be included with the great multitude seen coming out of the great tribulation, just before God pours out His wrath (Main Harvest rapture).

*"And it shall come to pass*
*That **whoever calls on the name of the LORD** Shall be saved.*
*For in Mount Zion and in Jerusalem **there shall be deliverance**,*
*As the LORD has said,*
*Among the **remnant whom the LORD calls.** "*
(Joel 2:32[14] – NKJV)

# Silence in Heaven
## (for one-half hour)

Once the final seal is released, the entire scroll is also finally opened, revealing its entire contents. As the 7th seal is opened, a one half hour of silence is observed.

Silence in heaven means that all *"lightnings and thunderings and voices..."* (Rev 4:5) have ceased. The entire universe is silent for 30 minutes in reverent anticipation of coming judgment. A sense of awe permeates the atmosphere.

This pause in the action presents a good time to reflect on what has happened and what is about to take place:

> The lion from the tribe of Judah was worthy to take the scroll from the right hand of the one who sits on the throne in control of all of creation. All authority has been given to the Lamb, who is now seen riding on the white horse, traversing the earth conquering men's hearts so that one day we will be able to rule and reign with Him as sons of God.

With the impending judgments about to be unleashed with the coming trumpets and vials, the reader will want to remember God's ultimate plan and design:

> To take back control of planet earth and redeem mankind so that truth and righteousness will be established in his eternal kingdom with Jesus Christ as the victorious King of kings.

Why not take 30 minutes right now and meditate on these great truths? The Lamb who was slain and overcame death wants you to be able to overcome by his mighty power and strength which is living inside of you.

Call upon him now and he will help you be the overcomer He wants you to be.

# The Seven Trumpets

*"1) And when he had opened the **seventh seal**, there was **silence in heaven about the space of half an hour**. 2) And I saw the seven angels which stood before God; and to them were given seven trumpets. 3) And **another angel** came and stood at the altar, **having a golden censer**; and there was given unto him much incense, that he should offer it with the prayers of all saints upon the golden altar which was before the throne. 4) And the smoke of the incense, which came with the prayers of the saints, ascended up before God out of the angel's hand. 5) And the angel took the censer, and filled it with fire of the altar, and **cast it into the earth**: and there were **voices**, and **thunderings**, and **lightnings**, and an **earthquake**. 6) And the seven angels which had the seven trumpets prepared themselves to sound."* (Rev 8:1-6)

The above picture is from **The Book of Revelation**, by Clarence Larkin, page 70, © 1919. Used with permission of the Rev. Clarence Larkin Estate, P.O. Box 334, Glenside, PA 19038, U.S.A., 215-576-5590, www.larkinestate.com

# Chapter 3 – 7 Trumpets

The silence in heaven is broken when the angel holding the golden censer filled with fire cast it into the earth. Immediately there were heard: *"voices, and **thunderings**, and **lightnings**, and an **earthquake**."* When the 4 living creatures were introduced in chapter 4 of Revelation (p. 51); *"**lightnings, thunderings, and voices**"* were heard around the throne. These four actions declared here as the 1st angel is about to blow his trumpet also occur when the 7th angel sounds his final trumpet (*cf.* Rev 11:15, 19) and finally once more as the 7th angel pours out his final vial (*cf.* Rev 16:17-18). God has distinctly designated these important events, leaving little doubt who is in charge of directing their actions. Remember, God allows these judgments to take place in order for people to learn righteousness (Isa 26:9). He loves all of mankind and wants them to turn to the Lamb, who was slain for their sins.

The first four trumpet judgments are all the result of natural causes aimed at the earth's environment: earth, trees, sea, rivers, sky (sun, moon and stars). These will be calamities aimed at man's resources in an attempt to bring about repentance. While these judgments will be severe, they will be limited to only one-third of the earth.

**Trumpet #1: Earth and Trees (Rev 8:7)**

> *"The **first angel sounded**, and there followed hail and fire mingled with blood, and they were cast upon the earth: and **the third part of trees was burnt up**, and **all green grass was burnt up**."* (Rev 8:7)

The first trumpet will cause one-third of the trees and all of the green grass in the area to be destroyed by fire. Most commentators agree these are literal devastating scenes, while some choose to spiritualize them (i.e., trees become men) to signify something that they may represent. We would take the literal approach and agree that these are judgments God allows by natural causes. While most concur that they are literal, not everyone agrees to their causes.

Most likely, the phenomena John saw in his vision were the result of major volcanic eruptions across a wide area of the earth's surface. Coincidentally, as this section of this book is being written, two major volcanic eruptions occurred: one in Iceland and the other in Papua New Guinea. The eruption in Iceland was near the volcano that erupted in 2010, which caused more than 100,000 planes to be grounded due to the heavy ash plumes that darkened the atmosphere. Both of these volcanic eruptions were preceded by thousands of earthquakes in the area.[1]

Remember that the 6th seal started the tribulation period with a great earthquake. This 1st trumpet is a continuation under the 7th seal as fire is cast to the earth along with *"voices, and* *thunderings, and lightnings, and an earthquake."* Pastor Tom McElmurry who is also a physical scientist and a meteorologist, has stated: "I assure you that sounds, thunderings, lightning and earthquakes are common occurrences in all major volcanic eruptions." He also observed that what John witnessed were probably: "…fiery volcanic rocks that looked as if they had been dipped in blood, and that blood-red liquid was lava…a perfect description of a literal volcanic eruption."[2]

The 1st trumpet judgment is most likely a series of volcanic eruptions caused by a continuation of thousands of earthquakes across the globe. Plumes of volcanic ash will be spewed into the air and hot molten lava will cause the earth's vegetation across one-third of the planet to be destroyed. This devastation will affect cities, forests and croplands, having a major impact on the food supply, as well as the normal routine of daily living.

When the devastation of 9/11 occurred in New York City, throngs of people returned to churches and thousands of people turned their life over to Christ. The plumes of smoke and ash witnessed in New York will pale in comparison to the effect of this 1$^{st}$ trumpet.

**Trumpet #2: Sea (Rev 8:8-9)**

> *"And the **second angel sounded, and as it were a great mountain burning with fire was cast into the sea**: and the third part of the sea became blood; And the third part of the creatures which were in the sea, and had life, died; and the third part of the ships were destroyed."* (Rev 8:8-9)

Most commentators view this large mountain being cast into the sea as a huge meteor falling through the atmosphere to wreak havoc with the sea, causing one-third of the fish to die and one-third of the ships to be destroyed. This author has held this view over the past several years and has been keeping track of recent, cosmic near-misses of large asteroids passing by our planet. Remember, Jesus warned us that there would be signs in the heavens to indicate when His return is drawing near. These recent fly-bys should certainly get our attention. The last major asteroid was about half the size of a football field and passed us by in February 2013, about 17,200 miles from impacting our planet. Since 2002, these large objects from space appear to be getting closer and closer.[3]

While an asteroid may be what John observed, there could be a more plausible explanation. In the above verse, John says *"as it were."* This could mean he was trying to describe an unfamiliar sighting using the best words that he knew to explain what he saw. Pastor McElmurry believes that John saw a large burning mountain spewing forth lava and volcanic ash into the sea. What appeared to John was actually a dormant volcano erupting from beneath the sea, making it appear to have just been cast into the water. With eruptions over a mass portion of the ocean floor, great quantities of molten magma would cause tremendous deaths to sea creatures. McElmurry believes: "the sea will be turned red by both oxidation and organism secretion....slowly spreading the blood-red shroud of poison across the oceans and the seas of the world."[4]

We believe the above explanation is more plausible than John witnessing a large meteor, as we had previous believed. Regardless of which scenario is correct, we are confident that what John actually witnessed will take place and produce the effects he describes under this 2nd trumpet.

### Trumpet #3: Rivers (Rev 8:10-11)

> *"And the **third angel sounded**, and there fell a great star from heaven, **burning as it were a lamp**, and it fell upon the third **part of the rivers**, and upon the fountains of **waters**; And the name of the star is called **Wormwood**[894]: and the third part of the waters became wormwood; and **many men died** of the waters, because they were **made bitter**."* (Rev 8:10-11)

The next blast from the 3rd angel brings a large object from outer space that appears to be burning as it enters the earth's atmosphere. Most commentaries describe this as a falling meteor; however, a more likely explanation would be that of a comet passing by our planet. The well-known tail of a comet appears as a *"burning lamp"* and scientists believe that if the earth were to encounter a comet, it could release various gases which would pollute the water supply for the area affected. These gases would be poisonous causing many people to perish upon drinking the water.

John named this future comet: Wormwood because he knows it

will make the water very bitter. The word for wormwood (#894) (*apsinthion*) is only seen in the New Testament in this verse and is derived from the name of a bitter herb. Because Israel had forsaken God's law, he brought them similar bitter water to drink:

> "...*thus says the LORD of hosts, the God of Israel,* "*behold, I will feed them...with* **wormwood** *and give them* **poisoned water to drink**." (Jer 9:15 – NAS)

This 3$^{rd}$ trumpet judgment will be sent on the world as a sign that he is not pleased and as a warning that future afflictions will follow on all of those who fail to repent.

## Trumpet #4: Sun, Moon, Stars (Rev 8:12-13)

> "*And the* **fourth angel sounded**, *and the third part of the* **sun** *was smitten, and the third part of the* **moon**, *and the third part of the* **stars**; *so as the third part of them was* **darkened**, *and the day shone not for a third part of it, and the night likewise*." (Rev 8:12)

The last of the first four trumpets to affect the environment cause the sun, moon and the starts to be darkened. Most of the commentators spend little time on this trumpet since it is puzzling as to how this could be fulfilled. We would partly agree with the assessment made by Robert Thomas: "The Creator of all things can certainly devise a means by which a partial eclipse can result in a shortening of duration from the light-bodies."[5] However, since this author was born in Missouri, the "show-me" state, a further investigation into the causes seems warranted.

One possible explanation as to how the duration of viewing the heavenly bodies is reduced by one-third of the time could be the result of the comet mentioned when the 3$^{rd}$ trumpet was sounded. If comet Wormwood, or another celestial body were to either hit or "flyby" our planet, it could speed up the rotation of the earth's axis, causing the length of our day to be reduced from 24 hours to 16 hours (i.e. shortened by 1/3). Readers may view such a scenario as too preposterous, however, those who are familiar with the writings of Donald Wesley Patten and others know that many of the events described in the Old Testament were astronomical in nature and that several were the result of what Patten termed a "Mars flyby." He believed that the orbit of planet Mars had been altered, causing it to flyby planet earth, creating numerous catastrophes and events such as: the Noachian Flood, the destruction of Sodom-Gomorrah, and the Long Day of Joshua, to name just a few.[6]

The shortening of the length of our present day from 24 hours to 16 hours is certainly a plausible explanation as to how the 4th trumpet events could occur. If so, it may also provide us with the reason Jesus spoke the following words in his discourse from the Mount of Olives:

> *"For then shall be **great tribulation**, such as was not since the beginning of the world to this time, no, nor ever shall be. And **except those days should be shortened**, there should no flesh be saved: but **for the elect's sake those days shall be shortened.**"*
> (Mat 24:21-22)

Jesus is telling us that once the great tribulation has begun the days would be shortened for the sake of the elect. If Jesus is telling us the **length** of the day is shortened, then the above explanation for the 4th trumpet could provide the solution as to how both of these perplexing Scriptures will be fulfilled.

One other solution to the 4th trumpet could be that the sun, moon and the stars would be only partially obscured from view for one-third of the time due to the heavy volcanic ash permeating the atmosphere. In other words, thick clouds of ash would obstruct people's view of the heavenly bodies for 8 hours every day. As the earth rotates these dense clouds of volcanic ash and debris would continue to place everyone into darkness one-third of the time.

Which of these explanations is correct is uncertain. Regardless of the exact cause, the affect on our planet will be devastating. Darkness is a symbol of God's judgment throughout the Old Testament (cf. Exodus 10:21, Amos 5:18, Isaiah 13:10, and Joel 2:2), and the terror created by these shocking developments should bring everyone to their knees.

Before the final 3 angels sound their trumpets, an eagle appears warning of the judgments about to arrive:

*"Then I looked, and I heard an **eagle flying** in midheaven, saying with a loud voice, "Woe, woe, woe to those who dwell on the earth, because of the remaining blasts of the trumpet of the three angels who are about to sound!"* (Rev 8:13 – NAS)

It is significant that the final 3 trumpets are introduced by the appearance of an eagle. We will learn more about this eagle in the next chapter of this book where the two wings of this great eagle[7] will protect God's people during these trying times.

## Trumpet #5: 1st Woe (Rev 9:1-12)

> *"And the **fifth angel sounded**, and I saw a **star fall from heaven** unto the earth: and to him was given the key of the bottomless pit."* (Rev 9:1)

The 5th trumpet begins with Satan being cast down from heaven to the earth (Beirnes, Hendriksen, Lee, Mize, Morris and Seiss) where he is temporarily given the key to the bottomless pit. He immediately opens the pit, allowing billowing smoke to darken the view of the sun, as hordes of demonic locusts are allowed a brief reprieve from their prison. They are given the power of scorpions to torment men for a period of five months. Whereas the four previous trumpet judgments were aimed at the earth's environment, these demonic beings are instructed to not harm the grass or the trees, but only those people who have not been sealed by God for protection.

> *"They were commanded not to harm the grass of the earth, or any green thing, or any tree, but only those men who* **do not have the seal of God** *on their foreheads."* (Rev 9:4 – NKJV)

They are not given the authority to kill anyone, but only to torment them: *"...Their torment was like the torment of a scorpion when it strikes a man....They had tails like scorpions, and there were stings in their tails."* (Rev 9:5, 10 – NKJV)

Satan's minions are allowed to torture men but not to kill them. People will want to die, but they won't be able to. God allows this horrible judgment to bring them to repentance before his final wrath is poured out.

It is important to note, these demonic beings are not allowed to harm those who have been sealed by God. This would include the 144,000 witnesses from the 12 tribes, who were given the *"seal of the living God,"* in addition to the great multitude of believers who enter the great tribulation. While John does not specifically exempt these believers, the Lord implies this in the Scripture below. As Satan is cast to earth, Jesus tells believers of their power over Satan and his cohort's ability to cause any harm:

> *"And he said unto them,* **I beheld Satan** *as lightning* **fall from heaven.** *Behold,* **I give unto you power** *to tread* **on** *serpents and* **scorpions,** *and* **over all the power of the enemy:** *and* **nothing shall by any means hurt you.**" (Luk 10:18-19)

Believers have all power over Satan and his demons because the one living inside of us is far greater (*cf.* 1 Jo 4:4). Also, all believers are sealed by the Holy Spirit (Eph 1:13, 4:30) and God will protect those who have the Spirit of the living God dwelling inside of them. Henry Morris shares a similar belief regarding the protection of believers during this time: "…they may have been martyred by this time. Still more probably, though the Scripture does not say, they also may have been sealed in virtue of their faith."[8]

Some commentators deal with the issue of who is affected by this 5th trumpet judgment by restricting the area being targeted to the region of Israel. They base this upon a reading of various Scripture which seems to imply these demonic locusts will be seeking to torment those in the Middle East (*cf.* Eze 9, Isa 11 – Lang) and (*cf.* Joe 1:6, 2:4-5, 25 – Lee). Presumably only the 144,000 servants of the tribes of Israel would escape their torment while the remaining people in the vicinity of Israel would face 5 months of torment.

We believe our Lord's reference to the believer's power at the time Satan descends to earth was made to encourage believers living at that time. This seems to be a more plausible rationale on why believers would not be harmed by these demon locusts; however, it is possible that these evil beings may only be directed at those living in Israel and neighboring countries.

John concludes his description of the 5th trumpet by telling us these demon locusts had a **king** over them *"And they had a **king** over them, which is the **angel of the bottomless pit**, whose name in the Hebrew tongue is Abaddon, but in the Greek tongue hath his name Apollyon."* (Rev 9:11)

Almost all commentators gloss over this verse; only noting this angel from the pit's name is Destroyer. A careful analysis of other Scripture reveals this *"angel"* could very well be the *Beast* that is seen *ascending out of the bottomless pit* in Rev 11:7 and Rev 17:8. In 2 Th 2:3, he is called the *"son of destruction,"* better known as the Antichrist, or the Beast who *"rises out of the sea"* as mentioned in Rev 13:1 (Bullinger, Lee).

John used the term angel to describe the pastors or ministers of the churches.[9] Angels are not always celestial beings. This angel of the abyss has many names and is described by John in many different ways. Remember, Jesus is seen as a: Lion, Lamb, Rider on the white horse, King of kings, etc. to name a few. Likewise, the Antichrist is known as: Angel of the abyss, Antichrist, Beast, Destroyer, son of destruction, etc. Satan likes to mimic God, but in reality he is the exact opposite. God wants to redeem mankind and bring in His righteous Kingdom, while Satan's objective is to kill and destroy.

### Trumpet #6: 2nd Woe (Rev 9:13-21)

> *"And the **sixth angel sounded**, and I heard a voice from the four horns of the golden altar which is before God, Saying to the sixth angel which had the trumpet, Loose the four angels which are bound in the great river Euphrates." And the four angels were loosed, which were prepared for an hour, and a day, and a month, and a year, for **to slay the third part of men**."* (Rev 9:13-15)

Once the 6th angel sounds his trumpet, the orders are given to release the four angels that have been bound. These instructions are probably coming from the Lamb himself. While five trumpets have already been sounded, many have still not come to repentance. The major purpose of the judgments of the first 5 angels was not designed to bring death. God wants all of mankind to be saved and has been patiently waiting – not wanting anyone to perish (2 Pet 3:15). The 2nd woe about to follow will reveal that his patience is almost up. The four bound angels are about to bring death to 1/3 of all mankind.

That these angels were bound in the Euphrates river tells us where this major war will begin, along with the fact that the ones directing the activities are four fallen angels that had been bound for this specific mission. Commentators are divided as to the phrase: *for an hour, and a day, and a month, and a year.* Some believe this is telling us the length of this great slaughter (Beirnes, Lee, Seiss) while others feel that it is merely stating the precise timing of when the campaign begins (Hendriksen, Ladd, Larkin, Mounce, Thomas). In other words, it either tells us that this horrible massacre will last a little while over 13 months (1 year + 1 month + 1 day + 1 hour) or that it will occur on the exact day and hour that had been determined by God.

John then goes on to give a detailed description of an army with over 200 million gruesome-appearing horsemen, whose horses spew forth *"fire and smoke and brimstone"* from their mouths and inflict injury from their tails (Rev 9:16-19). Some believe these are supernatural beings similar to the demonic locusts under the 5th trumpet, while others see them as instruments of modern warfare, capable of inflicting frightful injury and death. Regardless of how long this war lasts, or what instruments are employed, the final results will be devastating.

Despite the fact that 1/3 of mankind will perish in this colossal war, those who survive still remain unrepentant:

> *"The rest of mankind, who were not killed by these plagues, **did not repent** of the works of their hands, so as not to **worship** demons, and the **idols** of gold and of silver and of brass and of stone and of wood, which can neither see nor hear nor walk; and they did not repent of their **murders** nor of their **sorceries** nor of their **immorality** nor of their **thefts**."* (Rev 9:20-21 – NAS)

In spite of these 6 warning trumpets, impenitent men persist with their idolatry, murder, witchcraft, immorality and thefts.

## RECAP

The 6th trumpet sounding has brought incredible carnage and the death of over 2 billion people. John pauses before the final trumpet is blown with the insertion of chapters 10 and 11. The first 6 trumpets have taken us from the time the 7th seal was opened at the start of the tribulation period, which officially began when the 6th seal was opened. In other words, the 6th seal initiated the beginning of the tribulation and the sounding of the first 6 trumpets takes us near to the very end of 3 ½ years of unparalleled calamities and judgments. All of these trials have been aimed at teaching mankind about God's righteousness and their need to come to repentance. Sadly, after 42 months of incomparable trials and distress, men still remain impenitent.

Before John takes us to the 7th trumpet judgment, he pauses with a brief interlude to describe a "**little scroll**" (chapter 10), and to introduce the **two witnesses** (chapter 11). This pause in the action allows us to learn more important details about God's plan before the concluding trumpet sounds. This brief reprieve in the proceedings is similar to the previous chapter of this book where John paused to tell us about the 144,000 witnesses and the great multitude of believers between the 6th and 7th seals.

### Interlude: Little Scroll (Rev 10) and 2 Witnesses (Rev 11)

> *"And I saw another mighty angel come down from heaven, **clothed** with a **cloud**: and a **rainbow** was upon his **head**, and his **face** was **as** it were the **sun**, and his feet as **pillars of fire**: And he **had in his hand a little book [scroll] open**: and he set his right foot upon the sea, and his left foot on the earth..."* (Rev 10:1-2)

### Little Scroll (Rev 10)

Commentators are divided over this picture of an angel coming down from heaven, holding the opened scroll in his hand. Some believe this to be Jesus (Beirnes, Larkin, Lee, Mize, Morris and

Seiss), while others see him as a mighty angel (Hendriksen, Ladd, Lang, Mounce, Osborne, Thomas). Anyone who reads the glorious majesty of this mighty angel coming down from heaven can see the many descriptions of Christ mentioned earlier in this book. He appears: (1) *clothed with a cloud* and Jesus is pictured *"coming in the clouds"* (Rev 1:7), (2) with a *rainbow upon his head* (almost as a crown) and a *"rainbow encircles God's throne"* (Rev 4:3), (3) with a *face as it were the sun* compares to Jesus' *"countenance was as the sun shineth"* (Rev 1:16), and (4) feet as pillars of fire seen in Rev 1:15 where Jesus' feet are like *"..fine brass as if they burned in a furnace."*

The above description of this angel clearly shows him to be none other than our Lord Jesus Christ. The objection is made that Jesus is not identified as an angel elsewhere in Revelation, however, he appeared on numerous occasions as an angel in the Old Testament. Being an angel does not mean he is a created being since "Angel is a title of office, not of nature" (Seiss).

Remember that under the 5th trumpet we observed how the Antichrist was seen ascending as an *"angel of the bottomless pit."* The apostle John is now back on earth and is given a vision of this mighty Angel descending from heaven. Christ's appearance here is important. He now **holds the open scroll**, which he had previously opened (as the Lamb), and he is seen **standing on the earth and the sea**, which is a precursor to the time when he will return to take possession of the earth.

At this time, he lifts up his hand toward heaven and makes the **solemn pledge** there would be **no more delay** for the mystery of God to be finished once the 7th angel begins to sound his trumpet: *"...that there should be **time no longer**: But in the days of the voice of the seventh angel, when he shall begin to sound, the mystery[10] of God should be finished, as he hath declared to his servants the prophets."* (Rev 10:6-7)

This brief interlude before the 7th trumpet is sounded is given to assure us that Jesus is in complete control of the entire situation. He is the Lion from the tribe of Judah and he has opened the scroll and is ready to complete his mission of taking back possession of the earth. His grand **pledge** to the one who created the entire universe (heaven, earth and sea) is made to **assure us** that it won't be much longer before the redemption of mankind is finished so that his righteous Kingdom can be instituted with truth and righteousness established under his rule as the King of kings.

Before Jesus makes this important promise, John hears the voices of 7 thunders from heaven cry out. John is then instructed not to record what they say but is told to *"seal up"* the things these 7 thunders spoke. Since John was told not to record what these 7 thunders proclaimed we are not to know their message before they are announced. Any attempt to imagine what they said would be futile. While we won't know what the voices said, the following brief summary of where the 7 "thunderings" are recorded reveals God's perfection.

| 7 Thunders From Throne Room | | |
|---|---|---|
| After Door Opened | Rev 4:5 | Before 1st Seal |
| At 1st Seal | Rev 6:1 | Christ Rides Conquering |
| After 7th Seal | Rev 8:5 | Before 1st Trumpet |
| After 7th Trumpet | Rev 11:19 | Before 1st Vial |
| At Firstfruit Rapture | Rev 14:2 | Overcomers' Sheltered |
| After 7th Vial | Rev 16:18 | Before Final Hail |
| At Bride's Wedding | Rev 19:6 | Christ with His Bride |

Whether or not the above analysis relates to the 7 thunders John heard is not known. Some believe they relate to 7 additional judgments yet to come at the time John heard their message and some believe they relate to the 7 last vials about to be released under the 7th trumpet. We are not to know. Time alone will tell.

John is then instructed to take the little scroll and eat it, where he found it to be sweet as honey in his mouth, but made his stomach bitter after he had eaten it (*cf.* Eze 2 and 3). Once he ate the scroll he was told:

> *"...You must prophesy again about many peoples, nations, tongues, and kings."* (Rev 10:11 – NAS)

Eating the little scroll is a picture of taking in the Word of God, which is always sweet in our mouth (*cf.* Psa 119:103). John first must consume the words of the scroll in order to be able to proclaim its message. While God's word is sweet to our taste, it can make our stomachs bitter when we are required to experience trials and persecutions because of it. The wonderful promises in the word are like honey in our mouth, but the judgments about to occur makes one sick in the stomach. John has prophesied the first part of the scroll; he must now prophesy the remaining portion.

## 2 Witnesses (Rev 11)

The brief interlude between the 6th and 7th trumpets continues with the most widely debated and the most difficult portions of Revelation to interpret. How one views this section is determined by his or her approach to the book, as discussed in Appendix 1. For purposes of brevity, this will be limited to a review of the two most popular methods of interpretation: the Idealist and the Futurist approaches.

## Idealist View

The idealist understands the temple of God symbolically to be the church that represents spiritual Israel (i.e., as a *"real Jew"*). See the discussion on pp. 73-74 (the 144,000 witnesses), where believers being "real Jews" are referred to as spiritual Israel and therefore the idealist believes the church is the 144,000 witnesses in Rev 7:3-4. Likewise, the church is viewed as the temple of God in Rev 11:1 under the idealist's method.

Measuring the temple (*cf.* Jer 31:38-40 and Zec 1:16) under the idealist method, views the inner court as the true Church (real believers), with the outer court as mere professing Christians. The idealist believes the outer court, represented by false believers, will be trampled upon by the world. The 42 months (or 1,260 days) become a symbolic period of time during the entire church age, and the 2 witnesses are symbolic of the true Church (Hendriksen).

### Futurist View

The futurist view takes a more literal approach that can be divided into two schools. The dispensationalists believe the Jewish temple will be rebuilt in Jerusalem and that the gentiles, along with the Antichrist (Beast), will trample down the city of Jerusalem the last 42 month of great tribulation. The more moderate futurist school views the temple as representing true worshipers of God who are a faithful remnant of Israelites (Ladd), or figuratively, the temple is viewed as the church, or faithful believers (Mounce). Most of the futurist views see the 2 witnesses as two men who will prophecy for 1,260 days *"clothed in sackcloth,"* however, some take a figurative approach and see the 2 witnesses symbolizing the church.

---

*"1)Then I was given a reed like a measuring rod. And the **angel** stood, saying, 'Rise and **measure** the **temple of God**, the altar, and **those who worship there**. But **leave out the court** which is **outside the temple**, and do not measure it, for it has been given to the Gentiles. 2) And they will **tread the holy city underfoot for forty-two months. 3) And I will give power to my two witnesses**, and they will **prophesy one thousand two hundred and sixty days, clothed in sackcloth.** "* (Rev 11:1-3 – NKJV)

A proper understanding of the above Scripture begins by noticing that the same angel who gave Apostle John the little scroll in chapter 10, also instructs him to measure the temple. That this same **angel** is Jesus is confirmed in verse 3, where he declares that He will *"**give power to my two witnesses**..."* to prophecy for 1,260 days. These 2 witnesses represent *"...two olive trees and the two lampstands that stand before the Lord of the earth"* (Rev 11:4 – NAS). Zechariah confirms these 2 men are:

> *"...the two anointed\* ones who stand by the Lord of the whole earth."* (Zec 4:14 – ESV). [\* "sons of new oil"]

Scripture confirms for us that the angel (Jesus) gives power to these 2 holy men to prophecy for 1,260 days. They are filled with the Holy Spirit (oil) and are God's appointed instruments to witness for him over a period of 3 ½ years. During this same period of time, the city of Jerusalem will be *"tread...underfoot"* by the Gentiles, which indicates that those living there will be severely tested during that time. The Prophet Zechariah tells us the final outcome with only 1/3 of the people enduring (*cf.* Zec 13:9 and 14:1-2). God allows the nation of Israel to be chastised in order for them to turn to the Messiah, who they rejected when he came the first time.

### Identity of 2 Witnesses

The actual identity of these 2 holy men of God has been highly debated over the centuries. The early church believed Enoch and Elijah were the 2 witnesses because both had been raptured from the earth (*cf.* Gen 5:24 and 2 Ki 2:11), without experiencing death, which is implied as a requirement for all men to experience in Heb 9:27. While these two men are prime candidates, others believe Moses and Elijah would be more likely; since the miracles that they performed in their earlier appearances on the earth[11] were very similar to the powers John tells us they will have during their 1,260 days of ministry:

> *"...fire proceeds from their mouth... they have power to shut heaven, so that no rain falls...have power over waters to turn them to blood, and to strike the earth with all plagues..."* (Rev 11:5-6 – NKJV)

While Moses and Elijah appear to be possible contenders, others have suggested Lazarus and even the Apostle John himself.[12] The identity of these 2 witnesses will not be resolved in this short study because who they are is less important than understanding they will be used to testify for Christ during the world's darkest hours. Their earthly mission will be to testify of God's righteousness and his plan of salvation that is available to all who call upon him. Those who remain unrepentant will experience the numerous trials that are brought to the earth by the trumpet judgments described in this chapter. Their witnessing will last for a period of 1,260 days and the Antichrist will arrive during this same period of time to kill them, once they have completed their testimony:

> *"And when they have **finished their testimony**, the **beast that rises from the bottomless pit** will make war on them and conquer them and **kill them**..."* (Rev 11:7 – ESV)

Here we see the *"beast that rises from the bottomless pit"* who was first introduced to us during the 5th trumpet (pp. 87-88) and is better known as the Antichrist, who we will learn more about in the next chapter of this book. Here he is pictured as the beast from the Abyss, who will kill the 2 witnesses once they finish their testimony. They will not be buried, but their dead bodies will lie in the streets of Jerusalem. The world will rejoice over their deaths because these two prophets bring much torment and trouble during their 3 ½ years. But after lying in the street 3 ½ days, God will miraculously breathe life into their dead bodies and rapture them to heaven as the world looks on.

By the death of the 2 witnesses, the Antichrist believed he had thwarted God's plan and won the great battle. But God had the final say and wins the final triumph by bringing them back to life for the entire world to see. God is in complete control and he did not allow their death until they had finished their work. In the end, God will overcome Satan and win the final victory.

The brief interlude between the $6^{th}$ and $7^{th}$ trumpets has two encouraging reminders:

### Little Scroll

- Jesus makes a solemn pledge that there would be no more delay in bringing to completion God's mystery of redemption once the $7^{th}$ angel begins to sounds his trumpet. He will soon redeem the earth and establish his righteous Kingdom, where all overcomers will rule and reign with him as the King of kings.

### 2 Witnesses

- While Satan may be allowed to bring destruction and death during his brief appearance of 42 months, the Lamb has overcome death and holds the final victory in his hands, as witnessed by the rapture of God's 2 witnesses.

---

## Trumpet #7: $3^{rd}$ Woe (Rev 11:14-19)

*"The second woe is past. Behold, the third woe is coming quickly. Then the **seventh angel sounded**: And there were loud voices in heaven, saying, 'The kingdoms of this world have become the kingdoms of our Lord and of His Christ, and He shall reign forever and ever!'"* (Rev 11:14-15 – NKJV)

The sounding of the $7^{th}$ trumpet brings us to the very end of the tribulation period. The great trumpet blast will last over a period of days (Rev 10:6) as God's final design is fulfilled. The $2^{nd}$ woe will quickly proceed into the $3^{rd}$ woe as God's final wrath is poured out in the 7 vials.

Before the judgment of the vials begins, Jesus Christ takes control of the kingdom of this world and begins his mighty reign. The 24 elders fall down in worship – as the time for them to cast their crowns before the throne has come (see pages 51-52, where this important event is described in greater detail). These 24 angelic elders transfer their rule of the universe to Jesus, and his first official act is to decide the fate of the dead[13] and reward his servants with the crowns they earned for being the overcomers they had been called to be.  They will be revealed as the *"sons of God"* (Rom 8:19) and be given the remarkable opportunity to rule and reign with Jesus.  Once these *"called, chosen and faithful"* overcomers have been rewarded, he then prepares to bring the final wrath against mankind:

> *"The nations were filled with wrath, **but now the time of your wrath has come**...It is time to destroy all who have caused destruction on the earth."* (Rev 11:18 – NLT)

The 7th trumpet introduces the day of God's wrath which begins with the 7 vials that will be poured out as the final plagues.  These judgments represent the 3rd and final woe against those who have caused so much destruction on the earth.

The removal of the great multitude of believers described in the previous chapter of this book (see pp. 72-76) will have already taken place just prior to the time when God's final fury commences.  The Main Harvest rapture will protect all believers remaining on the earth before God pours out his wrath.[14]

The trumpets end as they began, with the four actions from the throne room, with the addition of *"great hail:"*

*"And opened was the sanctuary of God in the heaven, and there was seen the ark of His covenant in His sanctuary, and there did come **lightnings**, and **voices**, and **thunders**, and an **earthquake**, and **great hail**."* (Rev 11:19 – YLT)

---

### Summary of Seals, Trumpets and Vials

**Seals** – Cover the period from the Resurrection
To the Start of the Tribulation Period

**Trumpets** – Cover the Entire Tribulation Period

**Vials** – God's Final Wrath under the 7th Trumpet
(see Chapter 5 of this book – Rev 15 & 16)

The next chapter of this book will provide additional details of the many players seen throughout the Tribulation Period.

# Chapter 4 – 7 Visions

The previous chapter brought us to the very end of the tribulation period with the sounding of the 7th trumpet which is about to unleash the final 7 vials of God's wrath. Apostle John ends that section with a view of the throne room with the familiar four actions seen after the silence in heaven was broken as the trumpets began to sound (see p. 78). By this method, John is taking us back to the start of the 3 ½ year tribulation period to provide additional details of people, places and events during this final period of history before Jesus Christ returns as the victorious King to establish His righteous Kingdom over all the earth. The next 3 chapters of Revelation (Chapters 12, 13 and 14) include 7 very important visions that John saw to help us better understand God's plans.

## ① Woman & Dragon (Rev 12)

*"A great sign appeared in heaven: a **woman** clothed with the sun, and the moon under her feet, and on her head a crown of twelve stars; and she was with child; and she cried out, being in labor and in pain to give birth."* (Rev 12:1-2 – NAS)

This is a beautiful metaphor of the nation of Israel (woman) that is alluded to in Joseph's dream (Gen 37:9-11) where the sun, moon and stars represent Jacob (father), Rachael (mother) and 12 sons (11 brothers + Joseph), which represent God's faithful remnant of the nation of Israel. The passage in Rev 12:1-2 indicates that this woman (Israel) is about to give birth. This time was referred to by the prophet Isaiah: *"**Or shall a nation be born at once?** For as soon as Zion was in labor, She gave birth to her children."* (Isa 66:8 – NKJV) This describes the re-birth of the nation of Israel that occurred on May 14, 1948.

Ever since Israel was born (at once) she has been experiencing tremendous persecution from her Arab neighbors. This harassment will continue until the time when a faithful remnant from Israel is forced to flee into the wilderness, as described in Rev 12:6, and 14. Before then, a great red dragon appears:

> *"Then another sign appeared in heaven: and behold, **a** **great red dragon**...And his tail **swept away a third of the stars of heaven and threw them to the earth.** And the dragon stood before **the woman who was about to give birth,** so that **when she gave birth he might devour her child.**"* (Rev 12:3-4 – NAS)

This is a picture of Satan casting down 1/3 of his fallen angels to earth as he is ready to destroy the child about to be born. Most commentators incorrectly teach that this child is Christ, however a closer examination will show who he actually is.

> *"And she brought forth a **man child,** who was to **rule all nations with a rod of iron:** and **her child was caught up unto God, and to his throne.**"* (Rev 12:5)

While Christ will rule the nations with a rod of iron (*cf.* Psa 2:8, Rev 19:15), the context here is the birth of a *"man child"* just before Satan is cast down out of heaven to the earth to persecute the nation of Israel during the last 1,260 days (3 ½ years) of great tribulation (Rev 12:13-14). This could not be Christ since he died and rose from the dead almost 2,000 years earlier. Here this *"man child"* is born and immediately brought to the throne of God. The identity of this figure has already been alluded to in our discussion of the overcomers: *"And he who overcomes, ...to him I will give **power over the nations** He shall **rule them with a rod of iron**..."* (Rev 2:26-27 – NKJV)

The *"man child"* is the **overcomer,**[1] who will be caught up to the throne of God just before Satan arrives to persecute Israel and the rest of her offspring:

> *"And the dragon was wroth with the woman, and went to make war with* **the remnant**[3062] **of her seed, which keep the commandments of God,** *and* **have the testimony of Jesus Christ.** *"* (Rev 12:17)

After the overcomers are raptured to heaven, Satan will pursue *"the remnant of her seed."* The word for "remnant" #3062 is *loipos*, which means those remaining. In other words, the overcoming believers are caught up to the throne in heaven while the remaining believers are left behind to face a time of trial and testing during the tribulation period. Those remaining believers will quickly learn to be overcomers as they will be required to become martyrs for Christ (*cf.* Rev 14:12-13):

> *"And* **they overcame** *him by the* **blood of the Lamb,** *and by the* **word of their testimony;** *and they* **loved not their lives unto the death.** *"* (Rev 12:11)

After the rapture of the faithful overcomers, Satan will pursue the remaining believers who failed to be overcomers. They will become the Great Multitude described in chapter 2 (pp. 72-76).

The woman (God's faithful remnant of the nation of Israel) is then pictured fleeing into the wilderness[2] for a period of 3 ½ years, where she will be protected: *"But the two wings of the* **great eagle** *were given to the woman, so that she could fly into the wilderness to her place, where she was nourished... from the presence of the serpent."* (Rev 12:14 – NAS) This great eagle appeared right before the final 3 woes were announced (see p. 85). This eagle is a symbol of God's protection of his people when he delivered them from the Egyptians (Exo 19:4-6) and protected them in the wilderness (Deu 32:10-12). The Apostle John sees this great eagle here as a reminder that God will provide for and protect his people during this most difficult and troublous time.

The vision of the Woman and the Dragon is one of the most picturesque scenes in Revelation. It occurs at the half way point[3] in the book and tells us the good news that Satan has been cast out of heaven and he only has a short time until the Lamb defeats him entirely. The overcoming believer (male child) is taken to the throne of God in heaven, the faithful remnant of Israel (woman) is protected in the wilderness, and Satan (Dragon) is enraged and persecutes the remaining believers who have been left behind.

### ② 2 Beasts From Sea & Earth (Rev 13)

As Apostle John stood on the seashore he saw his second vision of two beasts. The first beast is seen rising from the sea having 7 heads and 10 horns with 10 crowns. This 10 horned beast is the beast described in chapters 2 and 7 of Daniel. Daniel 2 tells us about the 4 empires over a period of 2,600 years (Babylon, Medo-Persia, Greek, and Roman empires) while Daniel 7 describes 4 beasts (lion, bear, leopard with 4 wings, and a 4th more terrifying beast with 10 horns + a little horn – Dan 7:3-8).

John's beast is given its power by the Dragon and it appeared as a leopard with feet like a bear and a mouth like a lion. Many bible teachers believe that this beast will arise from the nations in the Middle East, as depicted by the following map.[4]

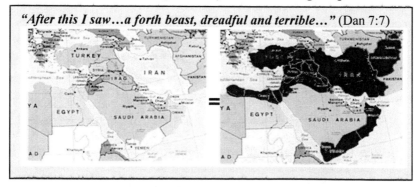

*"After this I saw...a forth beast, dreadful and terrible..."* (Dan 7:7)

Those who believe the *"beast out of the sea"* John saw will come from 10 Arab nations also see Syria as the *"little horn."* They view the 4th kingdom in Daniel's famous statue (Dan 2), as coming from the Seleucid kingdom (Syria/Iraq), which is seen as part of its legs/feet (Syria/Iraq and Egypt). Those who hold this view argue Rome is not part of the statue since Israel did not exist as a nation during the era of the Roman Empire.[5]

While the beast may arise from Israel's neighbors, many prophecy teachers believe that the beast out of the sea will come from a 10 nation confederacy of European nations, which will represent a revived Roman Empire. Some see Daniel's *"little horn"* as the United States, which is characterized later by John in his description of mystery Babylon (Rev 17 and 18).

Many of those who hold this view also see the leader of the United States as the most likely candidate for the Antichrist. If the U.S.A. represents part of this dreadful beast, then the person in the office of its presidency could be the most likely person to fulfill the role of the Antichrist. And if America is the political leader of Mystery Babylon[6], its religious partner may also be represented by Rome's spiritual head, which John describes as the *"beast out of the earth,"* which is also the False Prophet.

This diabolical duo will emerge on the world scene with an incredible entrance that will astonish and amaze all of mankind. Satan's plan is to completely counterfeit the death and resurrection of Jesus by making it appear that the Antichrist has come back to life after suffering a deadly wound to the head. The whole world will *"wonder after the beast"* (Rev13:3), who appears to have been miraculously brought back to life. It will be one of Satan's grandest masterpieces when this *"man of sin"* (2 Th 2:3) rises from the grave, mimicking Christ's resurrection.

*"And I saw one of his heads as if it had been mortally wounded, and his deadly wound was healed. And all the world marveled and followed the beast."* (Rev 13:3 – NKJV)

If the Antichrist is to come from the presidency of America, we cannot exclude the prospect that he could be a former president, who is brought back to life. As noted by Robert Thomas: "Whether the beast performs this marvelous feat through deception or through power permitted by God, it still brings him into the limelight as never before."[7] The Apostle Paul reminded us:

> *"For the mystery of lawlessness is already at work; only* **He who now restrains will do so until He is taken out of the way. And then the lawless one will be revealed.."** *The* **coming of the lawless one** *is according to the* **working of Satan, with all power, signs, and lying wonders***... And for this reason* **God will send them strong delusion***, that they should believe the lie..."* (2 Th 2:7-9, 11 – NKJV)

The coming of the Antichrist is the work of Satan to deceive the world into following him. God allows this grand deception because people rejected the truth found in Jesus Christ.

Also notice that the Antichrist arrives on the scene immediately after *"He who now restrains"* is removed. This writer contends that the presence of the **overcomer** on the earth is what is restraining the Antichrist from appearing.[8] Many believe that the Holy Spirit is removed when all believers are raptured, before the *"man of sin"* arrives. But all saints are not removed, as we learned when the *"man child"* was raptured to the throne, leaving the *"remnant of her seed"* (believers) behind to face the wrath of the Dragon. Also, once the restrainer (**overcoming believer**) is taken away, the Antichrist is given 42 months to reign, and allowed to pursue and kill the believers who remain:

> *"It was granted to him to **make war with the saints and to overcome them**..."* (Rev 13:7 – NKJV)

The *"**man child**"* is the *"**He** who now restrains,"* who is raptured before the Antichrist appears. After *his* removal the beast pursues the *"remnant of her seed"* / *"makes war with the saints."* Both picture the same event, only using different images and terminology. As we will see a little later in this chapter, John's 3rd (p. 106) and 6th (p. 110) visions tell the exact same story of how the **overcomers** are removed, leaving the remaining believers to face an additional time of trial or testing.

As observed by Grant Osborne: "In Dan 7:21 the little horn *'was waging war against the saints and defeating them...'* That is the pattern here...When the saints enter *'the fellowship of his suffering'* (Phil 3:10), they share his ultimate victory through seeming defeat."[9]

The false prophet will force everyone to receive a mark on their right hand or forehead, and compel them to worship the beast or be killed (Rev 13:15-18). True believers will refuse to worship the Antichrist and be martyred.[10] Because Jesus overcame death, they will be able to face death, proclaiming victory over Satan.

> *"And **they overcame** him by the **blood of the Lamb**, and by the **word of their testimony**; and they **loved not their lives unto the death**."* (Rev 12:11)

> **RECAP of PLAYERS in 1ST TWO VISIONS**
>
> Woman           Israel
> Dragon          Satan ①
> Male Child       Overcomer
> Remnant of her Seed   Believers who Remain
> Beast from the Sea     Antichrist ①
> Beast from the Earth   False Prophet ①
>     Empire With    ②    10 Arab Nations or 10
>       10 Horns    ②    Revived Roman Empire
>     Little Horn     ②    America ? Syria ?
>     ① Unholy Trinity ② Mystery Babylon ?

The first two visions tell the wonderful story of how God will remove the **overcomers** before the Antichrist appears. Those who remain will be given the opportunity to **overcome** Satan by demonstrating their faith in Jesus Christ by martyrdom. The five visions, which will be described next, cover the entire tribulation period and confirm this exact same scenario.

### ③ Lamb & 144,000 Firstfruits (Rev 14:1-5)

The third vision John saw was the Lamb standing on Mount Zion with 144,000 who had been redeemed from the earth before the tribulation period started (*cf.* Rev 14:6-7).

> *"Then I looked, and behold, a Lamb standing on Mount Zion, and with Him one hundred and forty-four thousand, having His Father's name written on their foreheads...who were redeemed from the earth."*
> (Rev 14:1, 3 – NKJV)

This is a figurative picture of heavenly Jerusalem with 144,000 believers who had been removed from the earth before the tribulation began.[11] They are described as a select company who were *"undefiled"* with *"no deceit* or *fault"* and purchased from among men as *"firstfruits"* to God and the Lamb (Rev 14:4-5).

The 144,000 seen in Rev 14 are clearly different from those pictured in Rev 7:

| Comparison of 144,000 | | |
| --- | --- | --- |
| | **Revelation 7**<br>**Tribes of Israel** | **Revelation 14**<br>**Firstfruit Believers** |
| **Foreheads** | Seal of Protection<br>(Rev 7:3) | Identification Mark<br>(Rev 14:1) |
| **Locations** | Earth in Tribulation<br>(Rev 7:3-4 & 9:4) | Heaven before Tribulation<br>(Rev 14:1 & 14:7) |
| **People** | Tribes of Israel<br>(Rev 7:4) | Redeemed from the Earth<br>(Rev 14:3) |
| **Associated** | With Demon Locusts<br>(Rev 9:3-4) | With the Lamb Jesus<br>(Rev 14:1) |

Those in Rev 14 are 144,000 **overcoming** believers in Christ who have been taken from the earth (raptured) prior to the tribulation. They are a special remnant in heaven before the throne of God (Rev 14:5). They represent the *"male child"* taken up to the throne before the Dragon can harm them and the *"He who now restrains,"* taken out of the way before the Antichrist (*man of sin*) can begin his 42 months of terror.

Before the hour of judgment commences, God removes his devoted, overcoming believers as a reward for their faithfulness and obedience.[12] They had made the necessary preparations and were found worthy of escaping the tribulation hour because they were found blameless, spotless and undefiled. The holy and pure life these overcomers led was because they **relied upon** the overcoming power of Jesus Christ to **rule and reign** in their hearts as they regularly prayed to him:

> *"Watch ye therefore, and pray always, that ye **may be accounted worthy to escape all these things** that shall come to pass, and to **stand before the Son of man.**"* (Luke 21:36)

God is **calling** all believers to be part of this **overcoming** group.

④ **Gospel Proclaimed (Rev 14:6-7)**

> *"Then I saw another angel flying in the midst of heaven, having the everlasting gospel to preach to those who dwell on the earth--to every nation, tribe, tongue, and people--saying with a loud voice, 'Fear God and give glory to Him, for the hour of His judgment has come; and worship Him who made heaven and earth, the sea and springs of water.'"* (Rev 14:6-7 – NKJV)

Immediately after the removal of the 144,000 **overcoming** believers in their Firstfruits rapture, God sends an angel to preach the everlasting gospel to the whole world (i.e. *"every nation, tribe and tongue and people"*). Please notice, an angel is used to proclaim this *everlasting gospel.* This is a unique time on the earth when the great tribulation period will be under way.

The gospel that the angel will declare appears to be different from the *gospel of grace* that is preached today: faith in our Lord Jesus Christ and repentance unto God. The eternal gospel that the angel announces is: **fear God and give him glory and to worship him who made heaven and earth**.

God's judgment is about to commence and he wants everyone on earth to be given the chance to recognize and worship the creator as opposed to placing their allegiance with the Antichrist and the false prophet. While not stated explicitly, the call to *"fear God and give him glory"* implies the call to repentance (Ladd).

Some may contend the fact that this angel does not preach the *gospel of grace,* it proves that the entire church has already been removed. This argument is easily disputed by the fact that believers are pictured in the 6th vision, which will be discussed shortly (Rev 14:9-12), as well as what we have already learned from our review of the first three visions in this chapter.

Also, remember that Jesus told us that the gospel of the kingdom would be preached to the whole world before the end comes:

> *"And this **gospel of the kingdom** will be preached in all the world as a witness to all the nations, and then the end will come."* (Mat 24:14)

While the angel of the Lord is preaching the everlasting gospel to the whole world, God's two witnesses, along with the 144,000 servants from the 12 tribes of Israel, will also be proclaiming God's good news of the coming kingdom. In the end, everyone on earth will have been given the opportunity to hear the good news of God's love for all of mankind. Before judgement arrives, God sends this angel to warn all men. Solomon ends Ecclesiastes with similar advice:

> *"Let us hear the conclusion of the whole matter: **Fear God and keep His commandments, For this is man's all.** For God will bring every work into judgment, Including every secret thing, Whether good or evil."* (Ecc 12:13-14 – NKJV)

⑤ **Babylon Fallen (Rev 14:8)**

> *"And another angel followed, saying, **'Babylon is fallen, is fallen**, that great city, because she has made all nations drink of the wine of the wrath of her fornication.'"* (Rev 14:8 – NKJV)

The fifth vision that John saw was that of an angel declaring that the great city of Babylon had fallen. While this prophecy is described in the past tense, as already taken place, the actual fall of Babylon does not occur until the very end of the tribulation period, as described in Rev 16:19 and Rev 18:1-3. This technique is frequently used in the Old Testament as well as other places in Revelation (*cf.* 10:7, 11:15, 18, and 18:2).

That the fall of Babylon is assured is a certainty felt by the double pronouncement of the great city's demise. John's mention of her causing the world to become drunk with her idolatrous excesses is a reference from Jeremiah:

> *"Babylon was a golden cup in the LORD's hand, That made all the earth drunk. The nations drank her wine; Therefore the nations are deranged."* (Jer 51:7 – NKJV)

How Babylon causes the nations of the world to become deranged will be discussed in great detail in the next two chapters of this book. Babylon the great is a multi-faceted seducer of mankind that encompasses the spiritual, financial and physical aspects of their lives. Revelation 17 and 18 provide a detailed look into Mystery Babylon and we will discover why God's fury and wrath will finally be poured out for all the misery and corruption that she caused.

## ⑥ Persecution by Beast (Rev 14:9-12)

John's sixth vision comes from another angel who warns us that anyone who worships the beast and receives the infamous mark (666) on his hand or forehead will suffer God's wrath and torment:

*"9) Then a third angel followed them, saying with a loud voice, 'If anyone **worships the beast** and his image, and receives his **mark on his forehead or on his hand**, 10) he himself shall also drink of the wine of the **wrath of God**.... He shall be tormented with fire and brimstone in the presence of the holy angels and in the presence of the Lamb.* (Rev 14:9-10 – NKJV)

The false prophet (*"beast out of the earth"*) will force everyone to worship the Antichrist (*"beast out of the sea"*) and take the mark of the beast as a symbol of their allegiance. Those who do will face the consequence of God's wrath as a result.

Remember, the **overcoming** believer was taken away in the Firstfruit rapture, leaving the *"remnant of her seed"* behind to face the Antichrist, who is given 42 months to reign. During this time, he is allowed to pursue and kill the believers who remain:

> *"It was granted to him to **make war with the saints and to overcome them**...*" (Rev 13:7 – NKJV)

John alluded to this earlier when he told us about the Dragon:

> *"And the dragon was wroth with the woman, and **went to make war** with **the remnant of her seed, which keep the commandments of God, and have the testimony of Jesus Christ.***" (Rev 12:17)

The Prophet Daniel confirms this beast will persecute the saints:

*"He shall speak words against the Most High, and **shall wear out the saints of the Most High**, and shall think to change the times and the law; and **they shall be given into his hand** for a time, times, and half a time [3 ½ years]."* (Dan 7:25 – ESV)

The believers who remain will be given this great trial of their life, requiring them to stand up to the beast and **overcome** him.

> *"Here is a call for the endurance of the saints, those who keep the commandments of God and their faith in Jesus."* (Rev 14:12 – ESV)

They will be able to triumph over Satan because Jesus overcame death for them:

> *"And **they overcame** him by the **blood of the Lamb**, and by the **word of their testimony**; and they **loved not their lives unto the death**."* (Rev 12:11)

They will learn to be overcomers and proclaim the final victory!

## Beatitude for Martyrs (Rev 14:13)

> *"And I heard a voice from heaven, saying, "Write,*
> ***'Blessed are the dead who die in the Lord from now***
> ***on!'"*** *"Yes," says the Spirit, "so that they may rest from*
> *their labors, for their deeds follow with them."*
> (Rev 14:13 – NAS)

The believers living in the last days of the church age, that miss the Firstfruit rapture, will face persecution by the beast. Their great hour of trial is reminiscent of the time when the early church of Smyrna underwent a similar period of testing. Those believers were given the wonderful promise that their martyrdom would be aptly rewarded: *"Be faithful unto death, and I will give you the crown of life.* (Rev 2:10 – ESV)

Between the 6th and 7th visions given to John, a voice from heaven tells him to be certain to write down this important Beatitude. Those believers who will be facing the trial of their lives need to remember that even though they may be confronted with such a difficult test, those who remain faithful will be greatly blessed.

God is calling believers living in these end times to prepare for the Bridegroom's soon return by being genuine **overcomers**. Those who fail to heed this important call will be given one final chance to overcome through death. By demonstrating their faith in Jesus, they will overcome Satan by their martyrdom. While he may take away their lives, Jesus will reward them with a glorious crown and the promise that they cannot be hurt by the second death (Rev 2:11).

---

**Lord Jesus, please help me be the overcomer you are calling me to be. Please count me worthy to escape the hour of trial that is coming upon this dying world that is not my home.**

## ⑦ 2nd Coming of Jesus (Rev 14:14-20)

The seventh and final vision given to John is the return of the Lord at the very end of the tribulation period. When Jesus returns he will be coming in the clouds, as announced at the very beginning of the book:

> *"BEHOLD, HE IS COMING WITH THE CLOUDS, and every eye will see Him, even those who pierced Him; and all the tribes of the earth will mourn over Him. So it is to be. Amen."* (Rev 1:7 – NAS)

### Harvest

Christ's second coming will actually occur in stages. First, Jesus will come in the clouds for the harvest:

*"Then I looked, and behold, **a white cloud**, and **on the cloud sat One like the Son of Man**, having on His head a golden crown, and in His hand a sharp sickle.*

> *And another angel came out of the temple, crying with a loud voice to Him who sat on the cloud, 'Thrust in Your sickle and reap, for the time has come for You to reap, for the **harvest** of the earth is ripe.' So He who sat on the cloud thrust in His sickle on the earth, and the earth was reaped."* (Rev 14:14-16 – NKJV)

The first part of the Lord's return is the final harvest, as the tribulation period is winding to a close. This is an agricultural picture used to show that the final harvest is now ripe and ready at the end of the summer heat. The firstfruits had been taken in an earlier season, but now that the summer was over, the remainder of the crop was ready to be reaped. This is the Main Harvest rapture where believers will meet the Lord in the air:

> *"For the Lord himself will come down from heaven, with a loud command, with the voice of the archangel*

*and with the trumpet call of God, and the dead in Christ will rise first. After that, we who are still alive and **who are left** will be caught up with them **in the clouds** to **meet the Lord in the air**. And so we will be with the Lord forever.* " (1 Th 4:16-17 – NIV)

The believers who remain at the very end of the tribulation period are taken in the air to the *clouds*. These believers had somehow not been required to become martyrs and are taken to meet Jesus just before God pours out his wrath on the rest of the world. After the remaining church is harvested is the vintage:

### Vintage

The final vintage of the grape season occurs when the grapes are trodden down in the winepress. This is superbly pictured as the final scene in Revelation 14:

*"Then another angel came out of the temple which is in heaven, he also having a sharp sickle. And another angel came out from the altar, who had power over fire, and he cried with a loud cry to him who had the sharp sickle, saying,*
    *'Thrust in your sharp sickle and gather the clusters of the vine of the earth, for her grapes are fully ripe.'*
    *So the angel thrust his sickle into the earth and gathered the vine of the earth, and threw it into the **great winepress of the wrath of God**.*
*And the winepress was trampled outside the city, and blood came out of the winepress, up to the horses' bridles, for one thousand six hundred furlongs.* " (Rev 14:17-20 – NKJV)

This is a preview of that great final battle of Armageddon at the very end of the tribulation period: *"...He treads the winepress of the fury of the wrath of God Almighty."* (Rev 19:15)

David M. Panton ably described John's final vision of the Lord's second coming in his book *The Judgment Seat of Christ:*

"The Field is the world; the Wheat is the church; the Reapers are angels (Matt. xiii. 39):–the Reapers first of all gather the Firstfruits, then garner the Harvest, and finally glean the Corners of the Field which had been deliberately left unreaped (Lev. xxiii. 10-22). So first-fruits are found in the Heavenlies *before* the harvest (Rev xiv. 4): and *after* the harvest (Rev. xvi. 15) the warning to watchfulness still goes forth (Rev xiv. 15). 'Only those who are devoutly looking and waiting for the Saviour's return shall be taken at first' (Seiss)."[13]

---

### 7 Visions

As an interlude between the 7 Trumpets and 7 Vials, John is given 7 Visions that provide very important details about the people, places and events that take place during the 3 ½ years of great tribulation.

| | |
|---|---|
| Dragon persecutes the woman | 1,260 days |
| Woman protected in wilderness | 3 ½ years |
| Beast given power to reign | 42 months |

John describes the length of this period three times and never mentions a 7-year tribulation period. Given the fact that the number 7 plays such a predominate role through-out the book of Revelation; logic would dictate that these 7 visions would be an appropriate time to introduce it. But to the contrary, the tribulation period is only described as 3 ½ years throughout these 7 visions (and throughout the entire Bible for that matter – please see Appendix 3).

The message of the seven visions is very clear: God is calling all believers to be **overcomers**. Those who are successful will be protected in heaven while the rest of the church experiences the trials of the tribulation. Those believers who remain will be given the opportunity to demonstrate their faith and **overcome** Satan by being martyrs for Christ.

---

# The Seven

# Vial Judgments

*1) Then I saw another sign in heaven, great and marvelous:* **seven angels** *having the* **seven last plagues***, for in them the* **wrath of God is complete***. 2) And I saw something like a sea of glass mingled with fire, and* **those who have the victory over** *the* **beast***, over his image and over his mark and over the number of his name,* **standing on the sea of glass***, having harps of God.*
*3) They sing the song of Moses, the servant of God, and the song of the Lamb, saying:*

> *'Great and marvelous are Your works, Lord God Almighty! Just and true are Your ways, O King of the saints! 4) Who shall not fear You, O Lord, and glorify Your name? For You alone are holy. For all nations shall come and worship before You, For Your judgments have been manifested.'"*

*5) After these things I looked, and behold, the temple of the* **tabernacle** *of the testimony* **in heaven** *was opened. 6) And out of the temple came the* **seven angels** *having the* **seven plagues***, clothed in pure bright linen, and having their chests girded with golden bands.* " (Rev 15:1-6 – NKJV)

# Chapter 5 – 7 Vials of Wrath

The 11th chapter of Revelation ended with the sounding of the 7th trumpet and the 3rd woe about to begin when the wrath of God is poured out on in the 7 vials. That scene ended with a view of the Ark of the Covenant in heaven (see pp. 97-98). Chapters 12, 13 and 14 provided us with a brief interlude in the action with the 7 Visions discussed in the previous chapter of this book. The action picks back up in chapter 15 of Revelation with a scene of the martyrs in heaven having won their victory over the beast (Antichrist). They overcame Satan by the blood of the Lamb and the word of their testimony (Rev 12:11).

They are standing on the sea of glass mentioned in Rev 4:6 (see pp. 51-52) which reveals a majestic scene in heaven. They are singing the songs of Moses (cf. Exo 15:1-8 and Deu 32:1-47) praising God for their victory over the beast as the children of Israel had sung when they were delivered from the hands of Pharaoh in Egypt and their journey into the Promised Land.

## Vial #1: Earth (Rev 15-16:2)

> *"7) And one of the four beasts gave unto the **seven angels seven golden vials full of the wrath of God,** who liveth forever and ever. 8) And the temple was filled with smoke from the glory of God, and from his power; and no man was able to enter into the temple, till the seven plagues of the seven angels were fulfilled."*
> (Rev 15:7-8)

There can be no doubt that the wrath about to be poured out on the earth is coming directly from the throne of God. It is his fury and wrath upon the beast's kingdom, and all those who worshiped him and remained unrepentant even after the 7 trumpets warning of judgment had been released.

Whereas the first four trumpet judgments were directed at the environment (earth, trees, sea, rivers and the sky), these final plagues are aimed directly at men.

> *"1) And I heard a great voice out of the temple saying to the seven angels, Go your ways, and pour out the vials of the wrath of God upon the earth. 2) And the **first** went, and **poured out his vial** upon the earth; and there fell a **noisome and grievous sore upon the men** which **had the mark of the beast**, and **upon them which worshipped his image.**"* (Rev 16:1-2)

The 1$^{st}$ vial of wrath from God is horrible sores on all those who had received the mark of the beast and worshipped him rather that the creator. God is furious over their decision and responds by sending these *"grievous sores"* upon their bodies. This plague will cause men much pain and suffering – being very difficult to bear and causing a great deal of agony. This vial is similar to the 6$^{th}$ plague that was inflicted by Moses in the land of Egypt (Exo 9:8-11) on all the Egyptians for failing to free God's people.

## Vial #2: Sea (Rev 16:3)

> *3) And the **second angel** poured out his vial upon the **sea;** and it became **as** the **blood** of a dead man: and **every living soul died in the sea.*** (Rev 16:3)

Whereas the 2$^{nd}$ trumpet caused 1/3 of the sea to become a blood-red color, the 2$^{nd}$ vial will kill all of the creatures in the oceans and seas. The first four trumpets were limited judgments covering only a third of the targeted element. The trumpets warned; but because mankind did not respond with repentance, God's wrath is now poured out with the corresponding vial. The chart on p. 72 depicts this in graphic detail as each trumpet is followed by subsequent devastation.

**Vial #3: Rivers (Rev 16:4-7)**

> *"4) And the **third angel** poured out his vial upon the **rivers and fountains** of waters; and they **became blood**.
> 5) And I heard the angel of the waters say, Thou art righteous, O Lord, which art, and wast, and shalt be, because thou hast judged thus. 6) For **they have shed the blood of saints and prophets**, and **thou hast given them blood to drink**; for they are worthy. 7) And I heard another out of the altar say, Even so, Lord God Almighty, true and **righteous are thy judgments**."*
> (Rev 16:4-7)

When the 3$^{rd}$ trumpet was sounded 1/3 of the rivers and fountains became bitter causing some people to perish upon drinking it. Here under the 3$^{rd}$ vial, all the rivers and fountains are turned into actual blood. This plague is similar to the 1$^{st}$ plague brought on Egypt when the Nile river was turned into blood (Exo 7:16-24), making fresh water used for drinking non-potable. Under this 3$^{rd}$ vial, **all** of man's sources of drinking water became unusable. Two angels who observed this deadly plague agreed that this judgment by God is righteous and true in recognition of the fact that the **blood** of the martyrs had been shed – a fitting drink for the ungodly as a recompense.

**Vial #4: Sun (Rev 16:8-9)**

> *"8) And the **fourth angel** poured out his vial upon the **sun**; and power was given unto him to **scorch men with fire**. 9) And men were scorched with great heat, and blasphemed the name of God, which hath power over these plagues: and **they repented not** to give him glory."*
> (Rev 16:8-9)

Whereas the 4$^{th}$ trumpet brought about darkness to 1/3 of the world, the 4$^{th}$ vial causes the sun to send forth a sweltering heat that actually scorches them.  Pastor Tom McElmurry has done an excellent analysis linking the 4th trumpet with the 4th vial. He believes that the darkening of the sun during the 4th trumpet is the result of thousands of volcanic eruptions occurring around the globe, sending tremendous amounts of hydrogen chloride gas in the atmosphere, causing a breakdown in the ozone layer. At the end of the 3 ½ tribulation period, these gases will have depleted the protective shield in the ozone layer, which "will allow ultraviolet radiation to pour through onto the inhabitants of the earth.   These occupants of the last days of Satan's kingdom on this earth will be scorched with the great heat..."[1] described in this 4th vial.  Despite this great judgment, men will still not repent.

### Vial #5: Beast's Kingdom (Rev 16:10-11)

> *"10) And the **fifth angel** poured out his vial upon the seat of the beast; and his kingdom was **full of darkness**; and they gnawed their tongues for pain, 11) And blasphemed the God of heaven because of their pains and their sores, and repented not of their deeds."*
> (Rev 16:10-11)

The 9th plague God brought on Egypt was complete darkness over the entire country for 3 days.  In spite of this, the Pharaoh's heart remained hardened and he would not let the children of Israel go (Exo 10:21-23, 27).  The 5th vial of God's wrath brings total darkness over the kingdom of the beast.   Because the Antichrist (beast) has authority over every nation on the earth (Rev 13:4) this vial brings darkness over the entire world.  The darkness created under the 4th trumpet only affected 1/3 of the earth has now spread across the entire planet.  This intense darkness will only intensify the pain being felt as a result of the previous judgments.  Darkness symbolizes the judgment of God (*cf.* Exo 10:21, Amo 5:18, Isa 13:10 and Joe 2:2) and despite all these torments, men's hearts remain hardened.

**Vial #6: Euphrates (Rev 16:12-14)**

> *"12) And the **sixth angel** poured out his vial **upon the great river Euphrates; and the **water** thereof **was dried up**, that the way of the **kings of the east** might be prepared. 13) And I saw three unclean spirits like frogs come out of the mouth of the dragon, and out of the mouth of the beast, and out of the mouth of the false prophet. 14) For they are **the spirits of devils**, working miracles, which **go forth unto the kings of the earth and of the whole world, to gather them to the battle of that great day of God Almighty.*** "* (Rev 16:12-14)

The 6th vial completely dries up the riverbed of the Euphrates river which will give the armies from the east a clear path to the final battle of Armageddon. The 6th trumpet released the four fallen angels who were bound in this same river. They are now given help by the demons that arise from the mouths of the unholy trinity: the dragon (Satan), the beast (Antichrist) and the false prophet (*"beast out of the earth"* – Rev 13:11-18). These demons are the *"spirits of devils"* that will be sent out to gather all the nations of the world as a united force.

This next-to-last vial paints a remarkable picture of how the evil forces of darkness will gather together in one final battle. This great day was anticipated by the prophets (Psa 2, Joe 3:2, and Zec 14:1-3) and shows how God's opponents completely reject truth, righteousness and His majesty.

> *"9) My soul yearns for you...When your judgments come upon the earth, the people of the world learn righteousness. But when grace is shown to the wicked, **they do not learn righteousness**; even in a land of uprightness **they go on doing evil** and **do not regard the majesty of the LORD**... Let them see your zeal for your people and be put to shame; **let the fire reserved for your enemies consume them.*** (Isa 26:9-11 – NIV)

### Beatitude for Watchful (Rev 16:15)

> ("Behold, I am coming as a thief! **Blessed is he who watches**, and **keeps his garments**, less he walk naked and they see his shame.")
> (Rev 16:15 – NKJV)

The timing of this Beatitude is most extraordinary.  The 6th vial of God's wrath had just been poured out, opening a path for the ungodly to traverse the Euphrates on their way to the final battle of the world.  The Main Harvest rapture had recently occurred, removing all believers from the earth before God poured out the first vial.  So who is this Beatitude addressing?

Apparently it has been inserted between the 6th and 7th vials to reveal the longsuffering of our great God!  He wants to bless a few remaining souls who have the opportunity to overcome right up until the very conclusion of the age.

Perhaps this Beatitude is addressed to those friends of believers who had only been raptured a few days earlier.  Having realized they were left behind, they were convicted in their hearts. Perhaps they picked up a Bible and realized what had just taken place and that Jesus really is the Lord and he really is getting ready to return at any moment.

Since these people had somehow managed to survive the last 42 months without bowing down to worship the Antichrist, they are given one final chance to call upon the name of the Lord for their salvation (Rom 10:13).  Someone may ask: "how can they obtain their garments at this late date?"

While Christ's robe of righteousness (Isa 61:10) is given to them when they call upon the Lord for salvation, they still have the time to acquire their own garments.[2]  In these closing hours, perhaps they furnish water or shelter to a widow or an orphan or a stranger (*cf.* Jas 1:27 & Mat 25:35)[3]. Maybe God uses them to supply a hot meal to someone in need. While time is short, there are always opportunities He provides. Also, as noted by Joseph Seiss: "There is a blessedness for them even down amid these last extremities of the judgment time; but it can only be secured, as in every other case, by constant watchfulness, prayer, and readiness for the summons when it comes."[4] Incredibly, God is calling out for overcomers until the very end!

### Vial #7: Armageddon (Rev 16:16-21)

> *"16) And he gathered them together into a place called in the Hebrew tongue Armageddon. 17) And the **seventh angel poured out his vial** into the air; and there came a great **voice out of the temple of heaven, from the throne**, saying, **It is done**."* (Rev 16:16-17)

The final vial brings us to the very end of the tribulation period. The armies of the world gather in the plain of Megiddo to fight the final battle mentioned in the 6$^{th}$ vial. The 7$^{th}$ vial brings the announcement form the throne of heaven *"it is done."* The final climax has arrived and the evil forces of this fallen world are about to meet their ultimate defeat. The familiar *"voices, and **thunders**, and **lightnings**..."* (p. 79) are accompanied by a mighty earthquake that devastates this planet.

> *"And there were **voices**, and **thunders**, and **lightnings**; and there was a great earthquake, such as was not since men were upon the earth, **so mighty an earthquake**, and so great....And **every island fled away**, and the **mountains were not found**."* (Rev 16:18, 20)

This great and mighty earthquake will cause the land masses around the globe to be violently shaken, creating destruction beyond any experienced before. This scene was alluded to with the opening of the 6$^{th}$ seal (pp. 68-69), which now culminates in a great crescendo.[5] This great shaking affects the entire world:

> *"And the **great city was divided** into three parts, and **the cities of the nations fell:** and **great Babylon** came in remembrance before **God**, to give unto her the cup of the wine of the **fierceness of his wrath.** "* (Rev 16:19)

The above verse shows three distinct areas: 1) the great city is Jerusalem (*cf.* Rev 11:8 and Zec 14:4), 2) the cities of the nations are cities around the world, and 3) the great city of Babylon is the headquarters of the beast. God's fury will be felt in towns and cities around the globe. His final wrath against rebellious mankind includes an arsenal of great hail raining down from heaven:

> *"And there fell upon men a **great hail out of heaven,** every stone about the weight of a talent: and men blasphemed God because of the plague of the hail; for **the plague thereof was exceeding great.** "* (Rev 16:21)

Men cursed God when he closed his final wrath with hail, weighing over 100 pounds each. To the very end, men remain defiant. But the afflictions brought on by these preliminary plagues are only the beginning of the end. God the Father has commanded these judgments as a prelude to his final tactic. His Son is preparing his great army for the ultimate show down.

In the next chapter of this book we will discover how God will finally defeat Satan and all of his evil cohorts. The rider on the white horse has now been given many crowns (Rev 19:12) and he will be returning with his great army of **overcoming** believers to fight the final battle.

> *"These shall make war with the Lamb, and the Lamb shall **overcome them**: for he is Lord of lords, and King of kings: and they that are with him are **called, and chosen, and faithful.** "* (Rev 17:14)

# Chapter 6 – 7 Voices from Heaven

The previous chapter of this book gave us a look at God's final wrath included in the 7 vials, which are summarized in Revelation 15 and 16. These vials cover the very final days of the tribulation period, as God's takeover of planet earth is about to be completed. In this chapter we will take a detailed look at the religious, political and economic systems that manipulate the world during its final stages. Chapter 13 introduced the Antichrist (*beast from the sea*) and the false prophet (*beast from the earth*). Chapter 17 portrays detail surrounding the religious aspects, while Chapter 18 depicts its political/economic facets. Chapter 19 gives important final announcements from heaven.

① **Harlot & Beast (Rev 17:1-6)**

> *"1) Then one of the seven angels who had the seven bowls came and talked with me, saying to me, 'Come, I will show you the judgment of the **great harlot** who **sits on many waters**, 2) with whom the kings of the earth committed fornication, and the inhabitants of the earth were made drunk with the wine of her fornication.' 3) So he carried me away in the Spirit into the wilderness. And I saw a **woman sitting on a scarlet beast** which was full of names of blasphemy, having **seven heads and ten horns**."* (Rev 17:1-3 – NKJV)

One of the angels carrying the vials of wrath tells John about a great harlot, who influences people around the globe (*peoples, multitudes, nations, and tongues*–Rev 17:15), with idolatry and spiritual fornication. A harlot is one who seduces and entices people to follow evil and falsehoods. This great harlot is pictured riding on the beast, which is Daniel's 4<sup>th</sup> beast that had been described earlier (p. 102 – Rev 13:1-2). This reveals how the false prophet and the Antichrist will be united in their great deception and blasphemy against righteousness and truth. Both make the people of the earth *drunk* and both cause them to commit *fornication* (*cf.* Rev 17:2 & 18:3). The harlot's wine is her false religious teachings, which captivate the world as the leader of "Christianity." Millions of people follow her and are deceived into thinking she represents Jesus Christ. Likewise, the beast's system has affected the entire world with the wine of materialism, causing mankind to place all forms of idols and lusts ahead of God. "In God we trust" has become a hollow slogan that was originally established as a bastion of faith and hope. Both are also *arrayed in purple and scarlet and adorned with gold and precious stones and pearls* (*cf.* Rev 17:4 & 18:16). *"And on her forehead a name was written:*

### *MYSTERY,*
### *BABYLON THE GREAT,*
### *THE MOTHER OF HARLOTS*
### *AND OF THE ABOMINATIONS OF THE EARTH.*
(Rev 17:5 – NKJV)

These names tell us that this figure represents a mystery, which includes multifaceted characters. To solve the identities of this mystery requires clues from other portions of the Bible. Babylon is first introduced in Genesis 10 and 11 and is well known throughout Scripture for being in opposition to God. Some of the important prophecies concerning Mystery Babylon can be found in Jeremiah 50-51, Isaiah 18, Habakkuk and Daniel (to name a few). Relevant examples include:

*"Your mother shall be utterly shamed, and she who bore you shall be disgraced. Behold, she shall be the last of the nations, a wilderness, a dry land, and a desert."* (Jer 50:12 – ESV)

This is a prophecy that the nation that birthed this New Babylon will be in existence and witness the total destruction of this great country at the close of the tribulation period.

*"Babylon hath been a golden cup in the LORD'S hand, that* **made all the earth drunken**: *the nations have drunken of her wine; therefore the nations are mad."* (Jer 51:7)

This shows how the Lord used this great nation at one time as his instrument (i.e. golden cup) to proclaim the Word of God. In the end, however, New Babylon causes the world to be led astray by offering them the wine of materialism and greed.

The prophecies in Daniel provide some of the most important keys in solving the mystery surrounding the identity of the beast in Revelation. In Daniel chapter 2, we are given the 4 great empires (Babylon, Medo-Persia, Greek, and Roman) that span some 2,600 years, until the very end of the tribulation period (Dan 2:44). Some contend that the 4th empire is the Seleucid kingdom (Syria / Iraq), which is seen as part of its legs/feet (Seleucid/Ptolemaic reign). Nevertheless, Daniel 7 presents a different perspective and provides the most important clues regarding the true identity of the beast in Revelation. Daniel 7 describes 4 beasts (lion, bear, leopard with 4 wings, and a 4th more terrifying beast with 10 horns + a little horn – Dan 7:3-8).

| Daniel sees 4 beasts: | Heads |
|---|---|
| 1st Lion (England) | 1 |
| 2nd Bear (Russia) | 1 |
| 3rd Leopard (below) | 4 |
| 4th Diverse BEAST | 1 |
| | 7 |

*"After this I beheld, and lo another, like a* **leopard**, *which had upon the back of it* **four wings of a fowl**; *the beast had also* **four heads**; *and dominion was given to it."* (Dan 7:6)
**(Egypt with Syria, Iraq, Jordan & Saudia Arabia or Iran?)**

Daniel's 3rd beast has 5 nations with only 4 leaders (heads).[1] These nations, along with England and Russia are **present** when

Daniel's 4th beast appears (which is the beast in Rev 13, 17-18):

*"After this I saw in the night visions, and behold a **fourth beast**, dreadful and terrible, and strong exceedingly; and it had great iron teeth: it devoured and brake in pieces, and stamped the residue with the feet of it: and it **was diverse from all the beasts that were before**[2] it; and it **had ten horns**.* (Dan 7:7)

Daniel's **four** beasts have 7 heads and 10 horns; exactly the same as John's beast described in Revelation 13:1: *"...And I saw a **beast** rising up out of the sea, having **seven heads and ten horns..."** Is this just a coincidence?[3]

② **Mystery Explained (Rev 17:7-18)**

The angel then tells John the clues to solve the mystery surrounding the harlot seen riding on the beast with 7 heads and 10 horns (Rev 17:7). On the facing page is a summary of the key verses, along with this author's speculation of the identity of the nations involved.

**Verse 8** – At the time John wrote this, the beast that "was" and "is not" must be Babylon, which fell in 539 B.C. It could not be Rome since the Romans came into power in 63 B.C. with Pompey's occupation of Jerusalem.

**Verse 9** – This verse will be discussed latter on in this section.

**Verse 10** – The 7 kings include the 5 who have fallen (Egypt, Assyria, Babylon, Persia and Greece, + Rome (which was in power at the time John wrote this), leaving the Beast, who has not yet come (which we believe is the New Babylon).

**Verse 11** – The Beast that "was" and "is not" is one of the 7 that are listed. From verses 8 and 10 above we see this must be from the Beast named New Babylon (the 7th). The actual Beast (Antichrist) is the *"little horn"* which comes out of the 7th one listed (*cf.* Dan 7:7-8). This *"little horn"* is the 8th and will be destroyed at the very end (*cf.* Rev 19:20).

## Mystery of Woman, Beast and 10 Horns

*"7) But the angel said to me, 'Why did you marvel?* ***I will tell you the mystery** of the **woman*** and of the **beast** that carries her, which has the **seven heads and the ten horns**.*

*8) The beast that you saw **was**, and is **not**, and **will ascend** out of the bottomless pit and go to perdition. **And those who dwell on the earth will marvel**... when they see the beast that was, and is not, and yet is."*

| Beast Was | Beast Is Not | Beast Will Ascend |
|---|---|---|
| Babylon | Babylon | *New Babylon* |

*9) 'Here is the mind which has wisdom: The seven heads are seven mountains on which the woman sits.*
*10) There are also seven kings. Five have fallen, one is, and the other has not yet come. And when he comes, he must continue a short time.'*

| 5 Kings Have Fallen | One Is | Not Yet Come |
|---|---|---|
| Egypt, Assyria Babylon , Persia Greece | Rome | Beast (*New Babylon*) |

*11) The beast that was, and is not, is himself also the eighth, and is of the seven, and is going to perdition.*

| <u>5</u> 5 Kings Have Fallen | <u>6</u> One Is | <u>7</u> Not Yet Come | <u>8</u> He is of The 7 |
|---|---|---|---|
| Egypt, Assyria Babylon , Persia Greece | Rome | Beast (*New Babylon*) [7 Heads & 10 Horns] | Little Horn (comes out of the 7) |

*"18) And the **woman*** whom you saw is that **great city which reigns over the kings of the earth**."*
(Rev 17:7-11, 18 – NKJV)
* Cities = New York City and Rome: the Headquarters for the United Nations and the Roman Catholic Church.

**Verse 9** – This verse, along with verse 18, reveal that the 7 heads are 7 hills or mountains upon which their headquarters are located.[4] Verse 9 states that understanding the true identity of this important city calls for wisdom. We know these cities will be the headquarters of the Beast and the harlot. Since the city of Rome is well known as *"the city on 7 hills,"* we know this is where the harlot is located.

The Beast will rule from the center of economic and political power. New York City is probably the greatest commercial and banking center in the world. It is also the headquarters for the United Nations, which will become the global government to place all sovereign nations under its control, in order to bring in the New World Order (NWO). Interestingly, New York will become **"the city on 7 mountains,"** since the Beast will have dominion over **"the seven continents"** of the world. Both the Beast and the harlot will rule the world from their strategic command centers: New York and Rome.

The Antichrist (Beast) will rule with "10 horns," the actual identity will not be speculated here. These 10 horns will turn on the harlot and destroy her headquarters located in Rome:

> *"And the **ten horns which you saw on the beast, these will hate the harlot,** make her desolate and naked, eat her flesh and **burn her with fire."** (Rev 17:16 – NKJV)*

Why these 10 horns annihilate her is not given. Chapter 13 of Revelation shows that the harlot (false prophet) will carry out the execution of believers (Rev 13:15-16). Perhaps the 10 horns will be horrified over the death of millions and seek vengeance.

> *"I saw the woman, drunk with the **blood of the saints** and with the **blood of the martyrs of Jesus**. And when I saw her, I marveled with great amazement."*
> (Rev 17:6 – NKJV)

③ **Babylon Has Fallen (Rev 18:1-24)**

*"1) After these things I saw another angel coming down from heaven, having great authority, and the **earth was illuminated with his glory**. 2) And he **cried mightily with a loud voice, saying, 'Babylon the great is fallen, is fallen,** and has become a dwelling place of demons, a prison for every foul spirit, and a cage for every unclean and hated bird! 3) **For all the nations have drunk of the wine of the wrath of her fornication,** the kings of the earth have committed fornication with her, and the **merchants of the earth have become rich through the abundance of her luxury.** '"* (Rev 18:1-3 – NKJV)

The angel coming down from heaven is believed to be Jesus (Beasley-Murray, Feinberg, Lee, Mize, Seiss) while others feel it is only another angel (Mounce, Newell, Osborne, Thomas). We feel this angel does represent Christ coming in his great glory to pronounce final judgment on the ungodly kingdom of Babylon, which causes the whole world to be corrupted.

Jesus cries with a loud mighty voice, a double pronouncement that Babylon has fallen. By repeating this declaration, he is asserting with great certainty their destruction and also alluding to both falls: the fall of the religious Babylon and the fall of the commercial and political Babylon. The annihilation of the harlot's kingdom occurred in chapter 17, and the Beast's kingdom is destroyed here in chapter 18.

The distinction between the two Babylon kingdoms is shown by the figures of a harlot and a beast. Both have many similarities, as already mentioned, however the wine of the harlot is one of false religion while the wine the Beast system offers is one of mammon. Here she is pictured bringing wealth and riches to the merchants of the earth as they supply the extravagant lifestyle of this New Babylon. Sadly, our great nation has become one that worships the god of materialism and has taught

the entire world to follow her path of luxury and greed. The
nation of America is the leading importer of goods that help
supply the profuse flow of money and merchandise to satisfy
her every desire. The fact that New Babylon's population is
less than 5% of the world population substantiates her opulence.
All the bankers, merchants, ship captains and suppliers of goods
have become wealthy and will weep when they witness her
sudden destruction:

> *"8) Therefore her plagues will come **in one day--death**
> *and mourning and famine.* **And she will be utterly**
> **burned with fire**, *for strong is the Lord God who judges*
> *her. 9)The kings of the earth who committed fornication*
> *and lived luxuriously with her will weep and lament for*
> *her, when they see the smoke of her burning...saying,*
> *'Alas, alas, **that great city Babylon**, that mighty city!*
> *For in **one hour your judgment has come.'** "*
> (Rev 18:8-9 – NKJV)

In one hour, such great riches come to nothing. The love of
luxury and pleasure will have come to naught. All those who
became wealthy will witness it all going up in smoke as
Babylon the Great is utterly devastated. The nation that once
boasted that she would never see sorrow (Rev 18:7) becomes a
heap of ruin (*cf.* Isa 21:9).

④ **Come Out of Her (Rev 18:4)**

> *"And I heard another voice from heaven saying, **'Come**
> **out of her, my people,** lest you share in her sins, and*
> *lest you receive of her plagues."* (Rev 18:4 – NKJV)

Any Christian living in modern America during these end times
should see how we represent Mystery Babylon. Readers are
encouraged to read Jeremiah 50-51, Isaiah 18, and Habakkuk
where they will see how we were once a great nation that was
greatly blessed and used by God, that has turned from him and

become corrupted. America has turned into a great cesspool of violence, sex, drugs, alcohol, idolatry and witchcraft, where the pursuit of riches and pleasure are the norm. The love of God has been replaced with the love of money.

Believers who fail to recognize this astonishing fact may be residing in the church of Laodicea (see pp. 44-48), which is blind to spiritual truth[5] and in love with mammon, which is a root of all kinds of evil (1 Ti 6:10).

America is now so anti-God and anti-Christian that standing up for biblical principles of truth and righteousness can result in being thrown into jail. This trend will continue until the time when the Antichrist appears and believers will be forced to renounce their faith in Christ or face martyrdom.

The admonition to come out of Babylon is appropriate for all of God's people throughout the ages. Believers are encouraged to recognize where their heart's affections lie (Col 3:3) and be reminded that we must keep ourselves from being polluted by the world (Jas 1:27), lest we become God's enemy:

> *"Don't you realize that friendship with the world makes you an enemy of God? I say it again: If you want to be a friend of the world, you make yourself an enemy of God."* (Jas 4:4 – NLT)

The overcomers will acknowledge this great peril and recognize that our **true citizenship** is not of this world and that we are merely **sojourners** simply passing through. Our hearts are longing for His righteousness and His coming Kingdom.

> *"Flee from the midst of Babylon, And every one save his life! Do not be cut off in her iniquity, For this is the time of the LORD's vengeance; He shall recompense her."*
> (Jer 51:6 – NKJV)

⑤ **Rejoicing in Heaven (Rev 19:1-5)**

*"1) After these things I heard a **loud voice** of a **great multitude in heaven**, saying, "Alleluia! Salvation and glory and honor and power belong to the Lord our God! 2) For **true and righteous are His judgments**, because He has **judged the great harlot** who corrupted the earth with her fornication; and He has **avenged on her the blood of His servants shed by her** 3) Again they said, 'Alleluia! Her smoke rises up forever and ever!' 4) And the twenty-four elders and the four living creatures fell down and worshiped God who sat on the throne, saying, 'Amen! Alleluia!' 5) Then a voice came from the throne, saying, 'Praise our God, all you His servants and those who fear Him, both small and great!'* (Rev 19:1-5 – NKJV)

The 5$^{th}$ voice from heaven is a great multitude singing praises to God for rightly judging Babylon for its idolatry and corruption on the earth and the martyrdom of millions of souls. This great multitude of heavenly hosts sings praise for the final destruction and burning of both the harlot and beasts' empires that brought so much pain and sorrow. God's vengeance is fitting and proper for their punishment, which is complete and final. The 24 elders and the 4 living creatures fall down in worship before the throne; in adoration and praise that is reminiscent of scenes described earlier in this book (see pp. 49-55). God is on the throne and in complete control. He deserves all of our praise and worship.

⑥ **Marriage of the Lamb (Rev 19:6-8)**

After John hears the voice of the great multitude singing praise and adoration to God for the complete destruction of Babylon, he again hears a great multitude singing additional praises that are accompanied by what resembles the sounds of many waters, along with the sound of *mighty thunderings*. This sound of the mighty thunders is highly significant as we learned earlier in our discussion of the 7 thunders (see p. 92). The sounding of the 7 thunders from the throne room in heaven only takes place at very crucial times. They were heard when the overcomers were taken before the throne in the rapture of Firstfruit believers in Rev 14:1-5 (pp. 106-107). They occur again here as the wedding of the bride to her Bridegroom is about to take place:

> *"6) And I heard, as it were, the voice of a great multitude, as the sound of many waters and as the **sound of mighty thunderings,** saying, "Alleluia! For the Lord God Omnipotent reigns! 7) 'Let us be glad and rejoice and give Him glory, for the **marriage of the Lamb has come,** and **His wife has made herself ready.**' 8) And to her it was granted to be arrayed in fine linen, clean and bright, for the **fine linen is the righteous acts of the saints.**"* (Rev 19:6-8 – NKJV)

This is the most important wedding event that will ever occur. It has been a long-anticipated design by God once his Son takes back the reign over all the earth. The bride makes herself ready for this great day by living her life with this wonderful time in mind. She devotes herself to Him and always lives her life in such a way to please Him. She prepares her wedding dress of *fine linen* by the righteous life that she leads and the many wonderful deeds she accomplishes because of her great love for her Bridegroom. She vividly exemplifies the **overcomer** by her devotion, faithfulness and obedience to righteousness.

To understand the preparation made by the bride, we should remember that the Apostle Paul instructed husbands to love their wives in the same manner as: *"...also the **Christ** did love the assembly, and **did give himself for it,** that **he might sanctify it, having cleansed it** ..."* (Eph 5:25-26 – YLT) Yes, Jesus sacrificed his very life because of his great love for his future bride! He sanctifies her by the *"washing of water with the word..."* (Eph 5:26 – AMP) This is a vivid picture of the bride allowing the Word of God to cleanse her life on a daily basis as she seeks nourishment and refreshment for her soul. Because of her love for her future Bridegroom, she steadfastly devotes her heart to Him so that he may present her to Himself:

> *"...in **glorious splendor, without spot or wrinkle** or any such things [that **she might be holy and faultless**]."*
> (Eph 5:27 – AMP)

The bride allows Jesus to rule and reign in her heart so that when he returns for their glorious wedding day she will be *"arrayed in fine linen, clean and bright"* without spot or wrinkle. Her preparation for that magnificent day will be fulfilled and the longing of her heart will be realized.

After the wedding of the bride to her Bridegroom takes place the 4th Beatitude is announced.

### Beatitude for Bride (Rev 19:9-10)

> *9) Then he said to me, "Write: **'Blessed are those who are called to the marriage supper of the Lamb!'** And he said to me, 'These are the true sayings of God.' 10) And I fell at his feet to worship him. But he said to me, 'See that you do not do that! I am your fellow servant, and of your brethren who have the testimony of Jesus. Worship God! For the **testimony of Jesus** is **the spirit of prophecy.'"* (Rev 19:9-10 – NKJV)

Most wedding ceremonies are usually followed by a reception where all of the friends and guests gather to celebrate the event together. The wedding of the bride to her Bridegroom is a monumental occasion, and being invited to such a colossal gathering is a tremendous blessing. Joseph Seiss observed "But there is a blessedness of being called to witness the marriage, and a blessedness of participation with the bridal company in the marriage banquet, as well as a more special blessedness of being the actual Bride of the Lamb. The call is indeed to make up the Bride."[6]

To be invited to the marriage supper of the Lamb is a great honor and blessing. The guests who are called to the marriage supper are the **great multitude** of believers (pp.72-76) who came out of the tribulation period. They became overcomers through martyrdom and will be invited to the wedding feast as honored guests. However, God is calling all believers to become part of the actual bride of Christ. Those **overcomers** who heed this great call will be given the opportunity of the highest honor and intimacy as the bride of the Bridegroom.

After the angel announced this great wedding, John fell at his feet to worship him. Because we are only to worship God, the angel then instructed him that he was only a servant of God, not to be worshiped. He then states that the motivating purpose of prophecy is to bear witness to Jesus. Inspired by the Spirit, all of prophecy tells how God is fulfilling his great plan through his Son. All believers should know and understand prophecy.

### ⑦ **Rider on White Horse (Rev 19:11-21)**

*"11) **Now I saw heaven opened**, and behold, a **white horse**. And He who sat on him was called Faithful and True, and in righteousness **He judges and makes war..12)** His eyes were like a flame of fire, and **on His head were many crowns...14)** And the **armies in heaven**, clothed in fine linen, white and clean, followed Him on **white horses.** 15) Now out of His mouth goes a **sharp sword,** that with it He should **strike the nations.** And He Himself will **rule them with a rod of iron.** He Himself treads the **winepress** of the fierceness and **wrath of Almighty God.** 16) And He has on His robe and on His thigh a name written: KING OF KINGS AND LORD OF LORDS."*
(Rev 19:11-16 – NKJV)

John sees a vision of Jesus returning from heaven, riding on His white horse, to fight the final battle against the nations. Here Jesus is wearing his many crowns (#1238 – *diadema*), which signify the majestic power and authority given to him by his Father. The final stage for this great war has been set with the preliminary artillery of God's 7th vial of wrath (pp. 123-124) and now Jesus returns with his great army of **overcomers** (*cf.* Rev 17:14) riding on their white horses, dressed in brilliant white linen apparel. All of the successful overcomers will accompany Jesus as he gains the final victory over Satan and his countless emissaries.

Jesus comes with a sharp sword (#4501 – *rhomphaia*) which is a large sword used in warfare. Here it represents the Word of God, which he will merely speak (*cf.* 2 Th 2:8) and all of the nations that have gathered for this ultimate conflict will be struck down and slain. This war was introduced in the 7th vision as the final **vintage**; as an allusion to the final grape harvest, which are trodden down in the winepress (pp. 114-115). Here Christ returns and *"He Himself treads the* **winepress** *of the fierceness and* **wrath of Almighty God.** *"* This is the great battle of Armageddon where Jesus brings God's final wrath against rebellious and unrepentant mankind.

The 7th and final voice from heaven then announces the great supper of God where the birds will devour all of the carnage left from those assembled to wage their last war.

> *"17) Then I saw an angel standing in the sun; and he* **cried with a loud voice,** *saying to all the birds that fly in the midst of heaven, "Come and gather together for the* **supper of the great God,\*)** *... 21) And the rest were killed with the sword which proceeded from the mouth of Him who sat on the horse. And all the birds were filled with their flesh. "* (Rev 19:17 and 21 – NKJV)
> \* NU-Text and M-Text read, **"the great supper of God."**

This battle will be decisive and final. All will be killed by the Lord's mighty sword (Word). The birds will come to feast on the bodies of all those who attempted to defeat the great **King of Kings and Lord of Lords**.

Included in this conflict will be the **beast** and the **false prophet**, who were responsible for deceiving mankind.

> *"19) And I saw the **beast**, the kings of the earth, and their armies, gathered together to make war against Him who sat on the horse and against His army. 20) Then the **beast was captured**, and with him the **false prophet** who worked signs in his presence, by which he deceived those who received the mark of the beast and those who worshiped his image. These **two were cast alive** into the **lake of fire burning with brimstone**."*
> (Rev 19:19-20   NKJV)

The Antichrist will accompany the false prophet as they are both cast into the **lake of fire** – an appropriate recompense for their evil lives. This is certainly a fitting end for all of the misery and heartache they brought mankind during their brief time of terror on the earth. These two individuals are the first ones to be thrown into the **lake of fire**. We will learn more about this infamous lake in the next chapter of this book.

The second coming of Jesus Christ ends with the final battle of Armageddon, where all of God's enemies are finally destroyed, including the two leaders who were responsible for controlling and manipulating events during mankind's darkest period. The rider on the white horse began His earthly trek almost 2,000 years ago. His great mission of conquering men's hearts with the good news that he is the sacrificial Lamb who overcame death and has risen in victorious life has now come to an end. He is accompanied by his army of **overcomers** on His final ride to take back control of the Earth. He is now the victorious King and ready to establish his Kingdom over all the Earth. Jesus is the final victor who conquered death and has now prevailed over all of his opponents. His triumph is complete; his sovereignty is established, and the Prince of Peace has now brought the Earth back under His power and authority.

The conclusion of chapters 17, 18, and 19 of Revelation brings us to the very end of the age. The new Millennium begins with chapter 20, followed by chapters 21 and 22, which outline the new Heaven and Earth and the ages beyond. Before we move on to the final chapter of this book, we should take a look back to review some of the major proceedings that have taken place.

---

### RECAP OF MAJOR EVENTS

The sounding of the $7^{th}$ trumpet (p. 97) brought us to the end of the tribulation period. The following is a summary of the main events that have occurred during this period.

- Kingdom of world becomes kingdom of Christ (Rev 11:15)
- Rapture of Great Multitude (Rev 7:7-14)
- 2 Witnesses raptured (Rev 11:7-12)
- Judgement seat of Christ (Rev 11:17-18)
- Overcomers revealed as "sons of God" (p.51-52)
- Marriage of the bride with the Lamb (Rev 19:6-8)
- Christ with overcomers win at Armageddon (Rev 19:11-21)
- Antichrist and false prophet to Lake of Fire (Rev 19:20)
- Harlot's empire destroyed by fire (Rev 17:16)
- Babylon the Great destroyed by fire (Rev 18:8-9)
- 7 Vials of God's wrath poured out (Rev 16:1-21)

---

*"Then I heard something like the voice of a great multitude and like the sound of many waters and like the sound of **mighty peals of thunder**, saying, '**Hallelujah! For the Lord our God, the Almighty, reigns.**'"* (Rev 19:6 – NAS)

# Chapter 7 – 7 Final Visions

The book of Revelation concludes with 7 visions the Apostle John had that make up its final 3 chapters (Rev 20, 21 and 22). As outlined in Appendix 2, the major focus for interpreting the book now changes to how one views the millennium. The second coming has just occurred with Jesus Christ winning the final victory by overcoming all of Satan's followers. Once the armies led by the Antichrist are defeated, the nations of the Earth are judged to determine the destiny of those remaining. The book of Revelation does not describe this judgment, which Jesus explained in his discourse from the Mount of Olives during the final week before his death. Please see Appendix 4 for a summary of this important address.

## ① Satan Bound (Rev 20:1-3)

*"1) Then I saw an **angel** coming down from heaven, having the **key to the bottomless pit** and a **great chain** in his hand. 2) He laid hold of the dragon, that serpent of old, who is the Devil and Satan, and **bound him for a thousand years**; 3) and he cast him into the bottomless pit, and shut him up, and set a seal on him, so that he **should deceive the nations no more** till the **thousand years** were finished. But after these things he must be released for a little while."* (Rev 20:1-3 – NKJV)

John first sees an angel coming down from heaven to remove the very last opponent. Satan, our greatest enemy, is finally abolished from the scene and given a temporary prison in the center of the Earth. He is securely bound there for a period of 1,000 years, in order to eliminate his ability to deceive and influence mankind during the millennium. During this time, he will not have any power to control or manipulate people or events. Jesus Christ has overcome and He now rules the Earth. ***Hallelujah! For the Lord our God, the Almighty, reigns.***

### ② Millennial Kingdom (Rev 20:4-10)

#### Start of Millennium

*"Then I saw* [1]*thrones, and they sat on them, and judgment was given to them. And I saw the* [2]*souls of those who had been beheaded because of their testimony of Jesus and because of the word of God, and* [3]*those who had not worshiped the beast or his image, and had not received the mark on their forehead and on their hand; and they came to life and reigned with Christ for a thousand years. The rest of the dead did not come to life until the thousand years were completed. This is the first resurrection."* (Rev 20:4-5 – NAS)

The millennium is launched with the resurrection of individuals who are all included in what is labeled *"the first resurrection."* As we will learn a little later on in Rev 20:6, to be included in this group is indeed a great blessing. Let's see who makes up this important company of believers.

The **first** party John describes in this second vision are those sitting on thrones given the authority to judge. These believers had already come back to life (they are sitting down) and are none other than the **overcomers**. These believers had been taken to heaven before the throne of God in the rapture of Firstfruit believers (Rev 14:1-5). Their authority to sit on their thrones was a promise Jesus made to his disciples (Mat 19:28), along with his promises to the **overcomers** in the 7 churches (see p. 22). They share the Lord's throne (Rev 3:21) and are given a *"rod of iron"* (Rev 2:26) to rule and reign with Jesus as the *"sons of God"* (see p. 52). The prophet Daniel also foresaw this time (Dan 7:9, 18, and 22) when the thrones will be set in place for these faithful saints.

The **second** group of **overcomers** John saw are described as the souls of those who had been martyred for their testimony of Jesus before the tribulation period began. These are all the souls of those believers who gave up their lives because of their faith and witness for Jesus Christ and the Word of God (Rev 6:9). From the church of Smyrna down through the entire church age, these courageous believers sacrificed their very life for Jesus.

The **third** and final company of **overcoming** believers is the Great Multitude who came out of the tribulation period because they had been martyred for their refusal to worship the beast and to take his mark (see pp. 72-76 and 110-112). These believers had entered the tribulation period, since they were not ready or properly prepared, and became overcomers by dying for Christ during the time of the Antichrist's rule.

All three categories of overcomers are part of what is known as "the first resurrection." While there are important distinctions among the various groups, all share in the magnificent blessing of being included in the first resurrection.

### Beatitude $1^{st}$ Resurrection (Rev 20:6)

> *"**Blessed and holy** is the one who has a **part in the first resurrection**; over these the **second death has no power**, but they will be **priests of God** and of Christ and will **reign with Him for a thousand years**."*
> (Rev 20:6 – NAS)

The resurrection of the dead will take place in two stages. The first is the resurrection of the "just," while the later resurrection is for the "unjust" (Act 24:15). John had previously recorded the Lord's teaching on this subject where he portrayed them as a resurrection of "*life*" and a resurrection of "*judgment*":

> *"...all who are in the tombs will hear His voice, and will come forth; those who did the good deeds to a **resurrection of life**, those who committed the evil deeds to a **resurrection of judgment**."* (Jhn 5:29 – NAS)

To be included in the first resurrection is a great blessing that all should aspire to. In the above verse, the Lord taught that how we live our life is very important. People who commit *"evil deeds"* in this lifetime will have their day of reckoning when they participate in the resurrection of judgment (unsaved). However, to be included in the first resurrection is a wonderful reward that embraces several facets as described below.

All overcomers will take part in the first resurrection and enjoy the millennial Kingdom. We will be given the remarkable ability to reign with the Almighty Lord during one of the most breathtaking eras in human history. In addition to this great blessing, we also obtain the assurance that we will not be affected by the *"second death,"* which relates to the lake of fire that will be discussed later in this chapter.

Finally, during the Kingdom age the overcomers are considered *"priests of God,"* which means Jesus is offering us the privilege of "unlimited access to and intimate fellowship with God" (Thomas). What an awesome opportunity awaits all those who hearken unto the Lord's call to be the overcomer he desires. Participation in the first resurrection represents an exceptional reward even the great Apostle Paul stove for (see 1Cr 9:24-27) and Apostle Peter called believers to pursue (1Pe 2:4-11, 16)[1].

## End of Millennium

*"7) When the thousand years are completed, Satan will be released from his prison, 8) and will come out to deceive the nations which are in the four corners of the earth, Gog and Magog, to gather them together for the war; the number of them is like the sand of the seashore."* (Rev 20:7-8 – NAS)

Once the millennium comes to a close, John said Satan *"... must be released for a little while"* (Rev 20:3 – NKJV). Satan had been tightly bound in his prison for 1,000 years, but God allows him to be released for a short period of time. The reason for his parole is not given, however commentators speculate various motives. Maybe God gave this once great leader of all the angels (*cf.* Isa 14:12 and Eze 28:14) one last chance to repent. Or perhaps God wanted to see how men who had lived for 1,000 years under Christ's reign would react when Satan emerged from his prison; to discover if mankind will follow Him or succumb to the deception of the Devil. Unfortunately, people from *"the four corners of the earth"* join Satan in the last war on planet Earth known as the battle of Gog and Magog. The term "the four corners of the earth" simply means that people from all around the world unite together with Satan in their opposition against God (Hendriksen, Mounce).

Many modern prophecy teachers believe the battle described in Ezekiel 38 and 39 is a war that takes place either before or during the tribulation period (Bullinger, Feinberg, Lee, Mize and Morris). This author once held this view where Russia invades Israel during the end times. Upon a thorough investigation and study, it becomes apparent that the Gog and Magog war in Revelation is the same war – with Ezekiel furnishing all the details (Beasley-Murray, Dahl, Hendriksen, Ladd, Mounce, Osborne and Thomas). James Matheny warned: "While much of the Christian world is awaiting a Russian invasion of Israel, Satan is busily conforming men, governments and religions to his standards, the level of which will usher in the Tribulation. Russia is merely a straw man, set up by Satan to confuse the world in the last days, to draw attention from his real activity."[2]

The **more important teaching** from this war relates to Satan's army. We should not lose sight of the fact that the people living on the Earth at the end of the millennium live during the most wonderful times the world will ever know. Jesus, along with his overcoming followers, rule with a rod of iron, guaranteeing peace on Earth. People were free from the devil's deception and yet a great multitude did not really recognize Jesus Christ as

King and never truly made Him the King of their hearts. They were all born with the flesh nature they had inherited from Adam; and even though Christ was present on the Earth, they did not really accept him and were easily won over by Satan. The Prophet Jeremiah taught: *"The heart is deceitful above all things, and desperately wicked: who can know it?"* (Jer 17:9) Without placing Jesus on the throne, man's heart remains desperately wicked. Their feigned obedience during Christ's reign is revealed when Satan is released and they join him in one last rebellion against God's Kingdom.

Christ came to conquer their hearts and allow Him to be the King of their hearts. Because they failed to do this, they were unable to resist the devil and defeat him. This presents us with an important lesson for today. Have we allowed Jesus to be the King of our hearts? If the answer is yes, then when the devil comes to tempt or test us we can be: *"...more than conquerors through him that loved us."* (Rom 8:37) We can do this by following the advice given to us by James: *"Submit yourselves therefore to God. Resist the devil, and he will flee from you."* (Jas 4:7)

Had those individuals living at the end of the millennium made Jesus the King of their hearts, they would have been able to resist Satan. Because they failed to make Jesus their Lord, they were destroyed by fire in an instant as they attacked Jerusalem:

> *"And they...surrounded the camp of the saints and the beloved city, and fire came down from heaven and devoured them."* (Rev 20:9 – NAS)

Satan then joins his two cohorts in the lake of fire:

> *"...and the Devil, who is leading them astray, was cast into the lake of fire and brimstone, where are the beast and the false prophet, and they shall be tormented day and night -- to the ages of the ages."* (Rev 20:10 – YLT)

③ **Great White Throne (Rev 20:11-15)**

Immediately after Satan joins the Antichrist and the false
prophet in the lake of fire, John introduces the topic of the Great
White Throne:

> *"11) And I saw a **great white throne,** and him that sat
> on it, from whose face the earth and the heaven fled
> away; and there was found no place for them. 12) And I
> saw **the dead,** small and great, stand before God; and
> the books were opened: and another book was opened,
> which is the **book of life**: and **the dead were judged** out
> of those things which were written in the books,
> **according to their works**…14) And death and hell were
> cast into the **lake of fire.** This is the **second death.** 15)
> And whosoever was not found written in the book of life
> was cast into the **lake of fire.** "*
> (Rev 20:11-12, 14-15)

In John's vision he sees multitudes of people standing before a
Great White Throne. He says they are *"the dead,"* which means
God raised everyone who remained in their graves. The first
resurrection of the "just" had already taken place 1,000 years
earlier (Rev 20:4), so this is the second and final resurrection of
judgment (Jhn 5:29) for the "unjust" (Act 24:15).

In other words, all those who are standing before Christ at this
judgment represent everyone who has lived and died without
Jesus Christ as their Lord and Savior. This is the second
resurrection, and it includes everyone who rejected Christ.
Because their names were not found written in the *"book of
life,"*[3] they were cast into the lake of fire.

Notice that unbelievers will be judged by their works. Whereas
the Judgement Seat of Christ judges the works of believers, the
Great White Throne judgment will judge the works of the rest

of mankind, where everyone will experience the *"second death"[3]* of being cast into the lake of fire. Apparently, the level of punishment people will experience will be based upon the things that they did during their life. Those who had committed the most heinous crimes will be judged accordingly.

> *"...and I will* **recompense them according to their deeds,** *and* **according** *to the* **works of their own hands.** *"* (Jer 25:14)
> *"30) For we know him that hath said, Vengeance belongeth unto me, I will recompense, saith the Lord... 31) It is a* **fearful thing to fall into the hands of the living God.** *"* (Heb 10:30-31)

The judgment at the Great While Throne is for all the ungodly, who rejected the love God offered them through his Son Jesus. God will then use fire to completely renovate our present Earth.

> *"7) But by His word the* **present heavens and earth are being reserved for fire, kept for the day of judgment and destruction of ungodly men.**
> *13)* **But according to His promise we are looking for new heavens and a new earth, in which righteousness dwells.**
> *14) Therefore, beloved, since you look for these things,* **be diligent to be found by Him in peace, spotless and blameless,** *"* (2 Pe 3:7, 13-14 – NAS)

Apostle Peter saw this new day dawning, and he encouraged his brothers to **be careful** to walk the walk of a **steadfast** disciple, looking forward to this **new dwelling place** of **righteousness.**

④ **New Heaven and New Earth  (Rev 21:1, 3-8)**

> *"1) Now I saw a* **new heaven** *and a* **new earth,** *for the first heaven and the first earth had passed away. Also there was no more sea."* (Rev 21:1 – NAS)

John then witnessed the reformation of our planet into a spectacular new heaven and new earth, completely different from our present environment.  Our new heaven and earth will be totally unique – unlike the present surroundings.  In the last sentence of Rev 21:1, he states *"there was no more sea."*  Almost all commentators take this to mean the new heaven and new earth will not have any oceans.  Thankfully, Joseph Seiss noted: "People only misread the text, and load themselves with endless perplexities, when they interpret it to mean the total abolition of all seas." He rightfully notices that John is saying "When the time to which the text refers arrives, the present sea *"no longer is,"* just as the first heaven and the first earth *"are gone."*[4] In other words, the sea will be re-created in a new way.  The old sea will be *"no more,"* but the new sea will be completely new and different (note: verse 5 below confirms this truth that *"**all things**"* [including the sea] will be made new).

---

Immediately after telling us about the new heaven and the new earth he introduces the subject of the holy city, the New Jerusalem in Rev 21:2.  This begins the 5$^{th}$ of 7 visions John saw – it will be fully discussed in the next section (see p. 152).  When John observed the 4$^{th}$ & 5$^{th}$ visions, he was probably so astonished and amazed by their marvelous brilliance, he felt impelled to introduce them both together.

---

John then hears a loud voice from heaven telling him the glorious and incredible news about this new heaven and earth:

> *"3) And I heard a loud voice from heaven saying, 'Behold, the tabernacle of God is with men, and **He will dwell with them**, and they shall be His people. **God Himself will be with them** and be their God. 4) And **God will wipe away every tear from their eyes**; there shall be **no more death, nor sorrow, nor crying**. There shall be **no more pain,** for the former things have passed away.'"* (Rev 21:3-4 – NKJV)

The wonderful news is announced that the God who created the entire universe will be coming to reside with mankind. The new heaven and the new earth will be the eternal home of Almighty God. We will be given the incredible opportunity to meet and abide in His loving presence for the ages to come. All of the former things in this fallen world will be gone. All the blood, sweat, tears and heartache we have endured during our pilgrimage will be forgotten. There will be no sickness or disease and no more mourning over the death of a loved one. God will sit on His throne overseeing the universe from this home base on the new heaven and earth, which He re-created to its magnificent splendor.

Given the amazing prospect being offered to mankind, he felt that it was extremely important to provide the Church with one final word of admonition and encouragement. God is making one final call to believers to stay faithful and remain steadfast, one final warning to make our calling and election sure. One final call for us to be the overcomers He is calling us to be.

### Admonition to the Churches
### CALLING ALL OVERCOMERS

*"5) Then **He who sat on the throne said**, 'Behold, I make all things new.' And **He said to me**, 'Write, for **these words are true and faithful.'***
*6) And He said to me, 'It is done! I am the Alpha and the Omega, the Beginning and the End. I will give of the fountain of the water of life freely to him who thirsts.*
    *7) **He who overcomes shall inherit all things, and I will be his God and he shall be My son.***
    *8) But the cowardly, unbelieving, abominable, murderers, sexually immoral, sorcerers, idolaters, and all liars **shall have their part in the lake which burns with fire and brimstone, which is the second death.'''***
(Rev 21:5-8 – NKJV)

In the messages John recorded to the 7 churches he revealed the 7 promises made available to those believers who are successful overcomers. All of those promises are combined in this final call in verse 7: *"He who overcomes shall inherit all things, and I will be his God and he shall be My son."*

God is reminding us that if we are victorious, we will be able to flourish and be considered his very own son (*cf.* Rom 8:18-19). If we allow Jesus Christ to rule and reign in our hearts during this life, we can overcome all the trials, temptations and tests we face. By relying upon His mighty power and strength living inside of us, we can be triumphant and be the overcomers he is calling us to be. If we succeed, our inheritance will be beyond all of our incomparable dreams and aspirations.

The next verse is an admonition to the Church, which has been obscured because almost all commentators fail to realize that this is meant for believers. Most view those described in verse 8, the *"cowardly, unbelieving, abominable, murderers, sexually immoral, sorcerers, idolaters, and all liars,"* as the unsaved.[5] Because they will have their part in the lake of fire, most conclude they could not be believers. But remember, believers who fail to be overcomers **can be hurt** by the second death.

> *"...He that overcometh shall **not be hurt** of the second death."* (Rev 2:11)

It would be foolish for Jesus to warn the Church about being hurt by the second death if it were not possible (Mize). Being hurt by the second death does not equate with being thrown in the lake of fire. It means believers can be adversely affected by it (i.e. have a part in it) by forfeiting their ability to rule and reign **during** the **millennium** with Christ. This is what believers can miss.[6] This is why God is pictured comforting them as the new heaven and earth are introduced: *"And **God** will wipe away every tear from their eyes"* (Rev 21:4 – NKJV).

One of the most prolific Biblical scholars in the 20th century was former Baptist pastor and teacher George Beasley-Murray. Regarding verse 8 he noted (from a pastoral heart): "It was intended especially for the man of faith, who is warned not to be of their number...This sure word of judgment is added as a plea to followers of Christ to make their calling and election sure...Everything of worth is at stake for the man of God."[7]

After John records the admonition for believers to overcome, he continues with the 5th vision of the holy city, the New Jerusalem. He began to record this earlier; however, he had paused to write the *true and faithful* call from God's heart first.

⑤ **New Jerusalem (Rev 21:2, 9-27)**

> *"2) Then I, John, saw the **holy city, New Jerusalem,** **coming down out of heaven** from God, **prepared as a** **bride adorned for her husband.** "*
> *9) Then one of the seven angels who had the seven bowls filled with the seven last plagues came to me and talked with me, saying, '**Come, I will show you the** **bride, the Lamb's wife.** '*
> *10) And he carried me away in the Spirit to a great and high mountain, and showed me the **great city, the holy Jerusalem,** **descending** out of heaven from God, "* (Rev 21:2, 9-10 – NKJV)

John's 5th vision is that of the holy city, the New Jerusalem coming down from heaven. He introduces it in verse 2, using a simile *"**prepared as a bride"** and in verse 9 he uses a metaphor *"**show you the bride, the Lamb's wife.** "*   Both refer to the *bride*, who we learned about when she was married to the Lamb, as described in the last chapter of this book (see pp. 134-137).  The bride of Christ represents the overcomers who went to be with her Bridegroom at the start of the millennium.  She, along with all of their wedding guests, will reside with Jesus for the next 1,000 years in the holy city, the New Jerusalem.

Once the bride's millennial reign with Christ has come to a close, John then calls her **the bride, the Lamb's wife** because she has been married for 1,000 years. John is then taken up on a high mountain where he sees this great and holy city coming down out of heaven. The New Jerusalem was apparently orbiting around planet Earth for 1,000 years for all earthly inhabitants to see. Once the re-creation of the new heaven and the new earth are completed, God brings this holy city down to the Earth where it will reside for all the ages to come.[8]

The beauty and splendor of this great city are pictured as a bride adorned for her husband because it appeared as a magnificent and brightly light city illuminated by the glory of God and the Lamb (Rev 21:11, 23). Most who have viewed a wedding ceremony know that the bride is always the focal point of beauty as she glows because of her great love for her husband. This holy city radiates the majestic glory of God and the Lamb because of their great love for mankind.

The remaining verses in Rev 21 go into great detail revealing all the dimensions and building material God used in preparing this wonderful home for His redeemed. Readers are encouraged to read the entire chapter, or even better, listen to it being read. Jesus promised us he was preparing this city for those who love him and obey his words. Both He and his Father will come and reside with us in the magnificent abode of the New Jerusalem.

> *"2) In my Father's house are many mansions: if it were not so, I would have told you. I go **to prepare a place for you**. 3) And if I go and prepare a place for you, I will come again, and receive you unto myself; that where I am, there ye may be also.*
> *23) Jesus answered and said unto him, If a man love me, he **will keep my words**: and my Father will love him, and **we will come unto him, and make our abode with him**."* (Jhn 14:2-3, 23)

To think that God, who created the universe, will actually come to reside with men is an incredible promise that Jesus made to those who love him and keep his word. We see its fulfillment here in John's vision (Rev 21:3). It fills one with awe and matchless wonder; contemplating intimate fellowship and communion with our heavenly Father and the Lamb.

The magnificent holy city will be an astonishing sight to behold – fashioned with a foundation of precious stones, walls of gold glistening as clear glass, and streets created with pure gold. The 12 gates made out of pearl will never be closed, providing unobstructed access. To be a resident in this glorious city and to call it our home is beyond anything we can ever imagine:

> *"But as it is written, Eye hath not seen, nor ear heard, neither have entered into the heart of man, the things which God hath prepared for them that love him."*
> (1 Co 2:9)

Entrance into this city will be granted to all those who have their names written in the book of life. In other words, **all believers** in Christ will be granted citizenship in God's eternal home:

> *"But there shall by no means **enter it** anything that defiles, or causes an abomination or a lie, but **only those who are written in the Lamb's Book of Life**."*
> (Rev 21:27 – NKJV)

God is calling us today to be one of the inhabitants in this new and holy city that He is in the process of preparing. The New Jerusalem will one day become a reality and the prospect of being one of its citizens should spur us on to be the **overcomers** he is calling us to be so we are granted an **abundant** entrance.[9]

> *"Therefore, brothers, **be all the more diligent** to confirm your calling and election, for if you practice these qualities you will never fall."* (2 Pe 1:10 – ESV)

# THE NEW JERUSALEM

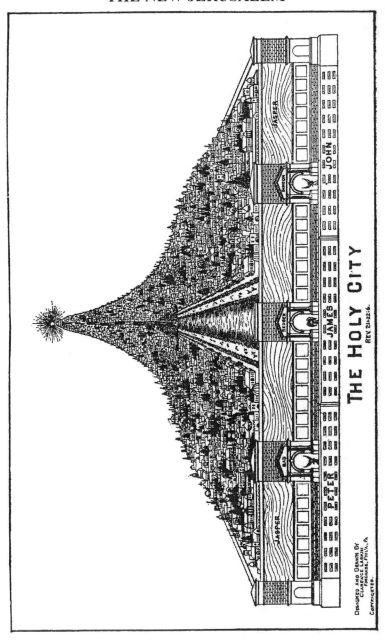

The above drawing is from **The Book of Revelation**, by Clarence Larkin, page 204,
© 1919.    Used with permission of the Rev. Clarence Larkin Estate, P.O. Box 334,
Glenside, PA  19038, U.S.A., 215-576-5590, www.larkinestate.com

> The rendering of New Jerusalem on the preceding page is shaped as a pyramid with the *"length, breadth and height"* all being equal (Rev 21:16). While this shape may be possible, most commentators picture the holy city as an enormous cube 1,500 miles in each direction, which could be extended from Maine to Florida and from the Atlantic Ocean to west of the Mississippi River, covering over half of the United States. Significantly, the holy of holies in the ancient temple was also a cube (*cf.* 1 Ki 6:20) which symbolizes the entire holy city as a temple; which explains why there is no temple in the city (Rev 21:22). **The entire city is the temple.**

### ⑥ River of Life (Rev 22:1-5)

*"1) And he showed me a pure **river of water of life**, clear as crystal, **proceeding from the throne of God and of the Lamb**.*
*2) In the middle of its street, and on either side of the river, was the **tree of life**, which bore **twelve fruits**, each tree yielding its fruit every month. The leaves of the tree were for the **healing of the nations**. 3) And there shall be no more curse, but the throne of God and of the Lamb shall be in it, and His servants shall serve Him. 4) They shall see His face, and His name shall be on their foreheads. 5) There shall be no night there: They need no lamp nor light of the sun, for the Lord God gives them light. **And they shall reign forever and ever.**"* (Rev 22:1-5 – NKJV)

The 6th and next to last vision that John witnessed begins with a crystal clear river of life flowing down from the throne. It is depicted in the drawing on the preceding page with the tree of life in the center of the street, as well as on both sides of this clean stream of water. The river of water of life will traverse down its center and will probably branch out in all directions to reach every corner of this vast capital. This pure water supplies all the inhabitants with life-sustaining water. Also, this pictures how the Spirit of God dwells in the hearts of all redeemed individuals (*cf.* Jhn 7:38). The Holy Spirit presently resides in all believers, and in the New city everyone will live in perfect harmony connected with the throne of *"God and the Lamb"* (Rev 22:1). This symbolizes how the Holy triune God (God, Lamb and Spirit) will all work together, supplying life-sustaining provision for all of the redeemed.

Readers will recall from our study of the 7 letters to the Churches that Adam and Eve were evicted from the Garden of Eden and no longer granted access to this tree of life because of their disobedience (see p. 23). The promise to the **overcomers** in the church of Ephesus (Rev 2:7) is to eat from this tree of life that is now seen here in the New Jerusalem. During the millennium all of the **overcomers** take pleasure in eating the various varieties of the 12 fruits; and once all of the redeemed inhabit the holy city – everyone will be able to enjoy them.

John tells us the **leaves** of the tree were for the **healing** of the **nations**. While the redeemed living in the holy city will eat the fruit from the tree of life, the nations will consume the leaves from the tree. The nations represent all the inhabitants on the new earth who live in bodies of flesh and blood. Apparently, these people will require the life-healing properties provided by the leaves in order to sustain their lives and thereby be able to live forever. Had Adam and Eve not sinned, this tree of life would have feed them for eternity.

Because of the Lamb's sacrificial death and resurrection, He conquered death and, as John explains, there is no more curse. God and the Lamb now share the throne and we will meet them face to face (*cf.* Mat 5:8) and be given His name on our foreheads. This speaks of an **intimate** personal relationship and fellowship everyone will enjoy throughout eternity. This was God's original plan when he created man and it will ultimately be fulfilled in the new and holy city he is preparing for us today.

John then tells us that there will be no night nor need of a lamp because the Lord God provides the light. Jesus is the light of the world (Jhn 8:12) and in the holy city the redeemed will not need any external light source. The people living outside the city, dwelling on the earth, will still experience night and day and will probably require their normal period to sleep in order to rejuvenate their bodies. The redeemed living inside the city will be living in their resurrected bodies and therefore will most likely not need to sleep.

John concludes this 6th vision by telling us those who dwell in the city will reign for eternity. Remember that the **overcomers** who take part in the first resurrection will rule (Rev 2:26) and reign (Rev 20:6) with Christ during the millennium as *"sons of God"* (see pp. 142-144). Once Satan is cast into the lake of fire and the new heaven and new earth begin, there will no longer be any need to rule with a "rod of iron." This is so, because when the New Jerusalem comes down out of heaven, **all** of the **redeemed** will now be residing in this holy city and will reign with God and the Lamb throughout eternity in perfect harmony.

This reign will extend throughout the galaxies for the eternal ages to come. What will the new heavens be like? Randy Alcorn put it this way: "Like being inside joy, as if joy were something tangible and you could wrap yourself up in it like a blanket." He continued saying: "we may see wonders God held back...that will cause us to marvel and drop to our knees in worship when we behold them in the new creation."[10]

To get just a slight glimpse of what God's marvelous creation will be like, readers are encouraged to visit NASA's website: APOD (Astronomy Picture Of the Day).[11] This site provides a new picture of God's great universe every day. The images and pictures provide a foretaste of what will be in store for all of the redeemed who will be blessed to call the New Jerusalem their home base throughout eternity.

**Introduction to John's Epilogue**

The prologue to this most wonderful book of Revelation began with Rev 1:1-2 as God's concluding message to mankind of the things Jesus will accomplish to fulfill His ultimate plan. John 7th and final vision in Rev 22:6-21 represents the **epilogue**, which the vast majority of commentators fail to properly comprehend.

The entire book of Revelation is addressed to the **believers** in the churches – admonishing them to be properly prepared for the return of our blessed Savior. All believers are called to be **overcomers**. Some will be successful overcomers prior to the start of the tribulation. The great multitude, on the other hand, will enter into the tribulation period because they had not been genuine overcomers prior to when it began. Many will finally become **overcomers** as they stand up for Christ during their final hour of testing (Rev 7:14). Many will be required to be martyred for Jesus in order to *wash their robes* in the precious blood of the Lamb (please see pp. 72-76, and 112).

Those believers finally become the **overcomers** they had been called to be. Had they been properly prepared (as those in the church of Philadelphia were) they would not have been left behind to undergo this additional time of trial and testing.

This great epilogue in Rev 22 is meant to address this most important issue: **the coming separation*** that will take place for those believers who are not genuine **overcomers**. Because most commentators fail to comprehend this issue of the coming separation,[12] they also misinterpret John's last word of warning in this important epilogue which closes out the book.

*(Please see pp. 209-213 in the Olivet Discourse for more information on this separation in the Church).

⑦ **Lord's Final Word (Rev 22:6-21)**

> *"6) Then he said to me, '**These words are faithful and true**.' And the Lord God of the holy prophets sent His **angel to show His servants the things** which must shortly take place."* (Rev 22:6 – NKJV)

The book of Revelation ends the same way that it began, with God sending His angel to reveal a vision of the future for the churches to know and understand (*cf.* Rev 1:1-2). The Lord's prologue had also introduced the first beatitude:

> *"**Blessed is** he who **reads** and those who **hear** the words of this prophecy, and **keep** those things which are written in it; for the time is near."* (Rev 1:3 – NKJV)

Now that John has completed most of the message in this book of prophecy, the 6$^{th}$ beatitude that he provides no longer needs to include the words "**reads**" and "**hears**" – for the book has reached its conclusion.

### *Beatitude for Overcomer (Rev 22:7)*

> *"Behold, I am coming quickly! **Blessed** is he who **keeps** the words of the prophecy **of this book**."*
> (Rev 22:7 – NKJV)

This next-to-last beatitude's blessing is to the believers who **keep** the things written in this book. The revelation has now been made, and the readers have already read and heard its vital message. The counsel Jesus makes to the believer now is to guard its words, to hold firmly to its teachings and to faithfully obey and **keep** all of its instructions. The believers who do so will be greatly blessed. The **overcomers** will hearken unto the Lord's word and remain steadfast; guarding the words of this important prophecy within their hearts.

After John had witnessed the river of life in the New Jerusalem and he is told the blessing for keeping the words of this book of prophecy, his natural tendency was to fall down in humble worship as he previously had done (*cf.* Rev 19:9-10).

> *"8) Now I, John, saw and heard these things. And when I heard and saw, I fell down to worship before the feet of the angel who showed me these things."*
> (Rev 22:8 – NKJV)

When we are confronted with such marvelous and wonderful revelations, the proclivity of most is to bow down in awestruck wonder. Since we are only to worship God, the angel again tells John that he is only God's servant and not to be worshiped.

### Book Not Sealed
John is then told the great importance of the message he has just been given in the book of Revelation. The significance of this book needs to be read and understood by all members of the churches because John is told that it is not to be sealed.

> *"10) And he said to me, "Do not seal the words of the prophecy of this book, **for the time is at hand**. 11) 'He who is unjust, let him be unjust still; he who is filthy, let him be filthy still; he who is righteous, let him be righteous still; he who is holy, let him be holy still.'"*
> (Rev 22:10-11 – NKJV)

Because the message in this book is not sealed, all members of the churches must be aware of what it teaches. Believers are warned that the time is near, and once the events outlined in this book commence, the condition of the believer's heart will determine his or her future destiny. The state the believers are found in when events begin will establish their future course.

The four states outlined at the outset of the tribulation are: 1) the unjust are the unsaved, 2) the filthy are those defiled by sin in their lives, 3) the righteous are those who are believers (whether defiled or sanctified) and 4) the holy are those believers who are sanctified. The state the individuals are found in once the tribulation begins will then determine their future. This important theme continues with our Lord's final alert:

> *"And behold, I am coming quickly, and **My reward** is with Me, **to give to every one according to his work**. 'I am the Alpha and the Omega, the Beginning and the End, the First and the Last.'"*(Rev 22:12-13 – NKJV)

Believers are saved by faith to accomplish the works He prepared for us to do (Eph 2:8-10). Once he returns, it will occur suddenly and every individual's status will determine their level of reward (or lack of reward).[13] The faithful believers will be greatly rewarded while the unfaithful may be seriously chastised (*cf.* Rev 3:19 and Heb 12:11). John then presents the second and final admonition to the churches.

## Coming Separation

The first concluding admonition to the churches was given from God's own heart during John's description of the new heaven and new earth (see pp. 150-152).[14] Rev 21:7 reveals the great promise for **overcomers** to be sons of God who will inherit all things, and Rev 21:8 records the **warning** for those believers who fail to be overcomers and thereby forfeit their ability to rule and reign with Christ during the millennium. While these unfaithful believers will miss millennial rewards, they **will be citizens** of the New Jerusalem throughout all the ages to come.

### *Beatitude for Overcomer (Rev 22:14)*

> *"14) Blessed are those who **wash their robes***, so that they may have the right to the tree of life and that they may enter the city by the gates."* (Rev 22:14 – ESV)
> \* *"do his commandments,"*

## Admonition to the Churches

The 7th and final beatitude is placed here at the very end of the book to encourage and remind believers to be the **overcomers** they are called to be. Those faithful and obedient believers who successfully "*wash their robes*" will automatically be given the right to enter the holy city and partake of the fruit from the tree of life. When Jesus returns, the **overcomers** will be greatly rewarded as we have seen throughout this book.

The overcomer lives his or her life in constant readiness and expectation of the Lord's return (Seiss). We long for Christ to return and try to keep our robes clean by living a holy and blameless life. Whenever we may stumble, we immediately go to the throne of Grace asking for forgiveness (1Jo 1:9) and thereby keep our robes washed. By allowing His mighty power and strength to direct and control us, we are able to lead a life that will be found pleasing to the Lord when he returns.

But not all believers are so obediently prepared and watching for the Lord's soon return. John then portrays some believers who are not living faithful lives.

> "*15) But outside are dogs and sorcerers and sexually immoral and murderers and idolaters, and whoever loves and practices a lie.*" (Rev 22:15 – NKJV)

Very few commentators correctly conclude these individuals are believers. However, a careful analysis reveals those listed here closely parallel those believers found in Rev 21:8.[15]

While these believers may be severely tried and tested for their infidelity, they will ultimately become **residents** in the holy city, where they will abide with God and the Lamb for eternity. Many may become martyrs during the tribulation period, where they will "*wash their robes*" (Rev 7:14) and become part of the first resurrection (Rev 20:4-6) while others may lose the chance to reign with Christ during the millennium and be found outside the city as described here by John. This grave outcome can still be averted by the unfaithful believer. Jesus is calling out today to all believers to repent while there is still time.

The final two chapters of Revelation provide two concluding admonitions to the churches. Both show the wonderful promises of reward to the faithful, as well as dire consequences to the unfaithful. God is crying out to the churches to get ready!

### Final Invitation
*"17) **And the Spirit and the bride say, 'Come!'** And let him who hears say, 'Come!' And let him who thirsts come. Whoever desires, let him take the water of life freely."* (Rev 22:17 – NKJV)

Because these concluding visions have revealed so much is at stake; the Holy Spirit[16] and the bride are crying out in unison – beckoning for everyone to be prepared. The final invitation is now being made to all those who will listen.

Let all those who have ears to hear – hearken unto this urgent call. Let all those who aspire to be an **overcomer** call upon Him today and ask him to help you be the **overcomer** he is calling you to be.

---

**Dear Lord Jesus,**

**I cry out to you today to help me be ready when you return. Please count me worthy to escape all the things that shall come to pass, and to stand before you. Please help me be the overcomer that you are calling me to be. May my life be pleasing to you.**

**Amen. Even so, come, Lord Jesus!**

# Epilogue

Throughout this writing, it has been the avid prayer of this author not to inadvertently add to or take away from the words of this Holy word of prophecy (Rev 22:18-19). May God forgive me if I have mistakenly distorted in any way what he wants to convey to the churches.

It is also our ardent prayer that this work might spark a renewed interest in this most important and intriguing book of prophecy. May believers discover that this book was meant to be a source of hope and comfort for all those undergoing the many trials we endure in this life. The incredible prospect of abiding with God and the Lamb in the holy city to come should spur all of us on to faithfully seeking His righteousness in our lives (Mat 6:33).

Finally, it is my fervent prayer that believers realize that it is only through God's marvelous grace that we can be enabled to overcome as he desires. Only by the grace of God can we overcome by allowing his life (Jhn 15:5) to rule and reign in our hearts as we abide in Him.

Jesus is indeed returning very soon. May this book help encourage you be the overcomer that he is calling you to be.

---

We are standing at the doorway to eternity...
With such monumental blessings in view...
God is calling men to be overcomers.
How will you answer the call?

Even so, come, Lord Jesus!
The grace of our Lord Jesus Christ be with you.

**O' Come Lord Jesus!**
**Count me worthy to escape**
**And be in your presence for**
**All the ages to come...**

*And the Spirit and the bride say, 'Come!'* (Rev 22:17)

# Reference Notes

**Prologue**
**1)** Morris, Henry M. – *The Revelation Record*, Tyndale House © 1983, adapted from pp. 28-30.

**Chapter 1 – 7 Letters to Churches**
**1)** Hendriksen, William – *More Than Conquerors – An Interpretation of the Book of Revelation*, Baker Books © 1940, 1967, 1998, pp. 25 and 62. Hendriksen noted "that in each separate instance Christ's self-designation has its bearing on the church to which the epistle is addressed." He also noted "All commentators note this fact." The following is a brief summary of this fact:

| Church | Attributes of Christ | Condition of Church |
|---|---|---|
| Ephesus | Holds 7 Stars (True ministers) | Encountered False teachers |
| Smyrna | First & Last Dead then Alive | Martyrs to receive Crown of Life |
| Pergamos | Sharp Two Edged Sword | Repent or He Will use Sword |
| Thyatira | Eyes – Flame of Fire Feet – Like Brass | Search / Crush False teachers |
| Sardis | 7 Spirits 7 Stars (Ministers) | Need to revive Dead Church |
| Philadelphia | Holy and True Key of David | Live for Christ To Open Door |
| Laodicea | Faithful and True Witness | Lukewarm with Christ outside |

**2)** The *Crown of Life* is one of five rewards God provides to those faithful, obedient believers who have pleased the Lord by allowing Him to accomplish the "good works" which he planned for us to do (Ephesians 2:10). To learn more about this subject, please see our book, *The Kingdom*, which can be freely downloaded at our website: www.ProphecyCountdown.com

## Chapter 1 – 7 Letters to Churches (continued)

3) Gallagher, Steve – *Intoxicated with Babylon*, Pure Life Ministries © 2006, pp.104: "….Bible teachers over-emphasize God's grace and de-emphasize the need for godliness and holiness [making] compromised living acceptable in the eyes of the average churchgoer….holiness in now politically incorrect."

4) Lee, Witness – *Holy Bible Recovery Version,* Living Stream Ministries © 2003, pp. 168-169.

5) Chambers, Oswald – *The Oswald Chambers Devotional Bible*, English Standard Version, Crossway © 2009, p. 1403: "When the world, the flesh, and the Devil do their worst, it is for us to understand were our true life is to be lived, not in the outer courts, but "hidden with Christ in God." *"...seek the things that are above, where Christ is...set your minds on things that are above, not on things that are on earth."* (Col 3:1-2)

6) An accurate, literal word-for-word paraphrase of Matthew 25:5 might be: *"While the bridegroom tarried, they all beckoned or slept."* The wise virgins were *"beckoning"* for the Lord to return while the foolish virgins were sleeping. This paraphrase was developed by Lyn Mize when he discovered that this verse had been grossly mistranslated. From a great article on the *Ten Virgins*, on his website: www.ffruits.org

## Chapter 2 – 7 Seals

1) The reader is encouraged to read Ezekiel's vision of heaven which is recorded in Ezekiel 1:1-28. The following are a few examples of similarities to John's vision of heaven:

### Sea of Glass

*"Now over the heads of the living beings there was something like an expanse, like the **awesome gleam of crystal**, spread out over their heads."* (Eze 1:22 – NAS)

### Living Creatures

*"And above the firmament that was over their heads [of the four **living creatures**] was the likeness of a throne, as the appearance of a sapphire stone: and upon the likeness of the throne was the likeness as the appearance of a man above upon it...."* (Eze 1:26)

**Chapter 2 – 7 Seals (continued)**
*"Each one had four faces: the first face was the **face of a cherub**, the second face the **face of a man**, the third the **face of a lion**, and the fourth the **face of an eagle**"* (Eze 10:14–NKJV)

### Rainbow

*"...As the **appearance of the rainbow** in the clouds on a rainy day, so was the appearance of the surrounding radiance. Such was the appearance of the likeness of the glory of the LORD. And when I saw it, I fell on my face and heard a voice speaking."* (Eze 1:28 – NAS)

Note: The appearance of the rainbow in both Ezekiel's and John's visions speaks to the fact that God will never destroy all life again by flood. (Genesis 9:9-17)

**2)** Thomas, Robert L., *Revelation 1-7: An Exegetical Commentary*, Moody Publishers © 1992, p. 348 states that the 24 elders are: "...a special class...of angels that belong to the court of God in heaven...(that) primarily assists in execution of the divine rule of the universe."

**3)** Arlen L. Chitwood, the Editor of *The Heavenly Calling*, has an excellent article on this important subject entitled: *The Time of the End – Part VII Crowns Cast Before God's Throne*. A PDF version of this article is available on our Prophecy Countdown website. Arlen Chitwood's website located at: www.lampbroadcast.org has this information under Pamphlets.

**4)** It is important to note that the King James translation of Revelation 5:9-10 is based upon a faulty Greek manuscript (Codex Sinaiticus) that added the word "**us**," which completely alters its meaning: *"...For You were slain, And have redeemed **us** to God by Your blood Out of every tribe and tongue and people and nation, And have made **us** kings and priests to our God; And we shall reign on the earth.* (Rev 5:9-10 – NKJV) This incorrect rendering has created much confusion over the true identity of the 24 elders and the correct rendering of these verses. The faulty insertion of "us" is attested to by: Bullinger (p. 242), Chitwood, Govett, Hendriksen (p. 91), Ladd (p. 74), Lang (p. 126), Mounce (p. 136) and Newell (p. 99).

## Chapter 2 – 7 Seals (continued)

**5)** This author is indebted to William Hendriksen and Steve Gregg for their significant insight in illuminating the 7 major divisions within the book of Revelation. Please see the Bibliography for information on their important writings.

**6)** The following chart reviews the use of *nikao* #3528 in Strong's and Vines' dictionaries:

---

**Strong's** G3528 *nikao* [A.V. Overcome]
Used 28 times in Authorized Version
   Overcome 24, Conquer 2, Prevail 1, Get the victory 1
      1) to carry off the victory, come off victorious
      2) of Christ, victorious over all His foes
      3) of Christians, that hold fast their faith even
         unto death against the power of their foes,
         and temptations and persecutions
      4) when one is arraigned or goes to law, to win
         the case, maintain one's cause

**Vines**
Overcome is used:
  (a) of God, Rom 3:4 (a law term), RV, "mightest
     prevail;"
  (b) of Christ, Jhn 16:33; Rev 3:21; 5:5; 17:14;***
  (c) of His followers, Rom 12:21 (2nd part); 1Jo 2:13,
     14; 4:4; 5:4, 5; Rev 2:7, 11, 17, 26; 3:5, 12, 21;
     12:11; 15:2; 21:7;

---

*** Vines' omits Rev 6:2 which includes #3528 two times.

**7)** Regarding Christ being the rider on the white horse in John's vision of the 1st seal, William Hendricksen states: "The identification of the rider upon the first horse in Zechariah's vision with the Christ is not improbable. (*cf.* also Hab. 3:8,9; Is. 41:2.)" op.cit., p. 96. In addition, Zane Hodges writes in his article, *The First Horseman of the Apocalypse*, "Thus here…is the pre-incarnate Christ, and so it happens that the first horseman of Zechariah is none other than the Son of God."

## Chapter 2 – 7 Seals (continued)

**8)** John introduces the second horse by stating *"another horse."* The word used for **another** (#243) seems to intimate there is a distinction being made or else he could have said, *"the 2ⁿᵈ horse..."* This same word for another (#243) is also used in 2 Cr 11:4 and Gal 1:7 where distinctions are being made.

**9)** Hendriksen, op. cit., pp. 101-103.

**10)** Pastor Tom McElmurry gives an excellent description of how the *"heaven departed as a scroll when it is rolled together..."* in his book ***The Key of the Bottomless Pit***, Bogard Press © 1987, pp. 33-36. Using diagrams he shows how the affects of volcanic smoke and ash could be trapped in the stratosphere over an extended period (i.e. 3 ½ years), causing it to appear like the heavenly bodies are slowly vanishing from sight as one would see if a scroll is gradually rolled together.

**11)** An article in the L.A. Times, dated December 27, 2004, by Thomas H Maugh II, reported that "it moved the entire island of Sumatra 100 feet." (http://articles.latimes.com/2004/dec/27/science/sci-tsunami27) (accessed February 6, 2015). The U.S. Geological Survey stated: "In places, the block of crust beneath the sea... is likely to have moved...10 meters to the west-southwest and to have been uplifted by several meters." (http://earthquake.usgs.gov/earthquakes/eqinthenews/2004/us2004slav/faq.php) (accessed February 6, 2015).

**12)** McElmurry, op.cit. pp. 44-49. He believes the stars John saw are the result of a comet ("name of the star is Wormwood" Rev 8:11) that passes by the earth during the 3ʳᵈ trumpet where: "pieces of space debris will...fall through the earth's atmosphere as meteors, billions of shooting stars. It will appear that all the stars of heaven are falling to the earth."

**13)** NASA Science News reported in an article titled, *Near Miss: The Solar Superstorm of July 2012*, by Dr. Tony Phillips http://science.nasa.gov/science-news/science-at-nasa/2004/23jul_superstorm/) (accessed February 6, 2015).

**14)** Joel's reference to deliverance on Mount Zion could refer to John's vision of heavenly Mount Zion in Rev 14:1-5 (p. 106).

## Chapter 3 – 7 Trumpets

**1)** Readers may want to Google "volcano eruption" to view some fairly startling pictures of the effects of volcanic eruptions. Just imagine thousands of these occurring around the globe and one can easily understand why John's vision states one-third of the earth's surface is affected.

**2)** McElmurry, op.cit. pp. 19-20.

**3)** Our website, at www.ProphecyCountdown.com has an article that has tracked recent near-misses:

| Date | Distance from Earth |
|------|---------------------|
| June 2002 | 75,000 miles |
| March 2009 | 45,000 miles |
| October 2010 | 29,000 miles |
| June 2011 | 7,500 miles |
| February 2013 | 17,200 miles |
| ???? | Rev 8:8 – Impact! |

**4)** McElmurry, op.cit. pp. 21-26. Pastor McElmurry holds a degree in physical science and is a certified meteorologist. In his book he gives an excellent explanation of how the effects of eruptions caused by the massive movement in the tectonic plates will cause the effects John witnessed under the 2nd trumpet including the destruction of one-third of the ships.

Incredibly; after this section was written, this author opened the morning newspaper to an article on the volcanic eruption that occurred in Papa New Guinea. It included a picture, which showed what appeared to be a mountain spewing forth a huge column of lava, smoke and ash right in the middle of a large body of water. It looked as if a mountain had been cast into the sea, precisely as John described in his vision of the 2nd trumpet!

**5)** Thomas, Robert L., *Revelation 8-22: An Exegetical Commentary*, Moody Publishers © 1995, p. 24

**6)** Patten, Donald Wesley, *Catastrophism and the Old Testament: The Mars-Earth Conflicts*, Pacific Meridian Publishing © 1998, p 107.

**7)** Protecting eagle: Rev 12:14 (*cf.* Exo 19:4, Deu 32:11-12)

## Chapter 3 – 7 Trumpets (continued)

**8)** Morris, op.cit, pp. 159-160.

**9)** Hendriksen, op.cit, p. 58.

**10)** The mighty angel (Jesus) makes the solemn pledge the *"mystery of God"* will be complete during the period of days that the 7th trumpet is sounded. This "mystery" includes the establishment of God's righteous Kingdom on the earth with Jesus reigning as the King of kings and the establishment of the new heaven and earth.

**11)** The prophet Elijah called fire from heaven (2 Ki 1:10) and stopped the rain from falling to the earth for 3 ½ years (*cf.* 1 Ki 17:1, Luk 4:25 and Jas 5:17). Moses had the power to turn the water into blood and brought many great plagues in the land of Egypt (*cf.* Ex 7:14-17 and Ex 8-11).

**12)** Beirnes, Rev. Wm. – **Revelation**, The Midnight Cry © n/a p. 126. "Many good people believe…John is to become one of the two witnesses during the last three and one-have years…"
And Leland Earls believes John and Lazarus are the 2 witnesses in his excellent booklet series: **The Manifested Sons – Book 2**, Shepherdsfield Publishers © 2011, pp. 13-18.

**13)** The judgment of the dead in Rev 11:18 is to determine who will share in the resurrection of life (*cf.* Joh 5:27-29) before the millennium (1 Cor 15:23; Rev 20:4-6), and who will appear before the great white throne judgment (Rev 20:11-12).

**14)** Rosenthal, Marvin – **The Pre-Wrath Rapture of the Church**, Thomas Nelson © 1990. Marvin Rosenthal does an excellent job of showing that God will rapture his church before his wrath is poured out sometime **after** the 6th seal. Please see pp. 163-167 of his book. The contention of this book is that Marvin is partially correct, but God's wrath is not poured out until the vial judgments begin in Rev 15 and 16 (see chapter 5 of this book). Also, he fails to see the Firstfruit rapture that takes place right before the tribulation period begins.

## Chapter 4 – 7 Visions

**1)** For a detailed discussion of the man child please see pp. 45-52, of **The Coming Spiritual Earthquake** that can be freely

**Chapter 4 – 7 Visions (continued)**

downloaded on our website: www.ProphecyCountdown.com
Also see G.H. Lang's *The Revelation of Jesus Christ Selected
Studies*, Schoettle Publishing © 2006, pp. 197-98 & 201-208.

2)   The Prophet Isaiah also alludes to the delivery of the male
child before Israel's time of testing in the wilderness: *"...Before
her pain came, She delivered a male child."* (Isa 66:7 – NKJV)

3)   There are 404 verses in Revelation.  The 202nd verse is
found in Rev 12:8 and states: *"And the dragon lost the battle,
and he and his angels were forced out of heaven."*  Satan is the
loser; the Lamb will be victorious.  We can overcome in Him!

4)   Dave Watchman developed the composite picture of the
beast from his studies in Daniel and Revelation.  He believes
the highlighted Arab nations surrounding Israel represent the
beast kingdom about to arise on the world stage.  His material is
available on his website: www.thewatchmanstime.com

5)   Colin Deal's *Revelation of the Beast*, © 1995, outlines
how the beast could arise from the Middle Eastern nations
represented by Syria/Iraq (Seleucid kingdom).

6)   Pastor Randy Shupe's book: *Babylon The Great*, © 2007
available at: www.PastorRandyShupe.com This excellent book
outlines how Mystery Babylon consists of three parts: America
as the political beast, Catholicism as the religious false prophet,
and the E.U. as the commercial ten horn empire (pp. 85-114).

7)   Thomas, op.cit, p. 159.

8)   See pp. 49-52, of *The Coming Spiritual Earthquake*
available at: www.ProphecyCountdown.com

9)   Osborne, Grant R. – *Revelation: Baker Exegetical
Commentary*, Baker Academic © 2002, p. 501.

10)   Ibid., p. 508. "Their victory against Satan is seen in their
deaths (Rev 12:11).  The two beasts both persecute and deceive
the saints, but God allows this to test them and bring out their
victorious response."

11) This passage in Rev 14:1 is a figurative picture of heavenly
Mount Zion, so the group of 144,000 is also **figurative**.  Please
see p. 83 of *The Coming Spiritual Earthquake*, as noted above.

## Chapter 4 – 7 Visions (continued)

**12)** Brubaker, Ray–*Rapture: Reward For Readiness*, © 2003, God's News Behind The News. Ray's book gives an excellent summary of why the rapture of believers is indeed a reward for those who are found ready when the Lord returns.

**13)** Panton, D.M. – *The Judgment Seat of Christ*, © 1984, Schoettle Publishing Co. Inc., p. 63 (This book is one of this author's favorite books – it should be read by all believers).

## Chapter 5 – 7 Vials

**1)** McElmurry, Pastor Tom – *The Key of the Bottomless Pit*, Bogard Press © 1987, pp. 51-56.

**2)** Lang, G. H. – *The Revelation of Jesus Christ Selected Studies,* Schoettle Publishing © 2006, on p. 258 stated: "…righteousness God puts on the believer, that is, imputes it to him…But the believer's own 'garments' are those habits, acts, and conduct which he *makes for himself,* by the grace of the Holy Spirit, and puts on himself...See Rom 13:11-14: Eph 4:20-24; 6:11-8: Col 3:18-14." For additional information on obtaining one's garments please see the discussions of the churches of Sardis (pp. 36-39) and Laodicea (pp. 44-48).

**3)** *"Pure and undefiled religion before God and the Father is this: to visit orphans and widows in their trouble, and to keep oneself unspotted from the world."*
(Jas 1:27 – NKJV)
*"…for I was hungry and you gave Me food; I was thirsty and you gave Me drink; I was a stranger and you took Me in…"* (Mat 25:35 – NKJV)

**4)** Seiss, Joseph A. – *The Apocalypse Lectures on the Book of Revelation*, Cosimo Classics © 2007, p. 379.

**5)** *"18)…For the windows from on high are open, And the* **foundations of the earth are shaken.** *19) The* **earth is violently broken, The earth is split open, The earth is shaken exceedingly.** *20) The earth shall reel to and fro like a drunkard, And shall totter like a hut; Its transgression shall be heavy upon it,* **And it will fall, and not rise again."** (Isa 24:18-20 – NKJV)

## Chapter 6 – 7 Voices

**1)** The leopard is pictured with four wings like a bird. The map below shows how four nations appear to be attached to the back of Egypt at the Sinai Peninsula (Syria, Iraq, Jordan and Saudi Arabia). Daniel says these 5 nations are given dominion  at the time of the end. Also, these 5 countries only have 4 leaders (heads), which would mean one of them is without a leader at the time they form an alliance. It is not certain which nation does not have a leader. It could be Syria since Damascus becomes a city in ruin around the time of the end in accordance with Isa 17.

**2)** The 4$^{th}$ beast was different from all of the beasts *"that were before it..."* The Hebrew word *qodam* (#6925) should have been translated as *"in front of"* or *"in the presence of"* as opposed to *"before."* The 3 beasts are in the presence of the 4$^{th}$.

**3)** Because many commentators claim Daniel's 4$^{th}$ beast comes on the world scene after Daniel's first 3 beasts are no longer present, this author is posing the question: is it a coincidence that the addition of the heads in Daniel's 4 beasts add up to 7?...the same number of heads that John says the beast out of the sea has (*cf.* Rev 13:1, 17:3). The purpose of this book is not to assert dogmatic identities of the nations associated with the harlot and the beast. The speculations in this book are only possible explanations. The final answer will be revealed in the near future as history plays out in these intriguing prophecies.

**4)** While many cities around the world claim to be built on 7 hills, the two most notable are Jerusalem and Rome.

**5)** Gallagher, op.cit. pp. 142 and 166: "...our lives have been shaped more by popular American culture than God's Word...How many American Christians have completely wandered away from a vibrant faith in Christ and yet are clueless about their spiritual condition?"

**6)** Seiss, op.cit. p. 428.

## Chapter 7 – 7 Final Visions

**1)** Both Apostle Paul and Peter were calling believers to live their lives in order to be the overcomers in the first part of the first resurrection. Their messages are of vital importance for us:

> *"Don't you realize that in a race everyone runs, but only one person gets the prize?* **So run to win!***... Otherwise, I fear that after preaching to others* **I myself might be disqualified.***"* (1 Cr 9:24, 27 – NLT)

> *"9) But you are a chosen race,* **a royal priesthood,** *a* **holy nation,** *a* **people for his own possession,** *that you may proclaim the excellencies of him who* **called you out of darkness into his marvelous light...11)** *Beloved,* **I urge you** *as sojourners and exiles to abstain from the passions of the flesh, which wage war against your soul. 16) Live as people who are free, not using your freedom as a cover-up for evil, but* **living as servants of God.***"* (1 Pe 2:9, 11,16 – ESV)

**2)** Matheny, James F. – *Is There a Russian Connection? An Exposition of Ezekiel 37-39,* Jay & Associates © 1987, p. 72. In his 80-page booklet he explains how Eze 37 parallels Rev 20:4-6 as the reign of Jesus immediately before the Gog and Magog war in Eze 38 and 39. Osborne and Ladd offer similar views:

| Millennium | Eze 36-37 | Rev 20:4-6 |
| Gog-Magog | Eze 38-39 | Rev 20:7-14 |
| Eternal Kingdom | Eze 40-48 | Rev 21:1 to 22:5 |

Matheny concludes his study advising believers: "Christians are to look for...the blessed hope...not watching for...a revival of the Roman Empire, a Russian invasion of Israel...and so on. These are red herrings designed to distract the Church from its position of watchfulness and readiness." p. 71.

**3)** For a detailed discussion of the *"book of life"* and the *"second death,"* please see pp. 53-60, of *The Kingdom* that can be freely downloaded at: www.ProphecyCountdown.com

**4)** Seiss, op.cit. p. 488. In addition to the comments found on p. 149, Joseph Seiss also noted "And so there will be a sea in

## Chapter 7 – 7 Final Visions (continued)

the new world, the same as a new heaven and a new earth. If not, this is the only passage in all the word of God that tells us anything to the contrary…Many passages also…distinctly speak of *the sea* as being turned in their favour, and as taking part in the general acclaim over the ultimate accomplishment of the mystery of God. (See Isa 42:10, 60:5,9, Psa 24:2, 96:11, 98:6,7, 1Ch 16:32, Rev 5:13)."

**5)** Four commentators correctly interpret Rev 21:8 as very important admonitions for believers. See Lyn Mize exegesis on his website noted in the Bibliography. See George R. Beasley-Murray's comments on p. 152 in this book. Also, Steve Singleton observed: "This is no arbitrary list of sinners…, [they represent] spiritual compromises Christians in some of the seven churches of Asia were already making…" See p. 244 in Singleton's Preterist commentary. Finally, see pp. 483-487 in Arlen Chitwood's commentary for his discussion on how non-overcoming believers can be hurt by the second death.

**6)** One of the purposes of our book, *The Kingdom*, is to alert believers of the peril they can forfeit their inheritance of ruling and reigning with Christ in the millennium if they fail to be overcomers. Please see pp. 33-44 and 53-60, which can be freely downloaded at: www.ProphecyCountdown.com

**7)** Beasley-Murray, G. R. – *The Book of Revelation (New Century Commentary)* Marshall, Morgan & Scott ©1974 p.314

**8)** While most commentators believe the holy city, the New Jerusalem will come down to rest on planet Earth; Lang, Mize and Seiss believe it will remain in orbit based upon their understanding of Rev 21:24: *"And the nations…shall walk in the light of it."* This author would side with the majority on this.

**9)** Apostle Peter encourages us **to be eager** to *"make every effort to supplement your faith with virtue,… knowledge, and …self-control, …steadfastness, …godliness, …brotherly affection, …and love"* (2 Pe 1:5-7 – ESV) to ensure a **rich** and **abundant entrance** into the eternal home God is providing for his faithful and obedient **overcomers** (please see, 2 Pe 1:11).

## Chapter 7 – 7 Final Visions (continued)

**10)** Alcorn, Randy – *Heaven*, Tyndale House Publishers, Inc. © 2004, p.264. (This book will inspire you to be an overcomer.)

**11)** NASA's Astronomy Picture Of the Day website is located at: www. apod.nasa.gov. (This site will stir your heart for God).

**12)** The commentators who properly expound this issue of the coming separation include: Brubaker, Dahl, Govett, Lang, Lee, Mize, Panton, Peters, Seiss and Simpson (all are now deceased).

**13)** Believers will be rewarded according to their works:
> *"For we must all appear before the judgement seat of Christ; that every one may receive the things done in his body, according to that he hath done, whether it be good or bad."* (2 Cr 5:10)

**14)** Chitwood, Arlen L. – *The Time of the End: A Study About the Book of Revelation*, 2011, pp. 427-429. Chitwood brings out the important parallels between John's 2 concluding admonitions to the churches.

| Admonition | ① | ② |
|---|---|---|
| Section in chapter 7 | **4ᵗʰ Vision** | **5ᵗʰ to 7ᵗʰ Visions** |
| Scripture | Rev 21:1,3-8 | Rev 21:2, 9-22:21 |
| Overcomers' promise | Rev 21:7 | Rev 22:14 |
| Believers' warning | Rev 21:8 | Rev 22:15 |

Chitwood properly notes that these warnings to believers only relate to possible losses during the millennium (Messianic Era). While believers may lose the rewards of partaking from the tree of life and living in the holy city, these will only be temporary losses. Once the millennium concludes, God will wipe away every tear from the eyes of the believers (Rev 21:4) who failed to heed these important admonitions. **All believers will ultimately reside in the holy city** and eat from the tree of life throughout the ages to come.

**15)** Those believers described in Rev 21:8 and Rev 22:15 are very similar. Many believers may think that the list of sins described in these two verses could not be offenses any Christian would commit. However, a careful reading of the Lord's Sermon on the Mount shows that these are sins believers

**Chapter 7 – 7 Final Visions (continued)**
commit every day.  If anyone has any doubts, please see our
book on the Sermon on the Mount entitled *Overcomers Guide
to the Kingdom* that can be freely downloaded at our website.
Remember, the Lord's standard for murder, adultery, idolatry,
lying, etc. are much higher.  Anger toward a brother can be
murder and a lustful look at a woman can become adultery
(sexually immoral).  The "dogs"[2965] are a metaphor for a man
of impure mind, which is comparable to the abominable in Rev
21:8.  The following compares the two verses along with the
reference numbers in Strong's dictionary:

| **Rev 21:8** | **Rev 22:15** |
| --- | --- |
| Abominable #948 | Dogs #2965 |
| Murderers #5406 | Murderers #5406 |
| Immoral (sexually) #4205 | Immoral (sexually) #4205 |
| Sorcerers #5332 | Sorcerers #5333 |
| Idolaters #1496 | Idolaters #1496 |
| Liars #5571 | Practice a Lie #5579 |
| Cowardly #1169 | |
| Unbelieving #571 | |

- The abominable are the defiled or polluted which compares
  with the morally impure "dogs" in Rev 22:15 (*contra* holy).
- The murderers either commit actual physical murder or by
  anger or hatred against a fellow believer (Mat 5:22).
- The sexually immoral are those who practice unlawful
  sexual fornication, which could be adultery or what Jesus
  referred to as committing adultery in a person's heart by
  looking at a woman with lust for her (Mat 5:28).
- The term sorcerer comes from the Greek word *pharmakeus*
  from which we get the word pharmacy.  The sorcerer could
  either be those who practice witchcraft (magical arts – aka
  Harry Potter) or those who are drug users or alcoholics.
- Idolaters are those who worship mammon or those who
  place wealth and material possessions above spiritual
  matters (Mat 6:19-24) and (1Jo 5:21).

## Chapter 7 – 7 Final Visions (continued)

- The liars are those who are deceitful by intentionally lying or in the habit of not telling the truth.
- The cowardly refers to those believers who are timid and fearful while the unbelieving are those who are unfaithful and not trustworthy.

This analysis of these two verses reveals that they do depict unfaithful believers who continue in sins that are not confessed and repented. These believers are being warned by the Lord in the two concluding admonitions to the churches (see p 162). These warnings are being made because God loves them and he wants them to repent before it is too late.

> "The Lord is not slack concerning his promise...but is longsuffering **toward us**, not willing that any should perish but that all should come to repentance."
> (2Pe 3:9 – NKJV)  [**toward us** means **believers**]

If they repent they can avert the consequences described in these concluding admonitions to the churches.

Unfortunately, most have misinterpreted these passages to represent warnings to unbelievers because their penalties are so serious: having a part in the lake of fire and being outside the holy city.  As discussed earlier, these allude to severe chastisements by the Lord for their infidelity.  The believers found guilty of these major sins will forfeit their ability to reign with Christ during the millennium, but they will be restored at the end of the 1,000 years and be allowed to reside in the holy city with God and the Lamb for eternity.

The Apostle Paul offered similar warnings to believers during his ministry.  Readers are encouraged to take the time to read his admonitions that can found in the following scriptures:
    Gal 5:16, 19-21, Eph 5:3-6, Col 3:1-10 and 2 Th 1:5, 11.
Please see our book, *The Kingdom*, for more information on this important subject, which is available on our website.

### Chapter 7 – 7 Final Visions (continued)

**16)** God the Father, Son and Holy Spirit are all crying out to the churches to get ready. In the final two chapters of Revelation the first concluding admonition to the churches is made by the Father (Rev 21:7-8), the second concluding admonition is made by the Son (Rev 22:14-15) and the Holy Spirit's final one word plea in Rev 22:17 is urgently crying: *"Come!"* All three are calling out in unison for believers to get ready and to be the overcomers they are called to be.

### Appendix 1 – Approaches to Revelation

**1)** Mounce, Robert H. – *The Book of Revelation in The New International Commentary*, Eerdmans © 1977, p. 29

### Appendix 2 – Millennial Views

**1)** Riddlebarger, Kim – *A Case for Amillennialism Understanding The End Times*, Baker Books © 2013, p. 104

### Appendix 3 – 70th Week of Daniel

**1)** Watchman, Dave – *The Truth of Daniel 9:27*, Article from website at: WatchmansTime.com

### Appendix 4 – Olivet Discourse

**1)** Lang, op.cit., p. 191 observed: "In the End Times an angel will call upon all men to fear the Creator (14.7). The 'sheep' of the Lord's parable (Mt 25.31-46) had not espoused Him, but had shown in practice that they feared the God of Christ's distressed brethren." And on p. 291 stated: "Thus those 'sheep' who befriend the persecuted disciples of Christ will not be doing this consciously as to Him, but will say to Him, 'When saw we Thee afflicted?' But He will receive them as having done it to Himself in the persons of His brethren, and such will enter into His kingdom of peace."

### Appendix 6 – Overcomers

**1)** Bloomfield, Arthur – *How To Recognize The Antichrist*, Bethany Fellowship, Inc. © 1975, p. 94

**2)** Lang, op.cit., p. 91.

**3)** Govett, Robert – *Seek First His Kingdom and His Righteousness* Tract (please see the Supplemental Articles on our website).

# Bibliography

## Commentaries on Revelation
Key to Approaches used by the authors in commentaries listed:
H-Historical, P-Preterist, F-Futurist, I-Idealist, E-Eclectic

~Beasley-Murray, G. R. – *The Book of Revelation (New Century Commentary),* Marshall, Morgan & Scott © 1974 [F]*
~Beirnes, Rev. Wm. – *Revelation,* The Midnight Cry © n/a [F]*
~Bickel, B. & Jantz, S. – *Revelation: Unlocking the Mysteries of the End Times,* Harvest House © 2003 [F]
~Blackaby, H.R.T.M.N – *The Revelation of Jesus Christ: Encounters with God,* Thomas Nelson © 2008
~Bowman, Dr. Christopher G.–*I Don't Want This City: a verse by verse study guide to the Book of Revelation,* Morris © 2004
~Bullinger, E.W. – *Commentary on Revelation,* Kregel Classics © 1984 [H]*
~Chitwood, Arlen L. – *The Time of the End: A Study About the Book of Revelation,* The Lamp Broadcast, 2011 [F]
~Colclasure, Chuck – *The Overcomers: The Unveiling of Hope, Comfort & Encouragement in the Book of Revelation,* Thomas Nelson © 1981 [F]
~Dahl, Mikkel – *The Book of Revelation Unveiled,* Shepherdsfield Publishers © 2001 [F]
~Feinberg, Charles Lee – *A Commentary on Revelation: The Grand Finale,* BMH Books © 1985 [F]
~Gregg, Steve – *Revelation: Four Views, Revised & Updated (A Parallel Commentary),* Thomas Nelson © 2013 [unbiased]*
~Hendriksen, William – *More Than Conquerors – An Interpretation of the Book of Revelation,* Baker Books © 1998 [I]*
~Hunt, Gladys – *Revelation: The Lamb Who is the Lion,* Water Brook Multnomah © 2010
~Koester, Craig R. – *Revelation and the End of All Things,* Eerdmans © 2001 [I]
~Ladd, George Eldon – *A Commentary on the Revelation of John,* Eerdmans © 1972 [E = F+P]*

## Commentaries on Revelation (continued)

Key to Approaches used by the authors in commentaries listed:
H-Historical, P-Preterist, F-Futurist, I-Idealist, E-Eclectic

---

~Lang, G. H.--*The Revelation of Jesus Christ Selected Studies,* Schoettle Publishing © 2006 [F]*

~Larkin, Clarence – *The Book of Revelation*, Rev. Clarence Larkin Estate © 1919 [F]

~Lee, Witness – *Holy Bible Recovery Version*, Living Stream Ministry © 2003 [F]*

~Mize, Lyn – *Revelation (a verse by verse Exegesis)* © n/a, (Available at: www.ffruits.org) [F]*

~Mounce, Robert H. – *The Book of Revelation in The New International Commentary*, Eerdmans © 1977 [E = F+I]*

~Morris, Henry M. – *The Revelation Record*, Tyndale House © 1983 [F]*

~Newell, William R. – *Book of Revelation,* Moody ©1935[F]

~Osborne, Grant R. – *Revelation: Baker Exegetical Commentary*, Baker Academic © 2002 [E = F+H]*

~Ryrie, Charles C. – *Revelation: Everyman's Bible Commentary* Moody © 1996 [F]

~Seiss, Joseph A. – *The Apocalypse Lectures on the Book of Revelation*, Cosimo Classics © 2007 [F]*

~Singleton, Steve – *Overcoming: a study guide for the Book of Revelation*, Deeper Study Bookstore © 2006 [P]

~Stott, John – *Revelation: The Triumph of Christ*, InterVarsity Press © 2008 [F]

~Taylor, Dr. Charles – *Chronological Study of The Revelation*, Today in Bible Prophecy © n/a [F]

~Thomas, Robert L. –*Revelation 1-7 and 8-22 an Exegetical Commentary (2 volumes),* Moody Publishers © 1992 [F]*

~Van Impe, Dr. Jack – *Revelation Revealed Verse by Verse*, Jack Van Impe Ministries © 1982 [F]

~Wiersbe, Warren W. – *Be Victorious NT Commentary*, David Cook © 1985 [F]

* Most useful commentaries in the opinion of this author.

## Other Works Cited

~Alcorn, Randy – *Heaven*, Tyndale House Publishers, Inc. © 2004

~Bloomfield, Author – *How to Recognize the Antichrist*, Bethany Fellowship, Inc. © 1975

~Brubaker, Ray – *Rapture: Reward For Readiness*, God's News Behind The News, © 2003, (www.GodsNews.com)

~Chambers, Oswald – *The Oswald Chambers Devotional Bible*, English Standard Version, Crossway © 2009

~Deal, Colin – *Revelation of the Beast*, Rutherford College, NC (P.O. Box 455), © 1995,

~Earls, Leland – *The Manifested Sons–Book 2*, Shepherdsfield Publishers © 2011

~Gallagher, Steve – *Intoxicated with Babylon*, Pure Life Ministries © 2006, (www.EternalWeight.com)

~Hodges, Zane – *The First Horseman of the Apocalypse*, Bibliotheca Sacra, October 1962, volume 119 (article).

~Matheny, Th.M., James F. – *Is There A Russian Connection? An Exposition of Ezekiel 37-39*, Jay & Associated © 1987

~McElmurry, Pastor Tom – *The Key of the Bottomless Pit*, Bogard Press © 1987

~Panton, D.M. – *The Judgment Seat of Christ*, Schoettle Publishing Co. Inc., © 1984

~Patten, Donald Wesley, *Catastrophism and the Old Testament: The Mars-Earth Conflicts*, Pacific Meridian © 1998

~Riddlebarger, Kim-*A Case for Amillennialism Understanding The End Times*, Baker Books © 2013

~Rosenthal, Marvin – *The Pre-Wrath Rapture of the Church*, Thomas Nelson © 1990

~Shupe, Pastor Randy – *Babylon The Great*, © 2007, available at: www.PastorRandyShupe.com

~Strong, James H. – *Strong's Exhaustive Concordance*, Baker Books © 1992

~Vine, W.E. – *Vine's Complete Expository Dictionary Of Old And New Testament Words*, Thomas Nelson © 1996

# ABBREVIATIONS

## Books of the Bible

### Old Testament (OT)

| | |
|---|---|
| Genesis (Gen) | Ecclesiastes (Ecc) |
| Exodus (Exd) | Solomon (Sgs) |
| Leviticus (Lev) | Isaiah (Isa) |
| Numbers (Num) | Jeremiah (Jer) |
| Deuteronomy (Deu) | Lamentations (Lam) |
| Joshua (Jos) | Ezekiel (Eze) |
| Judges (Jdg) | Daniel (Dan) |
| Ruth (Rth) | Hosea (Hsa) |
| 1 Samuel (1Sa) | Joel (Joc) |
| 2 Samuel (2Sa) | Amos (Amo) |
| 1 Kings (1Ki) | Obadiah (Oba) |
| 2 Kings (2Ki) | Jonah (Jon) |
| 1 Chronicles (1Ch) | Micah (Mic) |
| 2 Chronicles (2Ch) | Nahum (Nah) |
| Ezra (Ezr) | Habakkuk (Hab) |
| Nehemiah (Neh) | Zephaniah (Zep) |
| Esther (Est) | Haggai (Hag) |
| Job (Job) | Zechariah (Zec) |
| Psalms (Psa) | Malachi (Mal) |
| Proverbs (Pro) | |

### New Testament (NT)

| | |
|---|---|
| Matthew (Mat) | 1 Timothy (1Ti) |
| Mark (Mar) | 2 Timothy (2Ti) |
| Luke (Luk) | Titus (Tts) |
| John (Jhn) | Philemon (Phm) |
| Acts (Act) | Hebrews (Hbr) |
| Romans (Rom) | James (Jam) |
| 1 Corinthians (1Cr) | 1 Peter (1Pe) |
| 2 Corinthians (2Cr) | 2 Peter (2Pe) |
| Galatians (Gal) | 1 John (1Jo) |
| Ephesians (Eph) | 2 John (2Jo) |
| Philippians (Phl) | 3 John (3Jo) |
| Colossians (Col) | Jude (Jud) |
| 1 Thessalonians (1Th) | Revelation (Rev) |
| 2 Thessalonians (2Th) | |

# Appendix 1 – Approaches To Revelation

| Historical | Preterist | Futurist | Idealist | Eclectic |
|---|---|---|---|---|
| Wycliffe | Sweete | Kuyper(1) | William Hendriksen(1) | Mounce |
| Luther | Mounce | Newell(1) | William Milligan | Beale |
| Calvin | Singleton(1) | John Stott(1) | Harvey Blaney | Osborne |
| Newton | | Henry Morris(1) | Leon Morris | G.E. Ladd(1) |
| Jonathan Edwards | | Zane Hodges(1) | | Harman(1)(2) |
| Charles Finney | | Joseph A. Seiss (1)(2) | | |
| Spurgeon | | Witness Lee(1)(2) | | |
| Bullinger | | Robert Govett(1)(2) | | |
| Alford(1) | | A.B. Simpson, Mikkel Dahl(2) | | |
| Matthew Henry(1) | | G.H. Lang, D.M. Panton(2) | | |
| | | Ray Brubaker, Lyn Mize(2) | | |
| | | Schofield, Ryrie, Walvoord | | |
| | | Baptists & Pentecostals | | |
| | | Most nondenominational evangelical churches | | |
| | | Some church fathers before Augustine (Justin, Irenaeus(1)) | | |

1) Taught that the Rider on 1st Horse is Christ / Gospel proclaimed.
2) Believed in 2 Raptures (Pre-Trib followed by Pre-Wrath / Post-Trib).

The chart on the previous page summarizes the 5 different approaches to interpreting the book of Revelation.

### Historical
The Historical approach views the book as a prophecy of Church history from the time it began until Christ returns at the end of the age. While this view has drawn many adherents in the distant past, very few modern bible teachers support this method of interpretation, since the book would have little relevance to the original audience.

### Preterist
The Preterist method of interpretation believes that the prophecies in the book were already fulfilled in the early church with the persecutions by the Roman Empire. This view is held by some scholars today, but fails to present relevance to today's church other than alluding to past fulfillments as types of future prophecies (i.e., the beast of Rome being a forerunner of the coming Antichrist).

### Futurist
Today, the most popular approach to Revelation is to view the prophecies as future events at the end of the age. There are 2 major futurist schools: Dispensational and moderate. The Dispensational view sees the 7 churches as 7 ages of church history. Some have suggested the following general overview:

|   | Church | Period |
|---|--------|--------|
| 1. | Ephesus | First Century |
| 2. | Smyrna | 100 – 312 AD |
| 3. | Pergamos | 312 – 606 AD |
| 4. | Thyatira | 606 – End of church age |
| 5. | Sardis | 1517 – End of church age |
| 6. | Philadelphia | 1750 – End of church age |
| 7. | Laodicea | 1900 – End of church age |

The Dispensationalist's see 7 actual literal churches, as well as, 7 different types of churches that have existed during the Church Age. Also, every Christian would fall into one of these 7 categories. In other words, these 7 churches, in addition to being literal churches, represent the entire body of the Church throughout history.

The Dispensational view also sees Israel as a major player in the end times once the rapture of the Church takes place, leaving Israel to be persecuted by the Antichrist.

The moderate futurist view does not recognize the rapture of the church until the end of the Church Age – hence the persecution by the Antichrist is to the church and not Israel. This view also does not view the 7 churches as 7 ages of church history.

Both Futurist views do agree, however, that the primary focus of the book of Revelation is to predict the ultimate victory of Christ and His church in overcoming the forces of evil.

### Idealist
The Idealist view (which has also been referred to as the Spiritual view) does not recognize any specific historical fulfillment in the book. Rather, the Idealists view the book of Revelation as a symbolic portrayal of the battle of good and evil with Christ's final victory over Satan.

### Eclectic
The above 4 approaches to interpreting Revelation have been the major methods utilized to help readers understand its meaning. Recently, many Bible scholars and teachers have developed what has come to be labeled as an Eclectic view, which represents the blending of two or more of the approaches. For example, Beal combines the Historical and Idealist views, Osborne blends the Historical with the Futurist methods, and Ladd understands the book to be a blending of the Preterist and

the Futurist approaches.  Robert Mounce made the following astute observations:

> "From this brief survey it is readily apparent that each approach has some important contribution to a full understanding of Revelation and that no single approach is sufficient in itself."  Later he added: "The author himself (Apostle John) could without contradiction be preterist, historicist, futurist, and idealist.  He wrote out of his own immediate situation, his prophecies would have a historical fulfillment, he anticipated a future consummation, and he revealed principles that operated beneath the course of history."[1]

The Eclectic approach to Revelation allows one to draw from the suitable aspects of each of the four major methods of interpretation to provide the reader with a clearer picture of the true meaning of the book.  While no one view may be entirely correct, the blending of the various methods allows one to better understand what the Apostle John was describing.

This author has adopted the Eclectic approach in this book.

# Appendix 2 – Millennial Views

Chapters 1 to 19 of the book of Revelation have been interpreted by the 5 different approaches as outlined in the first Appendix: Historical, Preterist, Futurist, Idealist or Eclectic. Once we reach Chapter 20, the major discussion has to do with one's view of the millennium. There are 3 major views that are generally taken: Premillennial, Amillennial and Postmillennial. The Premillennial camp can be further divided into: Historic Premillennialism and Dispensationalism.

**Postmillennial**
The Postmillennial view holds that the second coming of Jesus will take place **after** the millennium. Some hold to a literal thousand years while others view the millennium as spiritual. This teaching has been around since the early church, but has few proponents today. It was widely held in the 19th century with the optimistic prospect that the church would be the instrument to bring about peace and prosperity which would usher in the Lord's second coming.

**Amillennial**
The Amillennial view essentially means "no millennium" and teaches that there is no literal 1,000 year period, but rather a symbolic or spiritual reign of Christ from the time of His Ascension until the second coming. This view states that Satan was bound at Christ's first coming and that Christ is presently reigning in the hearts of believers. In other words, the Amillennial view sees the time between the 1st and the 2nd advents as the symbolic reign of Christ described in chapter 20 of Revelation. The Amillennial teaching believes Satan will be loosed just prior to the second coming to deceive the nations once more. This spiritualization of the millennium has been firmly established in the church since Augustine adopted its allegorical approach.

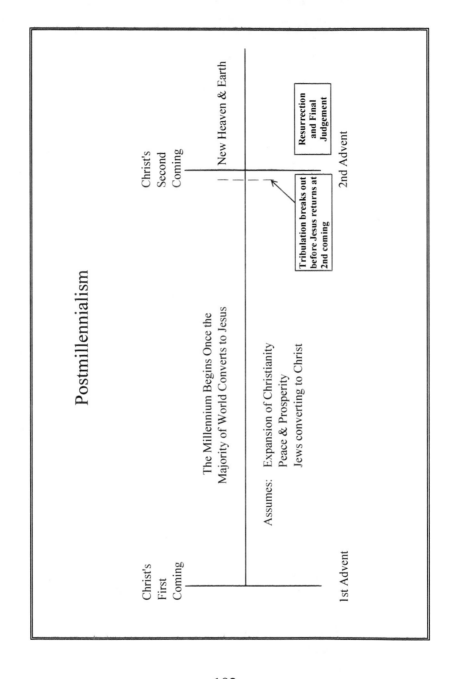

-192-

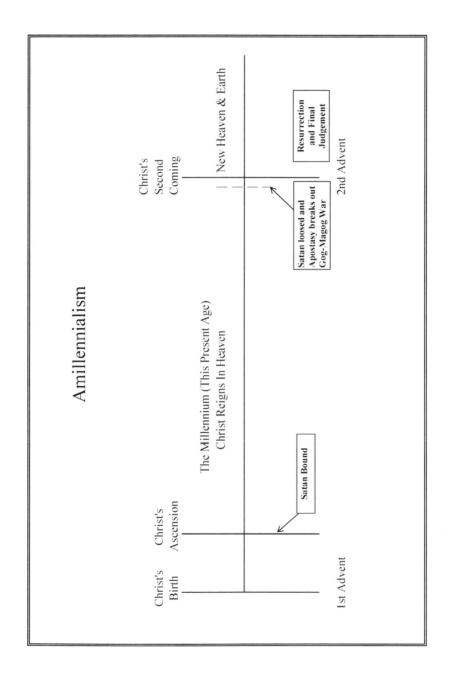

Amillennialism

Christ's Birth

Christ's Ascension

The Millennium (This Present Age)
Christ Reigns In Heaven

Christ's Second Coming

New Heaven & Earth

1st Advent

Satan Bound

Satan loosed and Apostasy breaks out Gog-Magog War

2nd Advent

Resurrection and Final Judgement

One of this author's favorite commentaries on the book of Revelation is William Hendriksen's: ***More Than Conquerors***. Hendrickson's presentation is easy to read and understand. His analysis of Christ as the rider of the 1$^{st}$ white horse is especially convincing and his division of the book of Revelation into 7 sections is quite helpful. He also takes the Amillennial view of interpretation and does a good job of explaining how he believes Satan was bound at the 1$^{st}$ coming of Christ.

Not being completely convinced by Hendrickson's understanding of the millennium, this author decided to investigate Kim Riddlebarger's: ***A Case for Amillennialism***. Riddlebarer's analysis is an excellent work; however, in trying to prove his case using what he terms the "two-age model," he reveals a striking flaw in the Amillennial view. In describing the ***age to come***, he acknowledges that Christ will reign in the age to come (Eph 1:21).[1]

However, a few pages earlier he stated: "For he must reign [from his coronation in his ascension] until he has put all his enemies under his feet [at the time of his return]. The last enemy to be destroyed is death [in the resurrection]."

Riddlebarger first claims Christ will reign from his ascension until the 2$^{nd}$ coming (i.e. the current age). He then also admits that Christ will reign in the age to come. In other words, he declares that Christ will reign over two separate ages.

> *"...and they lived and reigned with Christ for a thousand years. But the rest of the dead did not live again until the thousand years were finished. This is the first resurrection."* (Rev 20:4-5 NKJV)

Amillennialist would have us believe that we are reigning with Christ now, when Scripture clearly shows a 1,000-year gap between the 1$^{st}$ and 2$^{nd}$ resurrections.

The only manner for the Amillennial view to work is to suggest our reign with Christ is a spiritual reign instead of a literal reign. For this to be so, then the $2^{nd}$ resurrection of the rest of the dead would require a spiritual rising from the grave – a technique beyond the realm of feasibility. In other words, the dead would not literally rise from the grave. And if they do not literally come back to life, then they could not stand before the great white throne judgment seat as is described in Revelation 20:12.

**Premillennial**
The early church fathers believed in "chiliasm" or a literal "thousand year" reign of Christ. This view became known as the Premillennial view, which holds that the second coming of Jesus will take place **before** the literal 1,000 reign of Christ. At the end of this Kingdom age, Satan will be let loose from his prison in the bottomless pit to deceive the nations once again. God will then reign down fire from heaven and cast the devil into the lake of fire where he will join the Antichrist and the false prophet.

The Premillennial view has been further divided into two different types: the more traditional Historic Premillennialism and the Dispensational view. Dispensationalism differs from the Historic view in that Israel plays a major role in the end times because Dispensationalists believe that the church is raptured from the earth prior to the start of the tribulation period. With the removal of the Church, they believe that Israel becomes the major focus of the end times.

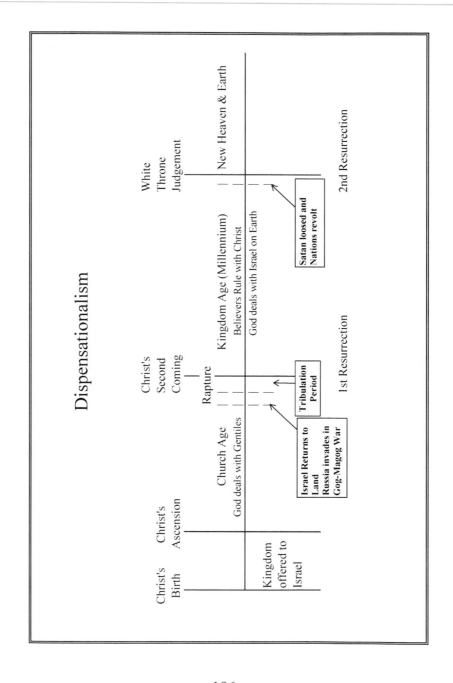

Dispensationalism

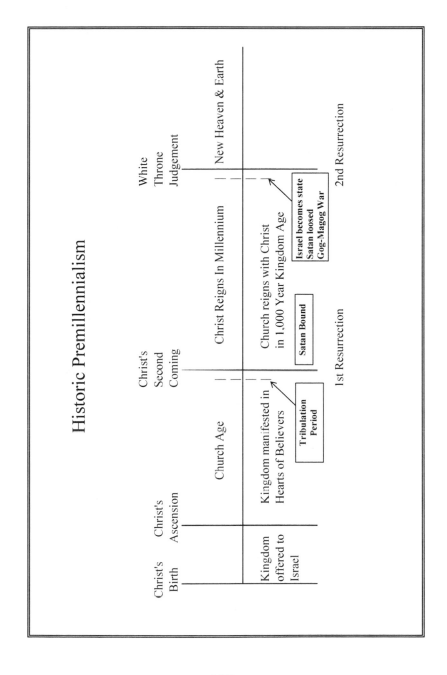

Historic Premillennialism

Christ's Birth

Christ's Ascension

Christ's Second Coming

Christ Reigns In Millennium

White Throne Judgement

New Heaven & Earth

Kingdom offered to Israel

Church Age

Kingdom manifested in Hearts of Believers

Tribulation Period

1st Resurrection

Church reigns with Christ in 1,000 Year Kingdom Age

Satan Bound

Israel becomes state
Satan loosed
Gog-Magog War

2nd Resurrection

**Ezekiel 33**

*"1) Again the word of the LORD came to me, saying, 2) 'Son of man, speak to the children of your people, and say to them: 'When I bring the sword upon a land, and the people of the land take a man from their territory and make him their watchman, 3) when he sees the sword coming upon the land, if he blows the trumpet and warns the people, 4) then whoever hears the sound of the trumpet and does not take warning, if the sword comes and takes him away, his blood shall be on his own head. 5) He heard the sound of the trumpet, but did not take warning; his blood shall be upon himself. But he who takes warning will save his life. 6) But if the watchman sees the sword coming and does not blow the trumpet, and the people are not warned, and the sword comes and takes any person from among them, he is taken away in his iniquity; but his blood I will require at the watchman's hand. 7) So you, son of man: I have made you a watchman for the house of Israel; therefore you shall hear a word from My mouth and warn them for Me. 8) When I say to the wicked, 'O wicked man, you shall surely die!' and you do not speak to warn the wicked from his way, that wicked man shall die in his iniquity; but his blood I will require at your hand. 9) Nevertheless if you warn the wicked to turn from his way, and he does not turn from his way, he shall die in his iniquity; but you have delivered your soul."*

(Eze 33:1-9 – NKJV)

# Appendix 3 – 70<sup>th</sup> Week of Daniel

As outlined in chapter 2, Christ is the most likely candidate to be the rider on the white horse in Seal #1, as opposed to the popular traditional view that the Antichrist is the rider. The early church fathers believed that Jesus was the one riding out to conquer the hearts of men with the Gospel.

In a similar manner, the prophecy in the 9<sup>th</sup> chapter of the book of Daniel surrounding the 70<sup>th</sup> week of Daniel has been tainted by the relatively new tradition that the Antichrist is coming on the scene to confirm a 7-year peace treaty, but after 3 ½ years he will break the treaty.

Back in 2007, we had our book published entitled: ***Don't Be Left Behind***, which thoroughly outlines why Jesus Christ is the person Daniel is referring to in the 9<sup>th</sup> chapter of his book and not the Antichrist. This revelation completely changes much of the traditional teaching found in bible prophecy today.

To properly understand this prophecy in Daniel, it is suggested that the reader review the entire 9<sup>th</sup> chapter of the book of Daniel.

Daniel begins in verse 2 of chapter 9, by saying that he came to understand *"by books"* i.e., the writings of Moses and the prophets, the teachings on the captivity of his people, the Jews. From the book of Jeremiah, Daniel understood that the Babylonian captivity was to last seventy years (see Jeremiah 25:11 and Jeremiah 29:4-10). The Prophet Daniel was a devout student of bible prophecy. He knew the Scripture and he sought the Lord for understanding. Because of Daniel's devotion, the angel Gabriel was sent to him:

> *"(20) And whiles I was speaking, and praying, and confessing my sin and the sin of my people Israel, and presenting my supplication before the LORD my God for*

*the holy mountain of my God;"*

Gabriel was sent by the Lord to give Daniel the answer to his prayer. Gabriel's answer is found in the last four verses of Chapter 9, upon which hundreds of books have been written.

> **"(27) And he shall confirm the covenant with many for one week: and in the midst of the week he shall cause the sacrifice and the oblation to cease, and for the overspreading of abominations he shall make it desolate, even until the consummation, and that determined shall be poured upon the desolate."**
> (Dan 9:24-27)

The very last verse which is highlighted above (v.27) is the key verse that has been misinterpreted and misunderstood by most in the Church. Notice that the verse says, *"he shall confirm the covenant with many..."* The questions we need to ask ourselves are "who is the 'he' that Daniel is referring to and what is the 'covenant with many'?"

We need to remember that this prophecy is dealing with Daniel's prayer:

> *"And I prayed unto the LORD my God, and made my confession, and said, O Lord, the **great and dreadful God**, keeping **the covenant** and mercy to them that love him, and to them that keep his commandments;"*
> (Dan 9:4)

The first thing we notice is the fact that Daniel mentions in his prayer before God that He is the **great God** who keeps the **covenant** to those that love him. In the NIV version of verse 4 it reads:

> *"O Lord, the **great and awesome God**, who **keeps his covenant of love** with all who love him and obey his commands,"* (Dan 9:4 – NIV)

Yes, the covenant that Daniel is referring to is the covenant of love and mercy that God made with His people.

Notice what Jesus had to say regarding this covenant at the Last Supper:

> *"And he said unto them, This is my blood of the **new testament (covenant)**[1242] which is **shed for many**."* (Mar 14:24)

At the Last Supper, the Lord was revealing how the wine the disciples were about to partake represented the blood of the new covenant. This shows that His blood actually strengthens the original covenant because there would no longer be any need to continue to offer sacrifices to God. His act of love and obedience on the cross made the original covenant a more durable covenant that would permanently bind His love to mankind.

What did Daniel say of the covenant in Daniel 9:27:

> *"(27) And he shall **confirm (strengthen)**[1396] the covenant with many..."*

Isn't this exactly what Jesus said that His blood would do? By shedding His own blood, Jesus strengthened the covenant of love and mercy that God had previously bestowed upon His people who love and obey His commands. By obediently going to the cross, Jesus shed His own blood to strengthen the covenant for many who will come to believe.

The precious life blood of Jesus Christ is like superglue that forever binds God's covenant of love and mercy to mankind. It creates an everlasting bond of God's love that can never be broken (see Heb 7:22-28).

At this point it is extremely important to mention that this prophecy in Daniel beautifully pictured how God sent his only son Jesus Christ to fulfill mankind's ultimate redemption. Through human "Tradition," Satan has twisted and perverted this Holy Scripture to mean that the "he" in Daniel 9:27 is the Antichrist! This grand deception has blinded mankind from the beautiful truth that God originally meant for this passage.

## ONE WEEK

Now let's look at the next part of the verse:

> *"And he shall confirm the covenant with many for one week: and in the midst of the week he shall cause the sacrifice and the oblation to cease, "* (Dan 9:27)

The original intention that God had for the Jewish people was the offer of the Kingdom. God sent His son Jesus Christ, however, the Jews rejected Him and after 3 ½ years of His ministry on this earth, they had the Romans crucify Jesus on the cross. This verse is showing that God sent Jesus for what would have been for 7 years (one week) but because of their hardness of heart and unbelief they rejected Jesus and had Him killed.

Daniel then says, *"and in the midst of the week he shall cause the sacrifice and oblation to cease..."* After 3 ½ years of ministry, Jesus' death on the cross forever ended God's requirement for man to offer animal sacrifices as atonement for sin. Jesus death on the cross literally caused the *"sacrifice and the oblation to cease"* forever more. Jesus paid the penalty for sin forever to all who will acknowledge Him by confessing Him as their own personal Savior.

Daniel's *prophecy clock* immediately stopped ticking when Jesus died on the cross. In God's eyes there will never be any need for animal sacrifices again. Jesus paid it all and sacrifices are no longer required. Daniel's final week or final 7-year period began when Jesus was baptized. His ministry lasted for a period of approximately 3 ½ years or in the "midst of the week." Daniel's *clock* has stopped half way through the final week.

There only remains about 3 ½ years until the end of this last week. In other words, Daniel's prophecy only has 3 ½ years to go. There is no 7 year tribulation period remaining!

**7 Year Tribulation Period**
The "Traditional" interpretation of Daniel says:

70<sup>th</sup> Week of Daniel = Tribulation Period = 7 years

The word of God does not mention a 7-year tribulation period. **The only one Scripture that does mention a 7-year period is Daniel 9:27!** The *"one week"* of Daniel 9:27 has already elapsed 3 ½ years with the ministry of Jesus. The first half of Daniel's final week has already been fulfilled!

There are several places in the word of God that do mention a period of 3 ½ years:

|  |  |
|---|---|
| Daniel 7:25 | 42 months |
| Daniel 12:7 | 42 months |
| Revelation 11:2 | 42 months |
| Revelation 11:3 | 1,260 days |
| Revelation 12:6 | 1,260 days |
| Revelation 12:14 | 42 months |
| Revelation 13:5 | 42 months |

The above summary is very enlightening. Each of the above references is referring to a period of approximately 3 ½ years – and there is not one Scripture that says there is a 7-year period of time remaining.

By distorting Daniel 9:27, human "Tradition" has created a doctrine that a 7-year Tribulation period is coming in the future before Jesus returns. This grand deception has created almost a fairy tale for all who are captivated by its scheme.

The time of the Tribulation period is rapidly approaching, however, there is no 7-year period mentioned in Scripture. The first half of Daniel's $70^{th}$ week has been completed by our wonderful Lord and Savior Jesus Christ.

**Creation of Popular Tradition**
This popular church tradition is a relatively new one. Dave Watchman wrote on this subject in an article entitled *The Truth of Daniel 9:27*. He notes that the error began in 1885 when the "Revised Version" (R.V.), was recommended to be the replacement for the Authorized King James Bible by the so called "textual critics" of that era!" He then compares the purified Authorized Version (A.V.) with the corrupted Revised Version (R.V.) which renders Daniel 9:27 falsely. The R.V. "makes" the "he" - the Antichrist, compared to the purified A.V. text which declares the "he" to be Jesus Christ:

| Authorized King James Bible | The Revised Version of 1885 |
|---|---|
| And he shall confirm the covenant with many for one week: and in the midst of the week he shall cause the sacrifice and the oblation to cease, and for the overspreading of abominations he shall make it desolate, even until the consummation, and that determined shall be poured upon the desolate. | And he shall make a firm covenant with many for one week: and for the half of the week he shall cause the sacrifice and the oblation to cease: and upon the wing of abominations shall come one that maketh desolate; and even unto the consummation, and that determined, shall wrath be poured out upon the desolator. |

"…the A.V. says "*and he* (Jesus) *shall confirm* (strengthen) *the covenant* (referring to the Abrahamic covenant already mentioned in Dan. 9:4, Gen. 12:1-3) *with many for one week* (7-years), whereas the R.V. says And 'he' (Antichrist) will make a firm covenant (peace) with many for one week (7-years)."[1]

His article goes on to point out that Sir Robert Anderson and C.I. Scofield were close friends who used the false rendering brought out by the Revised Version in their classic works: *The Coming Prince* and the *Scofield Bible*. "As time went on, other writers such as Larkin, Ironside, McClain, Pentecost, Green, Walvoord, etc. wrote prophetic books which 'also agreed' with Sir Robert's R.V. interpretation of Daniel 9:27 and formed the basis of our modern prophetic teachings we hear today!"

The modern interpretation believed and taught by the majority of the Church today has its roots in this change made to God's Word in 1885.

**3 ½ Year Tribulation Period**

Instead of there being a 7 year tribulation period, the word of God only mentions a period of 3 ½ years. The three primary views of when Jesus will return largely revolve around this faulty tradition. The *Pre-tibulational* view says Jesus will return before the 7-year tribulation begins. The *Mid-tribulational* view says Jesus will return half way through the tribulation. The *Post-tribulational* view says that Jesus will return at the end of the 7-year tribulation period.

Since the first half of Daniel's 70<sup>th</sup> week has already taken place with Christ's ministry, there only remains a period of 3 ½ years for the coming tribulation period. As outlined in this book, we believe that the coming raptures will take place before the tribulation ("Firstfruit Rapture") and right before the end of the tribulation when God gets ready to pour out his wrath ("Main Harvest Rapture") on the rest of mankind. The charts on the following page summarize these various views.

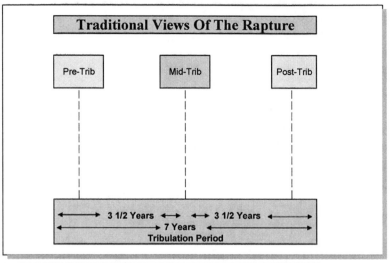

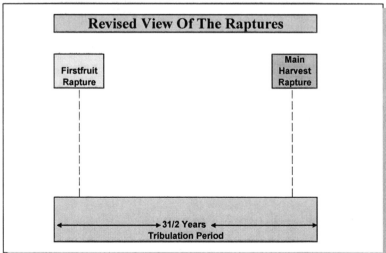

## Supplemental Articles

Please see the Supplemental Articles on our website under the tab for this book to find additional information on why there are only 3 ½ years remaining in the 70th week of Daniel for the tribulation period. (www.ProphecyCountdown.com)

# Appendix 4 – Olivet Discourse

As the entire book of Revelation is a prophecy given by God to Jesus Christ in order to make known what is to take place in the future, it is essential to remember those final things which Christ shared with his disciples immediately before his crucifixion. In Christ's last discourse on the Mount of Olives he shared a brief preview of things to come as well.

The Olivet Discourse can be found in Matthew 24 & 25, with similar accounts in Mark 13 and Luke 17 & 21. It is important to point out that the popular traditional interpretation states that Jesus was speaking to the Jews in his discourse and that it does not concern members of the Church. Others have stated that Jesus was only telling us what has already been fulfilled with the destruction of the Temple in Jerusalem back in 70 AD.

### Jews – Church – Gentiles

By properly dividing the word of truth (2Ti 2:15), we will find that Jesus was essentially speaking to all of mankind in this key address. The disciples in fact asked Jesus three questions and only Matthew recorded each of these:

> *"Now as He sat on the Mount of Olives, the disciples came to Him privately, saying, "Tell us, (1) when will these things be? And (2) what will be the sign of Your coming, and (3) of the end of the age?"*
> (Mat 24:3 – NKJV)

In both Mark's and Luke's accounts only two questions are mentioned, however, Matthew records three separate questions the disciples asked him. In answering these three queries, Jesus' response actually addressed three different groups of people. This division can be distinguished by making the following proper partition: Jews – Mat 24:4-31, Church – Mat 24:32 to Mat 25:30 and Gentiles – Mat 25:31-46.

**Jews – Matthew 24:4-31**

In answering the disciple's questions, Jesus addresses the Jewish people in verses 4 to 31 of chapter 24. A significant characteristic of this section is the fact that Jesus speaks in literal terms: a literal "temple" (i.e. holy place – v. 15), fleeing to the mountains (v. 16), houses (v. 17), fields (v. 18), nursing babies (v. 19), tribes of the earth (v. 30) and the four winds on the earth (v. 31). Throughout this section everything is literal. In both the Jewish section and the Gentile section of the Olivet Discourse the Lord deals in literal terms. This method all changes in the Church section where figurative language is utilized.

The Lord's answer to the Jews actually has three parts. The disciples were concerned when the temple would be destroyed: *"not one stone shall be left here upon another, that shall not be thrown down."* (Mat 2:2 – NKJV) This prophecy was fulfilled in 70 AD when the Romans came and destroyed the Jewish Temple – this was the answer to their 1st question. While this portion of the prophecy has already occurred, the disciple's 3rd question had to do with the "end of the age," which will not be fulfilled until the time of the end.

> *"Immediately **after** the tribulation of those days the sun will be darkened, and the moon will not give its light; the stars will fall from heaven, and the powers of the heavens will be shaken."* (Mat 24:29 – NKJV)

Once the tribulation is complete these cosmic manifestations will answer the disciple's final question. It is imperative to note that there are two similar places when the sun and the moon will be obscured: one **afterword**, as described in the above verse, and the occurrence **before** the great and terrible day: *"And I beheld when he had opened the sixth seal, and, lo, there was a great earthquake; and the sun became black as sackcloth of hair, and the moon became as blood"* (Rev 6:12)

The above verse describes the beginning of the 6<sup>th</sup> Seal, which will start with a great earthquake, to be followed by the darkening of the sun and the moon becoming as **blood**. This period of time **before** the great and terrible day of the LORD was described by Joel and was also mentioned by Peter:

> *"The sun shall be turned into darkness, and the moon into blood, before the great and the terrible day of the LORD come."* (Joel 2:31)

> *"The sun shall be turned into darkness, and the moon into blood, before that great and notable day of the Lord come:"* (Act 2:20)

While the sun will be turned to darkness and the moon into **blood** before the great and terrible day of the Lord with the opening of the 6<sup>th</sup> Seal, the Olivet Discourse describes an event that will take place at the very close of the tribulation when the sun and the moon will be **totally** darkened. It is noteworthy that Jesus mentioned these events in the Jewish section of his discourse. Right after these cosmic manifestations occur, the heavens are shaken even further and the Lord makes His glorious appearance at the very end of the great tribulation period. In answer to the disciples 2<sup>nd</sup> question, His glorious appearing will be preceded by an unknown sign of his coming in fulfillment of the prophecy in Zechariah 12:10-14.

**Church – Matthew 24:32 to Matthew 25:30**
The Church section of the Olivet Discourse begins with:

> *"Now learn this parable from the fig tree: When its branch has already become tender and puts forth leaves, you know that summer is near."* (Mat 24:32 – NKJV)

The partition of our Lord's discourse can easily be discerned by the fact that he immediately begins the Church section with the introduction of the first of several parables. Jesus uses figurative language throughout the description of his dealings with the Church. The first parable from the fig tree is the 1$^{st}$ of two signs that Jesus gives to the Church to signal that his return is drawing near. The fig tree represents Israel (Hosea 9:10 and Joel 1:6-7) and he lets the Church know that once Israel shows signs of life again, the generation alive to witness this will not pass away: *"Verily I say unto you, This generation shall not pass, till all these things be fulfilled."* (Mat 24:34)

With Israel becoming a nation in 1948, the Church has been put on notice that the Lord's return certainly must be very near.

The 2$^{nd}$ sign that Jesus gives the Church is the sign of Noah:
> *"But as the days of Noe were, so shall also the coming of the Son of man be. For as in the days that were before the flood they were eating and drinking, marrying and giving in marriage, until the day that Noe entered into the ark, And knew not until the flood came, and took them all away; so shall also the coming of the Son of man be."* (Mat 24:37-39)

Here the Lord is telling the Church that just prior to his return, things will be the same as they were back in Noah's day. A careful study of Genesis 4 to 6 will alert the reader to the fact that living in these end times is almost parallel to the time before the flood (note: please see Appendix 7 where one of the greatest specific signs of Christ's second coming is discussed).

After telling the Jews that the sign of his coming is linked to the time of His glorious appearing, and giving the Church two signs of his return, Jesus continues his discourse through the use of figurative language by warning of **the coming separation** that will occur (see pp. 159-164):

> *"But know this, that if the master of the **house** had known what hour the thief would come, he would have watched and not allowed his **house** to be broken into.*

> *Therefore you also be ready, for the Son of Man is coming at an hour you do not expect."*
> (Mat 24:43-44 – NKJV)

In the above passage, Jesus is warning the church leaders (*"master of the house"*) of the consequences of not properly preparing their flock for the Lord's soon return. Watchfulness is the primary key as also attested to in Luke's warning:

> *"Watch ye therefore, and pray always, that ye may be accounted worthy to escape all these things that shall come to pass, and to stand before the Son of man."*
> (Luk 21:36)

In addition to watching and praying, Jesus also notes that the faithful and wise servants will be distributing *"meat in due season"* (Mat 24:45-46) while the unfaithful servant will disregard the topic of the second coming and be chastised by the Lord as a result (Mat 24:48-51). The Lord continues this essential teaching with two more important parables.

### Parable of the Ten Virgins
The parable found in Matthew 25:1-13, has been misunderstood by many in the church. Some believe the book of Matthew is only addressing the Jewish people, while others feel Jesus was teaching on the need to be saved (i.e., the wise are saved and the foolish are lost).

In this parable we see that only the 5 wise virgins who were ready went into the wedding. All 10 virgins were Christians because all did possess their oil that represents the Holy Spirit, who was given to each of them upon their conversion. The 5 foolish virgins, however, did not carry along the extra measure of oil that the 5 wise virgins carried in their jars. The 5 wise virgins were ready because they were obedient to the word of God, which commands Christians to be *"filled with the Spirit"*

(Eph 5:18). Because the 5 wise virgins were filled with the Spirit, they allowed Him to direct and empower their lives. As a result, they were ready when the Bridegroom came.

However, the 5 foolish virgins were shut out of the wedding feast because they had not properly prepared themselves. This is a parable to teach believers of the need to get ready now while there is still time – before the separation occurs.

### Parable of the Talents

The parable of the talents found in Matthew 25:14-30, concludes the Church section of Christ's sermon on the Mount of Olives. In this portion of his discourse, Jesus used the parable of the talents to show the distinction between the faithful and unfaithful and the consequences for unfaithfulness.

> *"And I was afraid, and went and hid thy talent in the earth: lo, there thou hast that is thine. His lord answered and said unto him, Thou wicked and slothful servant, thou knewest that I reap where I sowed not, and gather where I have not strawed: Thou oughtest therefore to have put my money to the exchangers, and then at my coming I should have received mine own with usury. Take therefore the talent from him, and give it unto him which hath ten talents. For unto every one that hath shall be given, and he shall have abundance: but from him that hath not shall be taken away even that which he hath. And cast ye the unprofitable servant into **outer darkness**: there shall be weeping and gnashing of teeth."* (Mat 25:25-30)

Jesus had given three individuals talents to use. One received 5, the other received 2, and the third received 1 talent. The first two individuals were faithful and were able to double the talents that had been given to them. The third individual was called *"wicked and slothful"* because he buried his talent in the earth.

Because of his unfaithfulness, this individual was cast into *"outer darkness"* where he experienced *"weeping and gnashing of teeth."* It is important to understand that the parable of the talents is addressing Christians. Many try to interpret this parable to say Jesus was referring to non-believers; however, the entire **context** of this parable is to believers as it is found in the **Church section** of the Olivet Discourse.

The term *"outer darkness"* is only used three times in the New Testament. Jesus used this phrase in addressing three different classes of people: Jews – Mat 8:11-12, Gentiles – Mat 22:11-14, and Christians – Mat 25:14-30. To learn more about this topic and **the coming separation**, please see our book, *The Kingdom* that is available on our website www.ProphecyCountdown.com where it can be freely downloaded.

It is important to point out that being assigned to *"outer darkness"* is not punishment for sin, but it does represent the loss of reward for the believer. The Christian will still be with God in eternity, but will lose the opportunity of being able to rule and reign with Christ in the millennium.

**Gentiles – Matthew 25:31 to Matthew 25:46**
Jesus concludes his Olivet Discourse by addressing the final class of people: the Gentiles.

> *"When the Son of man shall come in his glory, and all the holy angels with him, then shall he sit upon the throne of his glory: And before him **shall be gathered all nations:** and he shall separate them one from another, as a shepherd divideth his sheep from the goats: And he shall set the sheep on his right hand, but the goats on the left."* (Mat 25:31-33)

The Lord returns to using literal language as he is seen coming with his angels, sitting on his throne and gathering the nations. This is his literal return to the earth at the very conclusion of the tribulation period. It represents Christ's second coming to the remaining Gentiles who survived the final battle of Armageddon and the judgments of God's final wrath. Some have labeled this portion of our Lord's Sermon on the Mount of Olives as a parable; however, a close reading of the text reveals that it is not really a parable at all, but rather an actual prophecy of events that will take place at the end of the tribulation period.

The reader is encouraged to read the account in Matthew 25:31-46. This is the famous sheep and goat judgement when Jesus returns at the end of the tribulation period. The sheep and goats represent Gentiles who are redeemed during the great tribulation at the very end of the age.

The sheep represent redeemed Gentiles who ministered to the Jewish people and Christians during the final part of the tribulation. Because the sheep were kind and helped these people, they are given the reward of entering into: *"the kingdom prepared for you **from** the foundation of the world."* (Matthew 25:34)   This represents a judgement of works for the Gentiles, and those found faithful (sheep), are richly rewarded by being able to enter into the earthly aspect of the coming Kingdom.

The goats, on the other hand, represent redeemed Gentiles who did not help the Jews and Christians during the last part of the tribulation. Because their works were found lacking (they did not feed, clothe, visit, etc.) they were chastised.

> *"44)...**Lord**, when saw we thee an hungered, or athirst, or a stranger, or naked, or sick, or in prison, and did not minister unto thee? 45) Then shall he answer them, saying, Verily I say unto you, In as much as ye did it not to one of the least of these, ye did it not to me. 46) And these shall go away into everlasting (#166) punishment: but the righteous into life eternal."* (Mat 25:44-46)

Please notice these are redeemed Gentiles (verse 44, shows they called Him Lord–II Corinthians 12:3). But because of their lack of concern for the Jews and Christians, they are sent away for punishment for the Kingdom age. The use of *aionios* (#166) by Jesus shows that this period of chastisement or punishment will only last for a limited time. Had Jesus meant to convey this to be eternal punishment, He would have used a different Greek word, such as *"aidios,"* if it were to be everlasting.

It is vital to understand that the sheep and goat judgement does represent Gentiles **redeemed** during the end of the tribulation. Those found faithfully helping the Jews and Christians (sheep) will be richly rewarded by entering the coming Kingdom for the 1,000-year reign of the earth. Those who did not help these people (goats) will be chastised during this same period.[1]

This judgement is similar to the one that will take place when Jesus comes to judge the Church as described earlier in the Church section of this summary of the Olivet Discourse. In like manner, the judgement of the sheep and goats is a separation of redeemed Gentiles based upon their works. While the faithful sheep are rewarded, the goats are chastised.

A fascinating observation about how these Gentiles may have been redeemed is found in Revelation 14:6-7 (ESV):

> *"6) Then I saw another **angel** flying directly overhead, with an **eternal gospel** to proclaim to those who dwell on earth, to **every nation and tribe and language and people.** 7) And he said with a loud voice, "Fear God and give him glory, because the **hour of his judgment has come**, and worship him who made heaven and earth, the sea and the springs of water."*

As described in Chapter 4, the rapture of the Firstfruit believers takes place in Revelation 14:1-5. Immediately after this, God sends an angel to preach the eternal gospel to the Gentiles (i.e., *"every nation, kindred and tongue and people"*). Please notice, an angel is used to proclaim this *eternal gospel*. This is a unique time on the earth when the great tribulation period will be under way. The gospel that the angel will declare appears to be different from the *gospel of grace* that is preached today: faith in our Lord Jesus Christ and repentance unto God. The eternal gospel that the angel announces is: fear God and give him glory and to worship him who made heaven and earth. Finally, the reader will note that the Jewish section of the Olivet Discourse mentions the gospel of the Kingdom being preached:

> *"And this gospel of the kingdom will be preached in all the world as a witness to all the nations, and then the end will come."* (Mat 24:14)

It is beyond the scope of this book to go into all of the nuances and differences among the three gospels that are mentioned. In the end, everyone on the Earth will have been given the opportunity to hear the good news of God's love for all of mankind.

**Summary**
The Olivet Discourse presents a comprehensive overview of how God will deal with all of mankind during the end times: a remnant of the Jewish people will be delivered by fleeing into the wilderness, the watchful and praying Christians will be delivered via Raptures before final judgments commence, and the caring and compassionate Gentiles who came to the aid of the Lord's brethren (Mat 25:40) will be granted entrance into the earthly aspect of the coming Kingdom.

God has a plan to reach every person with the gospel of his love for everyone. How each individual responds will determine their destiny when the Lord finally returns to set up his eternal Kingdom.

# Appendix 5 – 7 Beatitudes of Revelation

**Overcomers**
*"Blessed is he who **reads** and those who **hear the words** of this prophecy, and **keep those things** which are **written in it**; for the time is near."* (Rev 1:3 – NKJV)

**Martyrs**
*"Then I heard a voice from heaven saying to me, "Write: 'Blessed are the **dead who die in the Lord** from now on.' "Yes," says the Spirit, "that they may rest from their labors, and their works follow them."* (Rev 14:13 – NKJV)

**Watchful**
*"Behold, I am coming as a thief. Blessed is he who **watches**, and **keeps his garments**, lest he walk naked and they see his shame."* (Rev 16:15 – NKJV)

**Bride of Christ**
*"Then he said to me, "Write: 'Blessed are those who are **called to the marriage supper of the Lamb!**' "And he said to me, "These are the true sayings of God."*
(Rev 19:9 – NKJV)

**Part of 1ˢᵗ Resurrection**
*"Blessed and holy is he who **has part in the first resurrection**. Over such the second death has no power, but they shall be priests of God and of Christ, and shall reign with Him a thousand years."* (Rev 20:6 – NKJV)

**Overcomers**
*"Behold, I am coming quickly! Blessed is he who **keeps the words of the prophecy of this book**."* (Rev 22:7 – NKJV)

**Overcomers**
*"Blessed are those who **wash their robes***, so that they may have the right to the tree of life and that they may enter the city by the gates."* (Rev 22:14 – ESV)
* *"**do his commandments**"*

*"43) But know this, that if the goodman of the house had known in what watch the thief would come, he would have watched, and would not have suffered his house to be broken up.*

*44) Therefore be ye also ready: for in such an hour as ye think not the Son of man cometh.*

*45) Who then is a faithful and wise servant, whom his lord hath made ruler over his household, to give them meat in due season?  46) Blessed is that servant, whom his lord when he cometh shall find so doing.  47)Verily I say unto you, That he shall make him ruler over all his goods. "* (Mat 24:43-47)

# Appendix 6 – Overcomers

One of the main purposes of this book is to help Christians become the overcomers God wants us to be. As we have pointed out throughout this book, many of the teachings taught in the church today are based upon human tradition.

Paul gives us a strong warning about "Tradition" as shown in the following translations of Colossians 2:8:

> *"Beware lest any man **spoil you** through philosophy and vain deceit, after the **tradition of men**, after the rudiments of the world, and not after Christ."* (KJV)

> *"See to it that no one **takes you captive** through hollow and deceptive philosophy, which depends on **human tradition** and the basic principles of this world rather than on Christ."* (NIV)

Traditions come about through human philosophy that can cause us to completely miss what God is telling us. One of the popular teachings in today's church is that all Christians are automatically *"overcomers"* when they become a believer. While we love Mandisa's catchy hit tune, **Overcomer**, we would take exception to the implication that we are automatically overcomers. Rather than singing, *"You're an overcomer,"* we would change the lyrics slightly to: *"Be an overcomer."*

Being an overcomer is what being a Christian is all about. Granted, accepting Christ is vital to becoming an overcomer, it is really only the first step.

> *"For whatsoever is born of God overcometh the **world**: and this is the victory that overcometh the **world**, even our faith. Who is he that overcometh the **world**, but he that believeth that Jesus is the Son of God?"* (1Jo 5:4-5)

### Beware of Traditions

"The only defense against false
teaching is truth…(and) false doctrine
is like a disease germ; it sets up a
mental block to truth.
A person once infected is very difficult
to reach.  It seems as if one simply
cannot get through to him."[1]
      Arthur Bloomfield
      *How To Recognize The
      Antichrist*

"Given sufficient time,
cherished traditions
become dogmatic beliefs."
Amaury De Reincourt

"Minds are like parachutes.  They
work best when open."
Thomas Dewar

*"See that no one shall be **carrying you
away** as spoil **through philosophy** and
**vain deceit**, according to the
deliverance of men, according to the
rudiments of the world, and not
according to Christ."*
      Apostle Paul
      (Colossians 2:8 – YLT)

The first two times the word "overcometh" is used is found in the above Scripture. John is telling us that only those who are born of God, and believe that Jesus is the Son of God, have overcome the *world* by their faith. All that is required to overcome the *world* is the believer's faith in Jesus Christ.

**Overcome the Flesh and the Devil**
But to be considered a successful overcomer at the Judgement Seat of Christ, the Christian also must also be able to overcome the flesh and overcome the devil.

> *"For all that is in the world, the lust of the flesh, and the lust of the eyes, and the pride of life, is not of the Father, but is of the world."* (1 Jo 2:16)

> *"For we wrestle not against flesh and blood, but against principalities, against powers, against the rulers of the darkness of this world, against spiritual wickedness in high places."* (Eph 6:12)

Once a person receives Christ as their personal Saviour, they overcome the world by their faith in Jesus. At this point, a battle begins for the believer's soul. The flesh wants to gratify itself and the devil will attempt to destroy the new Christian's soul. Remember, the whole **goal** of our faith is the salvation of our soul: *"Receiving the **end** of your faith, even the **salvation of your souls.**"* (1 Pe 1:9)

In order to be a successful overcomer at the Judgement Seat of Christ, the Christian needs to ensure that his soul is saved by winning the victory over his flesh and the devil. Remember that your spirit was saved when you believed in Christ. The salvation of the soul requires the defeat of the world, the flesh and the devil. Only once all three are defeated will the Christian be considered a true overcomer. This requires a daily victory that won't end until life's journey is complete.

The world, our flesh and the devil will attempt to defeat us every single day. In order to be successful overcomers we must learn to **continually die to self** and allow the Holy Spirit to direct and empower our lives. In order to be an overcomer, we must continually seek the Lord's help, realizing that relying on our own strength will not work:

> *"I am the vine, you are the branches. He who abides in Me, and I in him, bears much fruit; for without Me you can do nothing."* (Jhn 15:5 – NKJV)

The overcomer learns to place his life in Christ's hands, and only by abiding in Jesus and being filled with the Holy Spirit can we exhibit the fruit of his life to this fallen world.

> *"28) Come to Me, all you who labor and are heavy laden, and I will give you rest. 29) Take My yoke upon you and learn from Me, for I am gentle and lowly in heart, and you will find **rest for your souls**. 30) For My yoke is easy and My burden is light."*
> (Mat 11:28-30 – NKJV)

---

**Learning to be an overcomer is perhaps the most difficult thing to do on this earth as a human being. The overcomer is born through the victory they receive by trusting in Jesus Christ.**

To learn more on the subject of what being an overcomer is all about, the reader is encouraged to see the author's previous books: *The Kingdom* and *Overcomers' Guide To The Kingdom*. Both of these books may be freely downloaded from our website: www.ProphecyCountdown.com

"The assertion that all believers are overcomers is so plainly contrary to fact and to Scripture that one wonders it ever has been made. It involves the false position that no believer can be a backslider. It avoids and nullifies the solemn warnings and urgent pleadings of the Spirit addressed to believers, and, by depriving Christians of these, leaves him dangerously exposed to the perils they reveal."[2]

G. H. Lang
***The Revelation of Jesus Christ***

"It has been pointed out that the Lord names overcomers in every one of His seven letters to the Churches (Panton). What a remarkable encouragement and revelation is this fact, especially for those of us who have been overcome, and have failed Him so often in the past! If we repent, and honestly and genuinely seek His help and strength to obey His word, we also can be overcomers. Let's not allow ourselves to be side-tracked by those 'who consider reward to be beneath the notice of a CHRISTIAN.' Let's be like Paul and *"press on toward the goal to win the prize..."* (Phil. 3:14)[3]

Robert Govett
***Seek First His Kingdom and His Righteousness*** (Tract)

### Ephesus

*"Remember therefore from whence thou art fallen, and* **repent,** *and do the first works ("first love"- NIV); or else I will come unto thee quickly, and will remove thy candlestick out of his place, except thou repent."*
(Rev 2:5)

### Smyrna

*"Fear none of those things which thou shalt suffer: behold, the devil shall cast some of you into prison, that ye may be tried; and ye shall have tribulation ten days:* **be thou faithful unto death,** *and I will give thee a crown of life."* (Rev 2:10)

### Pergamos

**"Repent;** *or else I will come unto thee quickly, and will fight against them with the sword of my mouth."*
(Rev 2:16)

### Thyatira

*"But that which ye have already* **hold fast** *till I come."*
(Rev 2:25)

### Sardis

" **Be watchful,** *and* **strengthen the things which remain,** *that are ready to die: for I have not found thy works perfect before God."* (Rev 3:2)

### Philadelphia

*"Behold, I come quickly:* **hold that fast which thou hast,** *that no man take thy crown."* (Rev 3:11)

### Laodicea

*"As many as I love, I rebuke and chasten: be zealous therefore, and* **repent.** *"* (Rev 3:19)

The above admonitions by our Lord require little commentary. Jesus is instructing the 7 Churches on what is needed for them to become overcomers. May we all meditate on these passages as reminders of areas in our lives that may require our attention for any necessary correction and repentance (1 Jo 1:9) and always remember the following promises for overcomers.

# Promises To Overcomers
## Ephesus
*"He that hath an ear, let him hear what the Spirit saith unto the churches; To him that **overcometh** will I give to eat **of the tree of life,** which is in the midst of the paradise of God.* (Rev 2:7)
## Smyrna
*"He that **overcometh** shall not be hurt of the **second death.** "* (Rev 2:11)
## Pergamos
*"He that hath an ear, let him hear what the Spirit saith unto the churches; To him that **overcometh** will I give to eat **of** the **hidden manna**, and will give him a **white stone,** and in the stone a **new name** written, which no man knoweth saving he that receiveth it. "* (Rev 2:17)
## Thyatira
*"And he that **overcometh**, and keepeth my works unto the end, to him will I give **power over the nations"*** (Rev 2:26)
## Sardis
*He that **overcometh**, the same shall **be clothed in white raiment;** and I will **not blot out his name out of the book of life**, but I will confess his name before my Father, and before his angels.* (Rev 3:5)
## Philadelphia
*"Him that **overcometh** will I make a **pillar in the temple** of my God, and he shall go no more out: and I will write upon him the **name of my God**, and the **name of the city** of my God, which is new Jerusalem, which cometh down out of heaven from my God: and I will write upon him **my new name.*** (Rev 3:12)
## Laodicea
*"To him that **overcometh** will I grant to **sit with me in my throne,** even as I also overcame, and am set down with my Father in his throne.* (Rev 3:21)

*"He that **overcometh** shall **inherit all things;** and I will be his God, and he shall be my son. "* (Rev 21:7)

### Excerpt from THE COMING SPIRITUAL EARTHQUAKE

An overcomer is a believer who has had an authentic experience with God. Though thrown into the furnace of affliction, they have come forth as pure gold. The overcomer is born through the victory they receive by trusting in Jesus Christ. Learning to be an overcomer is perhaps the most difficult thing to do on this earth as a human being. Possessing impressive credentials and degrees offer little solace when it comes to where the "rubber meets the road." Every professing Christian must learn to be an overcomer through faith and total trust in their Savior. In Matthew 11:28-30, Jesus urges: *"Come unto me, all ye that labour and are heavy laden, and I will give you rest. Take my yoke upon you, and learn of me; for I am meek and lowly in heart: and ye shall find rest unto your souls. For my yoke is easy, and my burden is light."* The overcomers take their agony and burdens to the mighty counselor. Through prayer and trust, Jesus leads the downcast believer to "green pasture." The sting of the adversary is somehow turned to sweet victory. Christ alone is able to provide the peace that passes all understanding. While every believer will have trials and testing in this world, Christ reminded us to be of good cheer because He overcame this world. As believers, we find our sweet victory in Him! Overcomers are believers who find their strength and help in Him--not through man, but by the power of the Son of God. A genuine overcomer follows in Christ's footsteps. They learn to "take it on the chin" and to "take it to the cross." Whatever the world dishes out is handled with prayer and placed on the altar before God. By offering everything to Christ, they find hope and sufficiency in Him. Being an overcomer is what being a Christian is all about. Through the trials of this life, the overcomers' faith is put on trial and thereby confirmed as Holy evidence before a mighty God, it is authentic. As our example, Jesus endured the cross for the joy set before Him. Overcomers have the victory because of His victory. Through His victory, the overcomer is able to walk in newness of life. The overcomer knows: they have been crucified with Christ and their old life is gone (Gal 2:20). By dying to self, the overcomer experiences the joy of Christ's triumph in their life. Finally, an overcomer is grateful and humble: for they know of God's rich mercy and marvelous grace. If it wasn't for Christ, they would be doomed. Out of this gratitude, rises the song of gladness and praise. An overcomers' heart bursts forth with praise and adoration unto their God for the victory He provides. The overcomer knows, first hand, that while weeping may endure for the night: joy cometh in the morning!

# Appendix 7

## Sign of Christ's Coming

April 8, 1997

**Comet Hale-Bopp Over New York City**
**Credit and Copyright:** J. Sivo
http://antwrp.gsfc.nasa.gov/apod/ap970408.html

"What's that point of light above the World Trade Center? It's Comet Hale-Bopp! Both faster than a speeding bullet and able to "leap" tall buildings in its single <u>orbit</u>, Comet Hale-Bopp is also bright enough to be seen even over the glowing lights of one of the world's premier cities. In the foreground lies the East River, while much of New York City's Lower Manhattan can be seen between the river and the comet."

- - - - - - - - - - - - - - - - - - - - - - - - - - - - - - - - - - - - - - - - - -

**"As it was in the days of Noah, so it will be at the coming of the Son of Man."** (Matthew 24:37 – NIV)

These words from our wonderful Lord have several applications about the Tribulation period that is about to ensnare this world.

Seas Lifted Up
Throughout the Old Testament, the time of the coming Tribulation period is described as the time when the "seas have lifted up," and also as coming in as a "flood" (please see Jeremiah 51:42, Hosea 5:10, Daniel 11:40 and Psalm 93:3-4 for just a few examples).

This is a direct parallel to the time of Noah when the Great Flood of water came to wipe out every living creature, except for righteous Noah and his family, and the pairs of animals that God spared. While God said He would never flood the earth again with water, the coming Judgement will be by fire (II Peter 3:10). The book of Revelation shows that approximately three billion people will perish in the terrible time that lies ahead (see Revelation 6:8 and 9:15).

2 Witnesses
A guiding principle of God is to establish a matter based upon the witness of two or more:

> *"...a matter must be established by the testimony of two or three witnesses"* (Deuteronomy 19:15 – NIV)

In 1994, God was able to get the attention of mankind when Comet Shoemaker-Levy crashed into Jupiter on the 9th of Av (on the Jewish calendar). Interestingly, this Comet was named after the "two" witnesses who first discovered it.

In 1995, "two" more astronomers also discovered another comet. It was called Comet Hale-Bopp and it reached its closest approach to planet Earth on March 23, 1997. It has been labeled as the most widely viewed comet in the history of mankind.

Scientists have determined that Comet Hale-Bopp's orbit brought it to our solar system 4,465 years ago (see Notes 1 and 2 below). In other words, the comet made its appearance near Earth in 1997 and also in 2468 BC. Remarkably, this comet preceded the Great Flood by 120 years! God warned Noah of this in Genesis 6:3:

> *"My Spirit shall not strive with man forever, for he is indeed flesh; yet his days shall be one hundred and twenty years."*

Days of Noah

What does all of this have to do with the Lord's return? Noah was born around 2948 BC, and Genesis 7:11, tells us that the Flood took place when Noah was 600, or in 2348 BC.

Remember, our Lord told us: ***"As it was in the days of Noah, so it will be at the coming of the Son of Man."*** (Matthew 24:37 – NIV)

In the original Greek, it is saying: ***"exactly like"*** it was, so it will be when He comes (see Strong's #5618).

During the days of Noah, Comet Hale-Bopp arrived on the scene as a harbinger of the Great Flood. Just as this same comet appeared before the Flood, could its arrival again in 1997 be a sign that God's final Judgement, also known as the time of Jacob's Trouble, is about to begin?

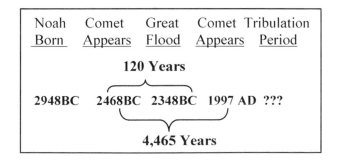

Comet Hale-Bopp arrived 120 years before the Flood as a warning to mankind. Only righteous Noah heeded God's warning and built the ark, as God instructed. By faith, Noah was obedient to God and, as a result, saved himself and his family from destruction.

Remember, Jesus told us His return would be preceded by great heavenly signs: *"And there shall be signs in the sun, and in the moon, and in the stars; and upon the earth distress of nations, with perplexity; the sea and the waves roaring..."* (Luke 21:25)

Just as this large comet appeared as a 120-year warning to Noah, its arrival in 1997 tells us that Jesus is getting ready to return again. Is this the **"Sign"** Jesus referred to?

---

Jesus was asked 3 questions by the disciples:
*"Tell us, (1) when shall these things be"* (the destruction of the city of Jerusalem), *" and (2) what shall be the __sign__ of thy coming, and (3) of the end of the world?"* (Matthew 24:3)

---

## Sign of Christ's Coming

The **first** question had to do with events that were fulfilled in 70 AD. The **third** question has to do with the future time at the very end of the age.

The **second** question, however, has to do with the time of Christ's second coming. Jesus answered this second question in His description of the days of Noah found in Matthew 24:33-39:

> [33] *"So likewise ye, when ye shall see all these things, know that it is near, even at the doors.* [34] *Verily I say unto you, This generation shall not pass, till all these things be fulfilled.* [35] *Heaven and earth shall pass away, but my words shall not pass away.* [36] *But of that day and hour knoweth no man, no, not the angels of heaven, but my Father only.* [37] ***But as the days of Noe were, so shall also the coming of the Son***

*of man be.* [38] *For as in the days that were before the flood they were eating and drinking, marrying and giving in marriage, until the day that Noe entered into the ark,* [39] *And knew not until the flood came, and took them all away; so shall also the coming of the Son of man be."*

Jesus is telling us that the **sign** of His coming will be as it was during the days of Noah. As Comet Hale-Bopp was a sign to the people in Noah's day, its arrival in 1997 is a sign that Jesus is coming back again soon. Comet Hale-Bopp could be the very sign Jesus was referring to, which would announce His return for His faithful.

Remember, Jesus said, *"exactly as it was in the days of Noah, so will it be when He returns."* The appearance of Comet Hale-Bopp in 1997 is a strong indication that the tribulation period is about to begin, but before then, Jesus is coming for His bride!

**Keep looking up! Jesus is coming again very soon!**
As Noah prepared for the destruction God warned him about 120 years before the Flood, Jesus has given mankind a final warning that the tribulation period is about to begin. The horrible destruction on 9/11 is only a precursor of what is about to take place on planet Earth. We need to be wise like Noah and prepare. Always remember our Lord's instructions:

## Watch and Pray

*"(34)And take heed to yourselves, lest at any time your hearts be overcharged with surfeiting, and drunkenness, and cares of this life, and so that day come upon you unawares. (35) For as a snare shall it come on all them that dwell on the face of the whole earth.(36)Watch ye therefore, and pray always, that ye may be accounted worthy to escape all these things that shall come to pass, and to stand before the Son of man"* (Luke 21:34-36).

# Footnotes to Appendix 7

(1) The original orbit of Comet Hale-Bopp was calculated to be approximately 265 years by engineer George Sanctuary in his article, *Three Craters In Israel*, published on March 31, 2001 that can be found at:

http://www.gsanctuary.com/3craters.html#3c_r13

Comet Hale-Bopp's orbit around the time of the Flood changed from 265 years to about 4,200 years. Because the plane of the comet's orbit is perpendicular to the earth's orbital plane (ecliptic), Mr. Sanctuary noted: "A negative time increment was used for this simulation…to back the comet away from the earth…. past Jupiter… and then out of the solar system. The simulation suggests that the past-past orbit had a very eccentric orbit with a period of only 265 years. When the comet passed Jupiter (*around 2203BC)* its orbit was deflected upward, coming down near the earth 15 months later with the comet's period changed from 265 years to about (*4,200)* years." (*added text for clarity*)

(2) Don Yeomans, with NASA's Jet Propulsion Laboratory, made the following observations regarding the comet's orbit: "By integrating the above orbit forward and backward in time until the comet leaves the planetary system and then referring the osculating orbital elements…the following orbital periods result:

Original orbital period before entering planetary system = 4200 years. Future orbital period after exiting planetary system = 2380 years."

This analysis can be found at:

http://www2.jpl.nasa.gov/comet/ephemjpl6.html

Based upon the above two calculations we have the following:

**265 [a] + 4,200 [b] = 4,465 Years**

**1997 AD – 4,465 Years = 2468 BC = Hale Bopp arrived**

(a) Orbit period calculated by George Sanctuary before deflection around 2203 BC.

(b) Orbit period calculated by Don Yeomans after 1997 visit.

# Special Invitation

This book hopes to bring people to a better knowledge of Jesus Christ. If you have never been saved before, would you like to be saved? The Bible shows that it's simple to be saved...

- **Realize you are a sinner.**
  *"As it is written, There is none righteous, no, not one:"* (Romans 3:10)
  *"... for there is no difference. For all have sinned, and come short of the glory of God;"* (Romans 3:22-23)
- **Realize you CAN NOT save yourself.**
  *"But we are all as an unclean thing, and all our righteousness are as filthy rags; ..."* (Isaiah 64:6)
  *"Not by works of righteousness which we have done, but according to his mercy he saved us, ..."* (Titus 3:5)
- **Realize that Jesus Christ died on the cross to pay for your sins.**
  *"Who his own self bare our sins in his own body on the tree, ..."* (I Peter 2:24)
  *"... Unto him that loved us, and washed us from our sins in his own blood,"* (Revelation 1:5)
- **Simply by faith receive Jesus Christ as your personal Savior.**
  *"But as many as received him, to them gave he power to become the sons of God, even to them that believe on his name:"* (John 1:12)
  *" ...Sirs, what must I do to be saved? And they said, Believe on the Lord Jesus Christ, and thou shalt be saved, and thy house."* (Acts 16:30-31)
  *"...if you confess with your mouth, 'Jesus is Lord,' and believe in your heart God raised him from the dead, you will be saved."* (Romans 10:9 – NIV)

**WOULD YOU LIKE TO BE SAVED?**

If you would like to be saved, believe on the Lord Jesus Christ (Acts 16:31) right now by making the following confession of faith:

> Lord Jesus, I know that I am a sinner, and unless you save me, I am lost. I thank you for dying for me at Calvary. By faith I come to you now, Lord, the best way I know how, and ask you to save me. I believe that God raised you from the dead and acknowledge you as my personal Saviour.

If you believed on the Lord, this is the most important decision of your life. You are now saved by the precious blood of Jesus Christ, which was shed for you and your sins. Now that you have believed on Jesus as your personal Saviour, you will want to find a Church where you can be baptized as your first act of obedience, and where the Word of God is taught so you can continue to grow in your faith. Ask the Holy Spirit to help you as you read the Bible to learn all that God has for your life.

Also, see the Reference Notes and Bibliography section of this book, where you will find recommended books and websites that will help you on your wonderful journey.

### Endtimes

The Bible indicates that we are living in the final days and Jesus Christ is getting ready to return very soon. This book was written to help people prepare for what lies ahead. The word of God indicates that the tribulation period is rapidly approaching and that the Antichrist is getting ready to emerge on the world scene.

Jesus promised His disciples that there is a way to escape the horrible time of testing and persecution that will soon devastate this planet. One of the purposes of this book is to help you get prepared so you will be ready when Jesus Christ returns.

# About The Author

Jim Harman has been a Christian for 37 years. He has diligently studied the Word of God with a particular emphasis on Prophecy. Jim has written several books and the four most essential titles are available at www.ProphecyCountdown.com: *The Coming Spiritual Earthquake, Calling All Overcomers, The Kingdom, and Overcomers' Guide To The Kingdom;* which have been widely distributed around the world. These books encourage many to continue *"Looking"* for the Lord's return, and bring many to a saving knowledge of Jesus Christ.

Jim's professional experience included being a Certified Public Accountant (CPA) and a Certified Property Manager (CPM). He had an extensive background in both public accounting and financial management with several well-known national firms.

Jim has been fortunate to have been acquainted with several mature believers who understand and teach the deeper truths of the Bible. It is Jim's strong desire that many will come to realize the importance of seeking the Kingdom and seeking Christ's righteousness as we approach the soon return of our Lord and Saviour Jesus Christ.

The burden of his heart is to see many come to know the joy of Christ's triumph in their life as they become true overcomers; qualified and ready to rule and reign with Christ in the coming Kingdom.

In 1996 the Lord opened the door for him to present the wonderful message of the return of our Bridegroom for His awaiting bride at Ray Brubaker's famous international prophecy conference. Sharing the same stage with some of the leading prophecy teachers and scholars of our time was both daunting and humbling at the same time for Jim.

His book table was adjacent to the well-known Tim LaHaye, who had just begun his popular *Left Behind* series that has since sold over 65 million copies. His message has captivated the church with the fascinating tale that a profession of faith in Christ is all that is needed to prepare one for the Rapture when the Lord comes for His own. While coming to know Christ as Savior is absolutely important, there are many admonitions given to believers to "watch" and "be ready" for our Lord's coming. The Apostle John reminds us in 1Jo 3:2-3:

> *"... when He shall appear, we shall be like Him; for we shall see Him as He is. And every man that hath this hope in Him, purify himself, even as He is pure."*

During the Philadelphian church age, great light was given to men of God who properly expounded the necessity for believers to sanctify their lives in order to be properly prepared when Jesus returns. Their teachings fostered the call to holiness for believers to be ready. Since that time, the Laodicean church age has emerged and almost all of the proponents of the coming separation (Mat 25:1-13) have gone to be with the Lord. This time of lukewarm Christianity was predicted by the Apostle Paul:

> *"For the time will come when they will not endure sound doctrine; but after their own lusts shall they heap to themselves teachers, having itching ears; And they shall turn away their ears from the truth, and shall be turned unto fables."* (2 Ti 4:3-4)

The lethargy in our modern church culture has blinded many from hearing the Word of God. The true message in the book of Revelation has been severely tainted by the desire of the church to be entertained rather than being taught and educated through diligent study and meditation of its contents.

God has recently been attempting to alert America in both song and the written word. The recent song by Casting Crowns entitled, *While You Were Sleeping*,\* contains chilling lyrics, which may represent a prophetic warning to all of us concerning the near-term future. Jonathan Cahn's *Harbinger* and his latest work, *Mystery of the Shemitah*, could also represent prophetic warnings to a nation that was once greatly used to uphold the Word of God. Readers who are familiar with his descriptions of America's demise will find strikingly parallel warnings in the Apostle John's predictions outlined in this book.

The book of Revelation holds vital ingredients that are necessary for the spiritual diet of believers living in these last days. Believers interested in their spiritual welfare need to ask the Holy Spirit to help them as they study the essential message in this final book of God's word. The book of Revelation does hold the secret of America's future, the future of the world and the reader's future, as well.

The message contained in this book may represent one final cry from the Lord to awaken His church while there is still time. It is the author's prayer that the reader will truly understand the magnificent future God has in store for all the faithful believers who have ears to hear what the Spirit is saying to the churches in these final days of the Church age.

**One Final Word**

The call from God's very own heart is for believers to be genuine **overcomers**.

The cry from the author's very own heart is for the Church to awaken to the incredible and awesome opportunity the very God of this universe is offering to all those believers who can hear the Spirit crying out in this final book of God's Word.

\* Please see the **Supplemental Articles** section of our website: www.ProphecyCountdown.com, where you will find a link to this song.

His prayer is that this book will help shed some of the many traditions that have obscured the vital message that Jesus Christ will be returning very soon – seeking out those **faithful** believers who really do love Him and whose **only** desire is to please Him and be ready for him when He returns.

The great earthquake is about to usher in end time events and our blessed Bridegroom is coming any day now for his beloved.

Remember, the Spirit and the bride are beckoning for the Lord to come (Rev 22:17).

Will you join in this urgent plea to encourage your other brothers and sisters in the Lord while time still remains?  Tell your friends and loved ones about this book that can be freely downloaded as a PDF file at: www.ProphecyCountdown.com

Incredible blessings await all those who answer the call to be the overcomer He is calling us to be.

To contact the author for questions, to arrange for speaking engagements or to order multiple copies of this book:

> Jim Harman
> P.O. Box 941612
> Maitland, FL  32794
> JamesTHarman@aol.com

---

*"The end of the age is coming soon.  Therefore be earnest, thoughtful men of prayer."*
(I Peter 4:7 – Paraphrase)

# Reader's Comments

James Harman's new book, **Calling All Overcomers**, does an excellent job of mapping out the process, from a Biblical perspective, for believers to enter into the coming Kingdom of the Heavens. I wholeheartedly congratulate Jim for providing God's people with a wonderful roadmap, of the book of Revelation, to help them on their spiritual journey. This outstanding literary work is a 'must read' for all believers in Christ, as the Church Age draws to a close and the Kingdom Age approaches.                    Tyler Cole – Asheboro, NC

Jim Harman has done a marvelous job of giving us searched out insight into one of the most complicated books of our Bible...because it contains the Past, the Present and the Future. Only the Spirit of God can quicken us with understanding...and one thing that stands out above all else...that is to set our Face, Heart and Life "as a Flint" towards "The Holy City of Jerusalem Coming down from our God in Heaven as a Bride adorned for Her Husband." May everyone who reads **Calling All Overcomers** be numbered among the Firstfruits of its Blessed, Overcoming inhabitants.   Jim's life and writings, through the years, have helped us much toward reaching forth for that Goal.                    Joan Olsen – Edmond, OK

**Calling All Overcomers** is wonderful "out of the box" insight into the unsealed book of Revelation. It is a must read that forces you out of your "religious," sometimes confident understanding of "what will soon take place." If you think, "I get it!" ...you may be further from understanding Revelation than you know. This book is definitely one to add to your collection of end-time study material. Remember: Jesus came offering the Kingdom of God and the majority of the religious teachers and leaders did not even get it, because of what they thought it would look like. His next coming will be no different. Strive to overcome!          Richard Fowler – Winter Park, FL

# Reader's Comments

While I have a few differences on certain interpretations in Jim Harman's latest book, the main message about being an overcomer is something that God is warning and calling for in all believers. Being an overcomer is not an option, but a requirement if one wishes to be a part of the rewards in the 1,000 year kingdom (Rev 20:4). *Calling All Overcomers* challenges many traditional religious teachings, and it should challenge the reader to discern for themselves what the Bible really teaches (Act 17:11). By studying the Bible and a book like Jims should bear fruit for the reader in the not too distant future. Lynn Navarre – Jensen Beach, FL


I do believe you will be blessed by Jim Harman's *Calling All Overcomers*, even though I can not endorse every interpretation it makes. What sets this book apart from the hundreds of others is Jim's great understanding of the important truths surrounding the accountability of believers, as outlined in the Scriptures. This book provides us with that much needed, often neglected balance between grace and works, eternal salvation and rewards, and a proper understanding of the age old debate between Calvinism and Arminianism. More importantly, Jim Harman is able to explain these things in an easy-to-understand, down to earth manner that is often missing in commentaries that seem to only want to impress other scholars. Brother Harman is a man of great faith in the Lord. With much zeal and diligence he has labored, in a labor of love, to awaken many to be the Overcomers they are called to be. It is my prayer that the Lord will continue to bless Jim's ministry, and may He continue to grow and perfect all of us, as the day of His coming draws nigh! Joey Faust, pastor, author – Theodosia, MO

# Reader's Comments

For the serious student of the book of Revelation, Brother Jim Harman's latest work, **Calling All Overcomers**, will prove to be a thought provoking read.        Charlie Dines – Marshfield, MO
Author of **Being Glorified Together with Him**


Jim Harman has dedicated his life to prepare the bride of Christ, for the fulfillment of all scriptures at hand! We are living in the days just preceding when *"....The kingdoms of this world are become the kingdoms of our Lord, and of his Christ; and he shall reign for ever and ever."* (Rev 11:15) **Calling All Overcomers** is a call to every believer to know the days we are living in on God's prophetic timeline, and to be prepared for all that is about to unfold. Thank you for your labor to prepare the church for things ahead!        Theresa Ruth – Orlando, FL


Christians often avoid reading the book of Revelation because it is too complex, confusing or frightening. Through many years of dedication to prophecy in scripture the author skillfully clarifies its symbolic language.  It is said that a picture is worth a thousand words; the charts and diagrams in this book simplify the chronology and progression of events in Revelation, and make this in-depth study "user friendly." I too have experienced "paradigm shifts," and I always wanted to believe that Rev 6 was Christ himself and not the Antichrist.  It was refreshing to read Jim Harman's interpretation. **Calling All Overcomers** gives great encouragement to all believers to become Overcomers who are prepared and looking for Christ's return. It's a wake-up call for any sleeping believer who has procrastinated in preparing their souls for the Lord's soon return.  I encourage all believers to read this edifying book – you will be blessed!        Judith Stack – Missionary in Central America with Christ for the City Int'l

# Reader's Comments

James Harman has a very unique gift from the Lord of making what could be considered difficult to understand, very simple. His book, *Calling All Overcomers*, has enriched my study time and has given me a hunger for more understanding on what the Bible says about the Kingdom. I recommend this book for reading enjoyment, study groups or a reference tool.

Pastor Marcus L. Jackson – Baton Rouge, LA

I have always been inspired by Jim Harman's writings. *Calling All Overcomers* is no exception. His love for the Lord and the Word mixed with his insight and wisdom resonates throughout this remarkable book.        Pastor Jeff Philips – Orlando, FL

The book of Revelation is much more than God's final prophetic word to mankind concerning the future; it is also a book that speaks to every Christian about their current walk with Jesus Christ. Author James Harman does an amazing job exploring the mysteries of this important book, while revealing God's heartbeat for His children to know, love and walk with His Son, and to be overcomers through the presence and power of the living Christ in their daily lives.

Pastor Tom Myers – Longwood, FL

Perplexed by the book of Revelation? Not sure what all the signs, symbols and metaphors really mean? Jim Harman's latest work unravels Apostle John's remarkable revelation of Jesus Christ and what's in store for the inhabitants of planet Earth. This extraordinary commentary is not another cookie-cutter, rehash of the popular teachings fostered by the *Left Behind* phenomena so prevalent in today's church.

This unique book outlines the 7 strategic sections of John's vision that are further divided into 7 segments. The reader will come away with a new and enlightened understanding of what the last book in God's Word is all about. Understand the book of Revelation and why it is so important for believers living in the last days of the Church age.

An electronic copy (PDF) of this book is available to be freely downloaded from our website. Permission is required for reproduction for resale. Permission is granted to save the PDF copy to your computer and e-mail to all your friends and loved ones to help them prepare for the glorious future He has in store for all those who are found faithful.

All of the books by Prophecy Countdown Publications are available to purchase at greatly reduced prices when your order 3 or more copies. See page 238 for information to contact us.

Download your FREE copy: www.ProphecyCountdown.com

Or from Amazon.com – Available in Paperback and or Kindle Edition

Once a person is saved, the number one priority should be seeking entrance into the Kingdom through the salvation of their soul. It is pictured as a runner in a race seeking a prize represented by a crown that will last forever.

The salvation of the soul and entrance into the coming Kingdom are only achieved through much testing and the trial of one's faith. If you are going through difficulty, then REJOICE:

> *"Blessed is the man who perseveres under trial, because when he has stood the test, he will receive the crown of life that God has promised to those who love Him."* (James 1:12)

The "Traditional" teaching on the "THE KINGDOM" has taken the Church captive into believing all Christians will rule and reign with Christ no matter if they have lived faithful and obedient lives. or if they have been slothful and disobedient with the talents God has given them. Find out the important Truth before Jesus Christ returns.

### MUST READING FOR EVERY CHRISTIAN

Jesus Christ is returning for His faithful overcoming followers. Don't miss the opportunity of ruling and reigning with Christ in the coming KINGDOM!

Download your FREE copy: www.ProphecyCountdown.com

Or from Amazon.com – Available in Paperback and or Kindle Edition

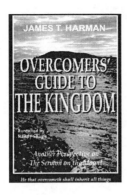

Get ready to climb back up the Mountain to listen to Christ's teachings once again. Though you may have read this great Sermon on the Mount many times, discover exciting promises that many have missed.

The purpose of this book is to help Christians be the Overcomers Jesus wants them to be and to help them gain their own entrance in the coming Kingdom. Learn what seeking the Kingdom of God is all about and be among the chosen few who will "enter into" the coming Kingdom. *"Whoever hears these sayings of Mine, and does them, I will liken him to a wise man who built his house upon the rock."* (Mat 7:24)

Also learn about:
- The link between Beatitudes and Fruit of the Spirit
- What the "law of Christ" really is
- The critical importance of the "Lord's prayer"
- How to be an Overcomer
- THE SIGN of Christ's soon Coming
- A new song entitled: LOOKING FOR THE SON which has the message of how vitally important it is to be Watching for the Lord's return and the consequences to those who are not looking.

Download your FREE copy: www.ProphecyCountdown.com

Or from Amazon.com – Available in Paperback and or Kindle Edition

# LOOKING FOR THE SON
## Lyrics by Jim Harman
### Can be sung to the hit tune: *"ROLLING IN THE DEEP"*

| Lyric | Scripture |
|---|---|
| *There's a fire burning in my heart* | Luke 24:32 |
| *Yearning for the Lord to come,* | Rev. 22:17, Mat. 6:33 |
| *and His Kingdom come to start* | |
| *Soon He'll come.....so enter the narrow gate* | Lk. 21:34-36,Mat.7:13 |
| *Even though you mock me now...* | II Peter 3:4 |
| *He'll come to set things straight* | |
| *Watch how I'll leave in the twinkling of an eye* | I Corinthians 15:52 |
| *Don't be surprised when I go up in the sky* | Revelation 3:10 |
| | |
| *There's a fire burning in my heart* | Luke 24:32 |
| *Yearning for my precious Lord* | Revelation 22:17 |
| *And His Kingdom come to start* | Revelation 20:4-6 |
| | |
| *Your love of this world, has forsaken His* | I John 2:15 |
| *It leaves me knowing that you could have had it all* | Revelation 21:7 |
| *Your love of this world, was oh so reckless* | Revelation 3:14-22 |
| *I can't help thinking* | Philippians 1:3-6 |
| *You would have had it all* | Revelation 21:7 |
| | |
| *Looking for the Son* | Titus 2:13, Luke 21:36 |
| *(Tears are gonna fall, not looking for the Son)* | Matthew 25:10-13 |
| *You had His holy Word in your hand* | II Timothy 3:16 |
| *(You're gonna wish you had listened to me)* | Jeremiah 25:4-8 |
| *And you missed it...for your self* | Matthew 22:11-14 |
| *(Tears are gonna fall, not looking for the Son)* | Matthew 25:10-13 |
| | |
| *Brother, I have a story to be told* | Habakkuk 2:2 |
| *It's the only one that's true* | John 3:16-17 |
| *And it should've made your heart turn* | II Peter 3:9 |
| *Remember me when I rise up in the air* | I Corinthians 15:52 |
| *Leaving your home down here* | I Corinthians 15:52 |
| *For true Treasures beyond compare* | Matthew 6:20 |
| *Your love of this world, has forsaken His* | I John 2:15 |
| *It leaves me knowing that you could have had it all* | Revelation 21:7 |
| *Your love of this world, was oh so reckless* | Revelation 3:14-22 |
| *I can't help thinking* | Philippians 1:3-6 |
| *You would have had it all* | Revelation 21:7 |

*(Lyrics in parentheses represent background vocals)*

(CONTINUED)

© Copyright 2011-15, Prophecy Countdown Publications, LLC

| Lyric | Scripture |
|---|---|
| Looking for the Son | Titus 2:13, Lk. 21:36 |
| (Tears are gonna fall, not looking for the Son) | Matthew 25:10-13 |
| You had His holy Word in your hand | II Timothy 3:16 |
| (You're gonna wish you had listened to me) | Jeremiah 25:4-8 |
| And you lost it...for your self | Matthew 22:11-14 |
| (Tears are gonna fall, not looking for the Son) | Matthew 25:10-13 |
| You would have had it all | Revelation 21:7 |
| Looking for the Son | Titus 2:13, Lk. 21:36 |
| You had His holy Word in your hand | II Timothy 3:16 |
| But you missed it... for your self | Matthew 22:11-14 |

Lov'n the world....not the open door — I Jn. 2:15, Rev. 4:1
Down the broad way... blind to what life's really for — Matthew 7:13-14
Turn around now...while there still is time — I Jn. 1:9, II Pet. 3:9
Learn your lesson now or you'll reap just what you sow — Galatians 6:7
*(You're gonna wish you had listened to me)*
*You would have had it all*
*(Tears are gonna fall, not looking for the Son)*
*You would have had it all*
*(You're gonna wish you had listened to me)*
*It all, it all, it all*
*(Tears are gonna fall, not looking for the Son)*

*You would have had it all*
*(You're gonna wish you had listened to me)*
*Looking for the Son*
*(Tears are gonna fall, not looking for the Son)*
*You had His holy Word in your hand*
*(You're gonna wish you had listened to me)*
*And you missed it...for your self*
*(Tears are gonna fall, not looking for the Son)*

*You would have had it all*
*(You're gonna wish you had listened to me)*
*Looking for the Son*
*(Tears are gonna fall, not looking for the Son)*
*You had His holy Word in your hand*
*(You're gonna wish you had listened to me)*
*But you missed it*
*You missed it*
*You missed it*
*You missed it....for your self*

**Scripture Summary**

Jeremiah 25:4-8
Habakkuk 2:2
Matthew 6:20
Matthew 6:33
Matthew 7:13
Matthew 22:11-14
Matthew 25:10-13
Luke 21:34-36
Luke 24:332
John 3:16-17
I Corinthians 15:52
Galatians 6:7
Philippians 1:3-6
II Timothy 3:16
Titus 2:13
II Peter 3:9
II Peter 3:4
I John 1:9
I John 2:15
Revelation 3:10
Revelation 3:14-22
Revelation 4:1
Revelation 20:4-6
Revelation 21:7
Revelation 22:17

(See www.ProphecyCountdown.com for more information)

CPSIA information can be obtained at www.ICGtesting.com
Printed in the USA
BVOW02s1546210815

414028BV00001B/88/P